PARATEXTUALITY IN BALZAC'S
LA PEAU DE CHAGRIN
The Wild Ass's Skin

PARATEXTUALITY IN BALZAC'S
LA PEAU DE CHAGRIN
The Wild Ass's Skin

Jeri DeBois King

Studies in French Literature
Volume 11

The Edwin Mellen Press
Lewiston/Queenston/Lampeter

Library of Congress Cataloging-in-Publication Data

King, Jeri DeBois.
    Paratextuality in Balzac's La peau de chagrin : The wild ass's skin / Jeri DeBois King.
    p.   cm. -- (Studies in French literature ; v.11)
    Includes bibliographical references and index.
    ISBN 0-7734-9507-X
    1. Balzac, Honoré de, 1799-1850. Peau de chagrin. I. Title.
II. Series: Studies in French literature (Lewiston, N. Y.) ; v. 11.
PQ2167.P6K5 1992
843'.7--dc20   92-12238
                                                                          CIP

This is volume 11 in the continuing series
Studies in French Literature
Volume 11 ISBN 0-7734-9507-X
SFL Series ISBN 0-88946-572-X

A CIP catalog record for this book
is available from the British Library.

Copyright © 1992 The Edwin Mellen Press

All rights reserved. For information contact

The Edwin Mellen Press	The Edwin Mellen Press
Box 450	Box 67
Lewiston, New York	Queenston, Ontario
USA 14092	CANADA L0S 1L0

The Edwin Mellen Press, Ltd.
Lampeter, Dyfed, Wales
UNITED KINGDOM SA48 7DY

Printed in the United States of America

Dedication

To my husband, Sandy.

Table of Contents

Illustrations	i
Preface	ii
Acknowledgements	iv
Introduction	1

Part One : On the Threshold of *La Peau de chagrin*

Chapter One
Paratextuality in *La Peau de chagrin* — 11

Chapter Two
The Protean Face: A Paratextual History — 29

Chapter Three
Balzac's *Tristram Shandy*, 322
Sterne and *La Peau de chagrin* — 65

Chapter Four
Four Prefaces: Contention and Correction
among Chasles, Davin, and Balzac — 83

Part Two: Crossing the Threshold — 107

Chapter Five
Foedora, Job, and the Lazarus Grid — 109

Chapter Six
Dance of Death Tableaux
and the Self-Consuming Narrative — 129

Chapter Seven
The Serpent: Trajectory and Narrative Rhythm 153

Chapter Eight
Strewn Goblets and Fallen Crowns:
Balzac's Carnival 181

Conclusion 201

Appendix A
"Foedora"
Poem Written in Balzac's Youth 209

Appendix B
"Foedora"
Poem Copied by Lovenjoul 215

Appendix C
"Le Livre de Job"
Poem Written in Balzac's Youth 223

Appendix D
Paratextual Chart of
La Peau de chagrin editions 227

Bibliography 231

Index 245

Illustrations

Title Page, First edition
La Peau de chagrin 34

Title Page, 1838 edition
Balzac illustré, Vol. I 38

Title Page, 1838 edition
Balzac illustré, Vol. II 39

First Page, 1851-53 edition
Oeuvres illustrées 40

Lithograph, 1838 edition
Balzac illustré 128

Lithograph, 1851-53 edition
Oeuvres illustrées 180

Preface

In this study I wanted to apply modern literary theory to a work by Balzac. Balzac was my choice because he has been overlooked by many writers of contemporary literary criticism, perhaps because his name is almost synonymous with the traditional novel. I focused on *La Peau de chagrin* because it contains an interesting juxtaposition of reality and fantasy and because its history lends itself to a paratextual study. Inspired by the writings of Gérard Genette, I undertook to look at Balzac's novel from a different perspective, approaching it in much the same way that a viewer conceptualizes a painting, emphasizing the visual process of perceiving the entire work, becoming conscious of the medium, then concentrating on details. I wanted to document how our view of text and textual boundaries has evolved in the last one hundred years. Some may see this approach as one in which text is subordinated to theory, but my intention was to create a symbiotic environment in which one supported the other.

The most difficult part of this undertaking was the writing of the paratextual history, for it is easily confused with bibliography. In this study, the emphasis is on the visual aspect of the medium, and bibliographies are aids in creating a paratextual history, but not its equivalent. Bibliographies presented another problem because they provided conflicting information and sometimes contradicted the paratext. OCLC sometimes disputes the Bibliothèque nationale catalogue and both contradict Talvart and Place and the Balzac bibliographies by Royce and George. Where the paratext of the volumes seemed to contradict the bibliographies, I relied on the information in the paratext of the volumes that I had in hand from the Bibliothèque nationale, the Bibliothèque de L'Institut de France, and the volumes available from OCLC. Working with the holdings mentioned above, I concentrated on one novel, but more could be done. Scholars interested in expanding this work could do paratextual studies of other novels by Balzac and examine the Balzac manuscripts and old editions available at the Maison de Balzac in Paris and the Château de Saché.

Acknowledgements

I am grateful for the help I received in the preparation of this book. I thank Converse College which afforded me the time to start this project and the staff of the Bibliothèque nationale and the Bibliothèque de l'Institut de France for their kindness and cheerful cooperation during the course of my research.

The following people helped in the preparation of the manuscript: Anthony S. Scavillo, Kitty Mackey, and Karen Carmean. Special thanks are due Catherine Jones West and Mechthild Cranston for their close reading and many helpful suggestions. I also thank my husband, Sandy, whose encouragement and help proved invaluable in the final stages of this project.

Author's Note

I would like to thank the editors of *The Comparatist* for permission to use portions of my review of *Seuils* (vol. XII, 1988) and my article "Balzac's *Tristram Shandy*, 322" (vol. XVI, 1992).

All photos of lithographs and paratextual items are courtesy of the Bibliothèque nationale, and the poems "Le Livre de Job" and "Foedora" are transcribed with the permission of the Bibliothèque de L'Institut de France.

Introduction

This study has two primary objectives, one broad, the other specific. The broad goal is to question current ways of defining literary criticism by using, in a single study, a variety of vocabularies and systems. Literary theory is no longer just a useful tool in the study of literature; it has become an object of study in and of itself. Courses in literary criticism, anthologies, histories, and dictionaries of literary theory abound. One can only wonder whether literary theory is placed above literature, when it is logically dependent upon it.

Terms used to describe modern literary criticism, such as "poststructuralist" and "deconstructive," reveal how the critics have defined literary theory since Roland Barthes, which they see either as a series of binary oppositions (structuralism /deconstruction, subjective /objective, genetic / formalist), or as a chronologically ordered sequence of movements, with structuralism followed by deconstruction, semiotics, and the "new historicism," succeeding each other under the rubric of "post structuralist" criticism. The term "post" itself connotes a temporality, a historical categorization of all these "isms" which take their place on the linear time continuum. Why not abandon the traditional binary approach and the historical-hierarchical approach and try a more prismatic view? Why not envision a new correspondence in which critical theories overlap, relate, communicate? Rather than imitate a deconstructive or semiotic technique, I want to be free to select from the abundance of theories and vocabularies available to create my own method. In order to avoid the accusation of nihilism, I have chosen a rigid organizational structure and narrow topic which will provide a grounding for the broad methods and vocabulary I intend to use.

The blueprint for my approach resembles an eighteenth century fan. Most fans have a mount composed of hard sections that are joined at and pivot from one locus point called a rivot. The support structure that I have chosen is Gérard Genette's work on paratextuality as defined in his work, *Seuils*. Paratextuality, as its name implies, is the study of everything that surrounds the text: introductions, prefaces, illustrations, even epigraphs and editors' notes. A structuralist critical approach will provide the stable support structure of this fan-like process. In the broadest sense, then, this study is structuralist, even formalist because a structuralist critical perspective will provide its intellectual girders.[1] What makes Genette's work attractive as the basis of this study is that its implications subvert its own definition and pigeonholing, as we shall see.

The pivot point and subject of study is Balzac's *La Peau de chagrin*. Genette mentions this novel in his work on paratextuality, noting that it holds the record for the briefest appearance by a preface.[2] Because of its paratextual richness, seven different editions, some of which contain lithographs, it is a perfect subject through which to study the ramifications of paratextuality.

This book's more specific aim is to consider *La Peau de chagrin* from a different perspective. Although readers have become far more sophisticated, able to separate author from narrator, reader from narrataire, implied author and reader from real author and reader, their approach to reading is basically the same.[3] The reader goes right to the text, culling paratextual items to arrive at "what happens in the story." Critics study prefaces, but even the best critics tend to read prefaces after reading the work. I am proposing a new way to read *La Peau de chagrin*: to stop and look at the total work before entering the text, an approach that is analogous to pausing at the threshold and looking at the entire house before entering. The paratext is analogous to the painting's canvas or frame. As the novel develops, so does the reader's and author's awareness of the medium, and in some cases medium becomes part of the work of art.

Most students of literature know Genette for his work on narratology and his studies of Proust in *Figures I, II,* and *III,* works that place his name with such structuralists as Barthes and Todorov.[4] In his last three works, which treat all aspects of the literary text, Genette has explored enough permutations and combinations of "text" to challenge even Julia Kristeva.[5] He first coined the term "paratextuality" in 1979 in *Introduction à l'architexte.*[6] In *Palimpsestes,* Genette's forum for a presentation of his own version of "intertextuality," he provided a short preview of his study of paratextuality.[7] The term was also used by Claudia Reeder in her article entitled "Paradoxe du (para) texte" in *Esprit Créateur* 24 .2 (1984): 36-38. Reeder contends that Denis Roche first treated the concept of paratextuality in his two works, *Dépots de savoir et de technique* and *Notre Antéfixe.*[8] Genette mentions Claude Duchet's "La Fille abandonnée et la Bête humaine, éléments de titrologie romanesque" as an early study in paratextuality [9] along with Margherita Di Fazio Alberti's *Il titolo e la funzione paraletteraria,* and Arnold Rothe's *Der Literarische Titel: Funktionen, Formen, Geschichte.* Among the works mentioned by Genette, the most inviting is Marcel Bénabou's *Pourquoi je n'ai écrit aucun de mes livres* (Genette 376).

For Genette, the paratext, analogous to a threshold (*seuil*), constitutes the mixture of practices and discourses surrounding a literary work. These may include a variety of things that are often ignored, such as prefaces, titles, subtitles, advertisements, book jackets, even bands covering the latter. Using a spatial categorical principle, Genette divides the paratext into two parts, peritext and epitext. Peritext refers to all that which surrounds the work within the confines of the volume in which the work appears; epitext is everything in the paratext that is exterior to the volume. In other words, that which is not peritext is epitext and that which is not epitext is peritext. "Tout ce qui n'est point prose est vers, et tout ce qui n'est point vers est prose."[10]

Comprising eleven of his thirteen chapters, the peritext, of which the most common variety is the preface, constitutes the essence of Genette's study. He defines nine different types of prefaces, according to two criteria: the first is the identity of the preface's author, who may be the author himself, a second party, or a character within the work (*auctoriale, allographe, actoriale,* respectively); the second criterion relates to the degree of authenticity of the claimed author, who may be the actual author, the person who signed a ghost-writer's preface, or a fictional author (*authentique, apocryphe, fictive*). The purposes of the preface range from a simple entreaty to read the work to an artful refusal to write a preface, as seen in Marivaux's *antipréface* to *La Vie de Marianne*.[11] Other types of peritext include: titles, intertitles (Genette's word for subtitles or chapter headings), dedications, epigraphs, notes, and what Genette calls "editorial peritext," everything in a book between the cover and the first page of the preface. Only the last two chapters of *Seuils* are dedicated to epitext, which is defined as promotional material that exists outside of the volume: articles, television or radio interviews, and lectures. Public epitext, which is the largest category of epitext, may be classified under one of three subdivisions: that written by the publisher, that written by a third party, and that written by the author for public consumption (*editorial, allographe officieux, actoriale public*). Private epitext is usually by the author and is categorized as either intimate or confidential; in the former, the author is writing for personal benefit alone; in the latter, there is a person to whom he addresses his ideas.

At its inception *Seuils*, as Genette insists, is synchronic rather than diachronic. Convinced that there is much more to be studied in paratextuality, he calls *Seuils* an "introduction." This explains the broad scope of the book which abounds with examples from world literature ranging chronologically from Homer to Michel Tournier. To some degree Genette is amused by his new science. Consider, for example, his choice of title, *Seuils*, which serves as an apt title, yet provides publicity for the publishing house, thereby creating a paratextual pun; consider also the fact that he does not study his own use of paratextuality for *Seuils*, i.e., its advertisement in his previous book, *Palimpsestes*. This is his warning to the reader not to take him too seriously. Lest someone ignore these small hints and become overzealous for this new branch of literary criticism, Genette states at the end of *Seuils* that discourse on paratext is merely discourse on discourse on discourse. "Thresholds are only there to cross" (377).

Now with the fan's mount constructed and in place, it is time to explain why *Seuils* is a perfect choice to argue a new correspondance in literary theory. Genette's work subverts its own contentions, using a structuralist approach, but at the same time threatening structuralism's basic tenets by parodying itself. The pun on the title *Seuils* and the publishing house Seuils is almost deconstructively precious. Genette's last comments in which he makes light of his own study undermine the work, and his contention that the work is synchronic presents the ultimate contradiction. A structuralist must claim that his work is synchronic because diachronic works are not in the structuralist tradition. Genette's material is presented in a synchronic fashion, but what is put forward constitutes, to some degree, a diachrony as well. That an essentially structuralist study writes a history in spite of itself shakes the very foundations of structuralism and subverts any efforts to force structuralism into a binary diachronic/synchronic system. There will be no claims at the outset that this study lacks such contradictions. Each chapter in this book uses a vocabulary and critical system that creates its own system of binary oppositions. Each system in individual sections of the book subverts the stated goal of questioning logocentrism and monologism, yet achieves the goal when studied simultaneously with all its accompanying chapters. Considered together, they provide a multifaceted critical view of both methodology and the object of study.

Paratext, especially peritext, creates its own spatial metaphor, as does poetry.[12] Together with paper and binding, it makes of the medium an icon. It creates a frame, a giant lens through which we view the text. Different paratextual metaphors will highlight different tropes. While the first half of this book, entitled "On the Threshold of *La Peau de chagrin*," will identify these paratextual metaphors, the second half, "Crossing the Threshold," will contain studies of the text that reenforce each paratextual metaphor. Their character will determine the approach and vocabulary used, which will run the gamut from structuralist, deconstructive, semiotic, psychoanalytical, to narratological. Genette's definition of paratextuality will hold together the variety of critical vocabularies and methods used in this study. Each paratextual metaphor and its textual complement, then, will extend the fan's mount, which when opened, will reveal images where we may read something of our culture: our changing view of history, and our changing perception of art.

Notes

[1] See Jonathan Culler, *On Deconstruction: Theory and Criticism after Structuralism* (Ithaca: Cornell UP, 1982) 20: "On the one hand, a structuralism like Barthes's, Todorov's, or Genette's, that remains preeminently literary in its references, is accused of formalism: of neglecting the thematic content of a work in order to concentrate on its playful, parodic, or disruptive relation to literary forms, codes, conventions."

[2] Gérard Genette, *Seuils* (Paris: Seuils, 1987) 12.

[3] These terms are frequently used by Gerald Prince, "Introduction à l'étude du narrataire," *Poétique* 14 (1973): 178-96; "Notes Towards a Categorization of Fictional 'Narratees'," *Genre* 4 (1971): 100-05; "On Presupposition and Narrative Strategy," *Centrum* 1 (1973): 23-31. For an application of these terms to *La Peau de chagrin* read Michaël Lastinger's article, "Narration et 'Point de vue' dans deux romans de Balzac: *La Peau de chagrin* et *Le Lys dans la vallée*," *Année balzacienne* (1988): 271-90.

[4] Jonathan Culler, foreword, *Narrative Discourse: An Essay on Method,* by Gérard Genette, trans. Jane E. Lewin (Ithaca: Cornell UP, 1980) 8.

[5] Julia Kristeva, *Semioteke* (Paris: Seuil, 1969).

[6] Gérard Genette, *Introduction à l'architexte* (Paris: Seuil, 1979) 87.

[7] " le texte proprement dit entretient avec ce que l'on ne peut guère nommer que son paratexte: titre, sous-titre, intertitres; préfaces, postfaces, avertissements, avant-propos, etc.; notes marginales infrapaginales, terminales; épigraphes; illustrations; prière d'insérer, bande, jaquette. . . ." Gérard Genette, *Palimpsestes* (Paris: Seuil, 1982) 9.

⁸Reeder 36-38. Reeder states that the word in the title reveals something of the character of paratextuality. An *antéfixe* was a device that hid the openings of round roof tiles. These functional structures became more elaborate over time, evolving into life-size statues. Reeder seems to see paratextuality as the study of the vanishing line of demarcation between the work of art and external reality.

⁹Genette sees *titrologie* as a small area of study within the larger domain of paratextuality. Claude Duchet, "La Fille Abandonnée et La Bête humaine; éléments de titrologie romanesque," *Littérature* 12 (1973): 49-73.

¹⁰"What is not prose is poetry, and what is not poetry is prose," proclaims the linguistics professor in Molière's *Le Bourgeois gentilhomme*. Molière, *Oeuvres complètes* (Paris: Seuil, 1962) 515.

¹¹My term. Genette mentions this preface in *Seuils* (256).

¹²Donald Keesey in his work, *Contexts for Criticism* (Palo Alto: Mayfield, 1987) 122, states that formalists contend that the "soul" of a successful lyric poem is a "contextual pattern" with a spatial metaphor.

Part One
On the Threshold of *La Peau de chagrin*

Chapter One

On the Threshold of *La Peau de chagrin*

La Peau de chagrin, as Genette reminds us, holds the record for the briefest appearance of a preface, eliminated after one month in the novel's second edition, entitled *Romans et Contes philosophiques*.[1] That distinction, with frequent paratextual adjustments resulting from *La Comédie humaine's* numerous editions, make *La Peau de chagrin* and *La Comédie humaine* a tempting model for the study of paratextuality. Let us examine *La Peau de chagrin* in the light of Genette's critical work on the *Comédie humaine* in *Seuils*. If we take Genette's title and the analogy it implies at face value, (i.e., that paratext is the threshold of the work of art), then pausing on the threshold will give us a new perspective on Balzac, on the novel in general, and on the meaning of art. The purpose of this chapter is to consider several of the paratextual elements of *La Peau de chagrin* from Gérard Genette's point of view as it is expressed in *Seuils*.

Epigraphs, notes, and titles are often ignored when a work is studied, perhaps because they are not considered part of the text, or perhaps they are simply overshadowed by the most significant form of peritext, the preface. They are often overlooked because they are constantly changing through additions and deletions made by the author or editor. They are, nevertheless, an important part of the peritext.

Titles

Because Balzac continuously published new works with *La Peau de chagrin*, its name changed several times with each subsequent edition. When it first appeared it bore the title *La Peau de chagrin*. In a subsequent edition one month later, it was grouped with other works as part of *Romans et contes philosophiques*, lowering its priority to that of a caption within a larger work. In 1835 Balzac subordinated both of the previous appellations to another, the *Etudes philosophiques*. In 1842-48, when Balzac published his novels as *La Comédie humaine*, *La Peau de chagrin* fell lower within the hierarchy of subtitles to a "sub" subtitle. Actually, Genette would not approve of using the latter term which he reserves for special cases.[2] Works that contain several novels such as *Les Hommes de bonne volonté* have what Genette refers to as surtitles (*surtitres*), or stacked titles. He mentions *La Comédie humaine* in a discussion of surtitles, but notes that it is in a category by itself because Balzac organized it from previously published works, whereas others such as the Rougon-Macquart novels have a more rigorous organizational structure conceived before the work was written.[3] Genette supports his contention by mentioning other editions of Balzac's works published with differing organizational patterns.[4] If we use Genette's term ulterior title (*ultérieur*), to express his consternation with the special case that *La Comédie humaine* presents, and combine it with the category surtitle (*surtitre*), previously established, we have created a new term, postfixed surtitle (*surtitre ultérieur*).

Genette categorizes titles by the logical relation they have to the content of the novel. *La Peau de chagrin* is thematic (*thématique*), rather than rhematic (*rhématique*), which is to say that it describes a central theme rather than the work itself. (By contrast, Baudelaire's title, *Petits poèmes en prose*, is rhematic [Genette, *Seuils* 76-80]). Since the wild ass's skin is central to the work, it is clear that this title is neither proleptic nor metonymic (Genette, *Seuils* 78), (proleptic titles referring to the denouement; metonymic titles referring to something or someone not essential, but contiguous to the focus of the work). The novel also contains internal titles: *le Talisman, la Femme sans coeur*, and *l'Agonie*. For Genette these internal titles are intertitles (*intertitres*), and play an important role in that they often signal a shift in narrative voice. They provide a mechanism which allows the author to express irony or to engage in alternative methods of narration. Thus, following Genette's terminology, the title *La Peau de chagrin* may be defined as both surtitle and intertitle.

Together with the titles, notes and postfaces comprise part of the peritext. In *La Peau de chagrin* there are a curious note and postface that deserve examination. The postface is entitled, "Moralité de la Première édition," and Balzac uses it to draw the following parallel with Rabelais:

> L'auteur mérite d'être grandement vitupéré pour avoir osé de mener un corbillard sans saulce, ni jambons, ni vin, ni paillardise, par les joyeux chemins de maître Alcofribas, le plus terrible des dériseurs, lui, dont l'immortelle satire avait déjà pris, comme dans une serre, l'avenir et le passé de l'homme.
>
> Mais cet ouvrage est la plus humble de toutes les pierres apportées pour le piédestal de sa statue par un pauvre Lanternois du doux pays de Touraine.[5]

In this passage Balzac alerts the reader to several considerations. First, he demonstrates his desire to be compared to Rabelais while at the same time indicating that the novel should be read on a philosophical level, in much the same way that Rabelais in the prologue invites his reader to read *Gargantua*. The note from the editor found in the fourth edition is also curiously deceptive. On first examination it appears to be a clarification of the number of the edition. However, a closer reading reveals that it is most likely the author himself, claiming to be the editor, who makes this clarification. He indicates that the August 1831 preface has been eliminated in favor of that of the second edition and that the third edition has been erroneously labeled as the "fourth." The note concludes with the implication that Balzac has had some conflicts with the previous publishers, Canel and Gosselin. "Aujourd'hui, l'oeuvre entière prend le seul titre (*Etudes philosophiques*) que l'auteur avait voulu lui imposer dès l'origine, et auquel s'étaient opposées de mesquines considérations dont il est inutile de parler."[6] Balzac clearly indicates which of the titles he prefers for the novel and implies that he and his publisher were at odds on this issue. This note presents a contradiction, presenting itself as allographic (*allographe* i.e., authored by someone other than the novelist), while in fact it is authorial (*actoriale*).

Epigraphs, like a lintel at the top of a threshold, represent the last thing the reader sees before he enters the world of the text. *La Peau de chagrin* contains several different epigraphic elements, including a snake which is found in the space provided for the epigraph, between the title and the beginning of the text. In addition, there is a mysterious reference to Sterne's *Tristram Shandy*, Chapter CCCXXII, mysterious because there are numerous editions of *Tristram Shandy*, none of which contains Chapter CCCXXII. Is this a misprint? Is this a game on Balzac's part? Or is it a reference to a work Balzac mistook for Sterne's?[7] Like Rabelais, Sterne had the habit of making bogus references. Is Balzac underscoring his philosophical kinship to these two authors? These questions will be addressed in a later chapter. Like other peritextual elements, epigraphs may be stacked or deleted. In the seventh edition of *La Peau de chagrin*, Balzac added a dedication to Félix Savary, professor at the Ecole Polytechnique, and member of the Academy of Sciences whom Balzac consulted on scientific matters.[8]

The broadest category within the definition of epitext is prefaces. The first of *La Peau de chagrin*'s prefaces appeared at the beginning of the first edition of August 1831, and was eliminated by the author in the September edition. Since the August 1831 preface was the only one Balzac wrote to *La Peau de chagrin*, its short life makes it an interesting example for paratextual study. This short-lived preface is curious because it says little about *La Peau de chagrin*. Balzac officially claims authorship of his previous novel, *La Physiologie du mariage*, and announces that he, like Rabelais, is different from the picture readers have of him. This is an obvious attempt to establish a difference between himself and the implied author in that novel.[9]

> Il y a sans doute beaucoup d'auteurs dont le caractère personnel est vivement reproduit par la nature de leurs compositions, et chez lesquels l'oeuvre et l'homme sont une seule et même chose; mais il est d'autres écrivains dont l'âme et les moeurs contrastent puissamment avec la forme et le fond de leurs ouvrages; en sorte qu'il n'existe aucune règle positive

> pour reconnaître les divers degrés d'affinité qui se trouvent entre les pensées favorites d'un artiste et les fantaisies de ses compositions. (10: 47)

This preface could also be treated as peritext for *La Physiologie du Mariage*, since peritext is everything outside the work that tends to promote it. Balzac defends the novel's suggestive language as an effort to resurrect the novelistic style of the eighteenth century.

> *La Physiologie du mariage* était une tentative faite pour retourner à la littérature fine, vive, railleuse et gaie du dix-huitième siècle, où les auteurs ne se tenaient pas toujours droits et raides, où, sans discuter à tout propos la poésie, la morale et le drame, il s'y faisait du drame, de la poésie et des ouvrages de vigoureuse morale. L'auteur de ce livre cherche à favoriser la réaction littéraire que préparent certains bons esprits ennuyés de notre vandalisme actuel, et fatigués de voir amonceler tant de pierres sans qu'aucun monument surgisse. Il ne comprend pas la pruderie, l'hypocrisie de nos moeurs, et refuse du reste aux gens blasés, le droit d'être difficiles. (10: 54)

This preface is epitext only to the degree that it meets the spatial criteria. The reference to Rabelais is but one of many found throughout the *Comédie humaine,* and it highlights numerous similar allusions throughout the novel, including a note at the end. Balzac identified with Rabelais as another author who was essentially different from the image projected in his work. Consequently, Rabelais references run the gamut from short quotes in the text to claims of an aesthetic similarity in the preface.

The second edition of the novel went on sale in September of 1831, just one month after the appearance of the first edition of *La Peau de chagrin.* It introduced a larger work, entitled *Romans et contes philosophiques,* and this time Balzac did not sign the preface. A classic case, according to Genette, of allographic writing, the preface is attributed to Philarète

Chasles, a distinguished literary scholar of the period and a good friend of Balzac. There could be some discussion concerning whether or not the preface is authentic or allographic, a point which ultimately depends upon who "edited" Chasles' preface, Balzac, or someone else. In any case, there is no doubt that Chasles wrote it, and it is also certain that he had the benefit of Balzac's advice and aid in its preparation. There was perhaps some evolution in the attitude toward identifying the preface's author; it was signed "P" in the September 1831 edition, but "P Ch" in the fourth edition of *Romans et contes philosphiques*.[10] There are several points in Chasles' preface that Balzac could not have made without causing an uproar. It is more credible for a critic to admonish a public incapable of appreciating an author's work because an accusation from the author has no authority. Chasles analyzes the period and states that it is too analytical for a novel like *La Peau de chagrin*. He implies that the 1831 reader was too inquisitive and would not accept a work of fiction without extensive inquiry concerning its origins. "Ils vous demanderont par quel procédé chimique l'huile brûlait dans la lampe d'Aladin. Ils ont demandé à M. de Balzac ce qui serait advenu, si Raphaël eût souhaité que *la Peau de chagrin* s'étendît!" (10: 1187) Chasles also criticizes the blasé nature of Balzac's reading public (10: 1187). This egotism, evident from the "irony, indifference, ennui and lassitude," pervades all levels of society, from the lower classes to the intellectual elite (10: 1186). "Je jure que le plus habile critique de 1800 à 1820 ne se ferait pas une idée nette sur un pareil ouvrage. Il briserait sa toise, jetterait son compas" (10: 1190). Chasles' preface afforded Balzac the vehicle to inform both reader and critic of his own interpretation of the novel, while strengthening his authority to impose his interpretation on the reading public and explaining through Chasles the allegorical quality of the novel: "le livre renferme un intérêt de philosophie allégorique qui s'attache aux plus minces détails et poursuit sans pitié cette science d'égoïsme que la civilisation fait naître" (10: 1189).

Quite expectedly, Chasles states that the subject of Balzac's novel is society, with three elements certain to attract readers: "satire, fantasy, and vivid tableaux" (10: 1191). He compares Balzac to Rabelais, giving more weight to Balzac's own identification with the latter. Just as Rabelais tells his reader to be with *Gargantua*, as a dog with his bone (suggesting that there is more to the novel than laughs), Chasles tells the reader that there is much more to *La Peau de chagrin* than the oriental tale which seems to dominate: "lisez *La Peau de chagrin*, vous en avez pour trois nuits d'images éclatantes et terribles . . . et pour un an de réflexion, si vous êtes né contemplateur, observateur et penseur" (10: 1191-92). Chasles' preface also provides the opportunity for a third party, seemingly objective, to announce the rapid and successful sale of the first edition, while underscoring the fact that the author disavowed the earlier preface to *La Peau de chagrin*. Chasles agrees with Balzac regarding the ideas presented in the original preface and states that Balzac's apology for *La Physiologie du mariage* was unnecessary (10: 1192). He then reproduces a large portion of Balzac's preface in his introduction. This act shifts the point of view within the preface and at the same time creates a contradiction: Balzac writes that the first preface is no longer to be included in the work, yet Chasles considers it worthy of incorporating in his preface. In the course of his analysis, Chasles draws a parallel between contemporary social events and the picture of society portrayed in *La Peau de chagrin*. A comparison is irresistible: Raphaël's impotence against the shrinking skin mirrors his failures in society, the satire and irony of all the works serving as a justification for the inclusion of the contes and *La Peau de chagrin* in the same volume (10: 1197).

The *Etudes philosophiques* appeared in December of 1834. Included in the volume was the fourth edition of *La Peau de chagrin*. Félix Davin, a young protégé, wrote the preface, but in all likelihood Balzac corrected it to suit his own ends.[11] With his prefaces to both volumes, Davin became the apologist and vulgarizer of Balzac's aesthetics. Since Balzac edited Davin's work liberally, the prefaces should properly be defined as simultaneously allographic and authorial. At the outset, Davin justifies a change in the surtitle *Etudes philosophiques* because it complements its companion volume, *Les Etudes de moeurs*. Davin, in referring to the ensemble of Balzac's works, compares it to a structure, an "édifice" with Balzac the architect (10: 1201, 1209). He minimizes what Balzac's critics call errors as incomplete areas glossed over in Balzac's rush to accomplish a project of far greater import, that of painting a picture of the society of his time (10: 1209-10). For Davin, the only work left to finish is the elaboration of these incomplete areas. He sees the first volume as separate from the second according to how each treats society's ills, the *Etudes de moeurs* treating its effects and the *Etudes philosophiques* treating its causes.

Davin's preface affords Balzac another opportunity to explain the philosophy behind his novel. Both Davin and Balzac believe that man's greatest weakness is his faith in thought. Comparing Balzac to Rabelais, who used *Gargantua et Pantagruel* to combat, "la pensée religieuse," Davin writes that Balzac's struggle is with "le sensualisme analytique" (10: 1211). "A mesure que l'homme se civilise, il se suicide" (10: 1211). Davin then explains the significance of the epigraph line, making us aware of Balzac's exasperation with the critics' imperviousness.

> Peu de personnes ont vu qu'après un tel arrêt porté sur notre organisation, il n'y avait d'autres ressources, pour la généralité des hommes, que de se laisser aller à l'allure *serpentine* de la vie, aux ondulations bizarres de la destinée. (10: 1213)

It is in this preface that he announces the third part of his work, the *Etudes analytiques*, a collection which includes *La Physiologie du mariage* and *Le Traité de la vie extérieure*. This preface is more than both authorial and allographic; it is simultaneously epitext and peritext. Genette defines this preface as pseudo-authorial (pseudo-auctorial or crypto-auctorial), basing his views on textual comparisons which prove that Balzac edited Davin's preface (Genette, *Seuils* 168).

Balzac's "Avant-propos" to the 1842-48 edition of *La Comédie humaine* expunges the earlier prefaces. Seeking to describe and defend his choice of title, he writes that the general purpose of *La Comédie humaine* was to depict the society of his time. One of the themes that appeared in the original preface to *La Peau de chagrin* continues in the "Avant-propos:" the defense of Balzac's personal morality, a defense he deemed necessary in light of the questionable morality of some of his characters.[12] Of the numerous novels in *La Comédie humaine*, Balzac singles out *La Peau de chagrin*, referring to it as a "bridge," connecting the *Etudes philosophiques* and the *Etudes de moeurs*.

> . . . *La Peau de Chagrin*, relie en quelque sorte les *Etudes de moeurs* aux *Etudes philosophiques* par l'anneau d'une fantaisie presque orientale où la Vie elle-même est peinte aux prises avec le Désir, principe de toute Passion.[13]

Balzac reiterates what Davin noted in his Preface, the *Etudes philosophiques* supplies the causes, the *Etudes de moeurs*, the effects. Balzac used the "Avant-propos" to two ends: to provide himself a reason to publish an inventory of the works he recognized as his own; and to disavow his earlier unsigned works for posterity.

Epitext: Publicity

In *Seuils* the second major paratextual category is epitext. It consists of publicity for the work existing outside the volume: other prefaces and articles in journals by the author, his editor, or his friends. The publicity campaign for *La Peau de chagrin* was well orchestrated for the times.[14] Gosselin and Balzac had friends on the editorial boards of a number of journals, and succeeded in placing excerpts in numerous reviews: "Le Dernier Napoléon" in *La Caricature* and "Une Débauche (fragment de *la Peau de chagrin*)" in *La Revue des deux mondes*, the latter containing the following note:

> Impatiemment attendue, l'oeuvre originale dans laquelle notre collaborateur a, dit-on, merveilleusement uni la peinture de la société moderne, son manque de croyance, son luxe, ses passions, aux plus hautes idées morales et philosophiques doit paraître dans quelques jours.[15]

Balzac also wrote publicity articles under a pseudonym, including a review in *La Caricature* for the August 11, 1831 issue, which he signed Alexandre de B . . . .**16** Genette, who refers to this category of epitext as original and autonomous public epitext (*épitexte public original et autonome*), uses an example by Stendhal to delineate its characteristics (Genette, *Seuils* 324).

> L'épitexte public original et autonome est une espèce plutôt rare, au moins sous une forme ouverte: Il s'agit d'un compte rendu produit, dans un journal ou une revue, par l'auteur lui-même. Nous avons vu comment Stendhal pratiquait la chose sous la forme plus ou moins voilée d'un article signé S., mais comme si ce S. n'était pas Stendhal. Beaucoup plus ouvertement auctoricale, quoique également rédigé à la troisième personne, le compte rendu du *Roland Barthes par Roland Barthes*, signé Roland Barthes, que publia *la Quinzaine littéraire* du 1er mars 1975(sic) sous le titre approprié "Barthes puissance trois."(Genette, *Seuils* 324)

Although Genette gives little attention to the study of other prefaces that function as epitexts, they are common in Balzac. Similarly, *La Peau de chagrin's* first preface defended *La Physiologie du mariage*. Analogously, Balzac's preface to *Les Contes philosophiques*, published in 1832, functions more as a publicity piece for *La Peau de chagrin* than as an introduction to les *Contes philosophiques*. This preface relates *La Peau de chagrin's* success, the number of copies sold, and information about the new edition of the *Contes philosophiques*, noting that this edition completes the set started with *La Peau de chagrin*.**17** Genette defines these editors' promotions as editorial epitext (*épitexte éditorial*) and spends little time treating the category because of his belief that authors rarely involve themselves in this type of epitext. He does, however, recognize that Balzac was an exception to the rule, since he often collaborated with his editors (Genette, *Seuils* 318-19).

Balzac's participation in advancing the sales of his novels created a special type of epitext. It falls under the category of editorial epitext, which Genette considers a precursor of the *prière d'insérer*.**18** Genette refers to the Prospectus of 1842 and 1846, and although he does not mention the catalogue that Balzac wrote in 1845 as a definitive guide to *La Comédie humaine*, it too belongs under the same category as the prospectus.[19]

> Il s'agit ici des affiches ou placards publicitaires, communiqués et autres prospectus, comme celui de 1842 pour *la Comédie humaine*, l'un des ancêtres de notre prière d'insérer, des bulletins périodiques destinés aux libraires, et des "dossiers de promotion" à l'usage des représentants. (Genette, *Seuils* 318-19)

Private Epitext

Genette separates private epitext from public epitext on the basis of the existence of a person to whom the author addressed his thoughts. Private epitext, then, includes correspondence, private confidences, and private journals. Genette defines private epitext addressed to an intermediary as confidential (*confidentiel*), while personal materials such as journals are intimate (*intime*) (342). Scholars have separated Balzac's correspondence in such a way that private epitext is to be found in the *Lettres à Madame Hanska*.[20] A good example of confidential epitext for *La Peau de chagrin* is Balzac's letter to Charles de Montalembert, wherein he thanks him for a favorable review of *La Peau de chagrin* in an August 1831 issue of the *Correspondant*, praising Montalembert for looking beyond the surface for the deeper meaning of his novel.

> Le but de profonde moralité caché dans mon livre, échappe à beaucoup de critiques malveillants, qui ne voient que la forme, et j'avoue que je suis vivement touché lorsque quelque critique veut bien dégager mes intentions de leur sauvage enveloppe. Tous nos maîtres ont mis la moelle dans un os, à l'exemple de la nature.[21]

Balzac tells Montalembert that the true meaning of the novel was allegorical. "*La Peau de chagrin* est la formule de la vie humaine, abstraction faite des individualités . . . tout y est mythe et figure" (567).

A Special Case: Illustrations

Due to the existence of at least two very famous illustrated editions of *La Peau de chagrin*, the question of whether or not illustrations are paratext must be decided before this study may proceed. Genette seems to avoid the question of illustrations in *Seuils*, but it seems clear that they would fall under the category of editorial peritext, within the realm of the editor's responsibility. Genette defines editorial peritext as follows:

> J'appelle péritexte éditorial toute cette zone du péritexte qui se trouve sous la responsabilité directe et principale (mais non exclusive) de l'éditeur ou peut-être, plus abstraitement mais plus exactement, de l'édition, c'est-à-dire du fait qu'un livre est édité, et éventuellement réédité, et proposé au public sous une ou plusieurs présentations plus ou moins diverses. (20)

Genette mentions illustrations only in passing during a discussion of what he calls, "Couverture et annexes," providing a list of items that could be on a cover. In that list are both a portrait of the author and a specific illustration (27). It is conceivable that this part of the text falls within his elaborations on format, although he does not discuss illustrations specifically within this context.

Illustrations that accompany an edition are rarely the work of an author. They are usually chosen by the editor, often symbolizing a particular interpretation of the text. They demonstrate authorial approval to differing degrees. The illustrated version of *La Peau de chagrin* published in 1838 and the illustrations published in the Furne edition were prepared with Balzac's active participation. The famous illustrated edition of Balzac's complete works by Marescq, however, appeared posthumously. In "Living On," Derrida discusses what he calls "invagination." Diegesis, or narration within a text constitutes a pocket, an invagination where the implied author (narrator, or narrator-author), enters the work of fiction. Similarly, illustration inserts diegesis in the form of editorial peritext. Since these illustrations may occur within the body of the text, rather than within the cover pages, they represent epitextual folds within the confines of the text.[22]

Since paratextuality is a study of both authorial and editorial choices, it is never-ending if its goal is to examine a work the size of *La Comédie humaine*. Each new edition brings changes in the paratext. The more vast the work, the more complicated must be the decision to retain or eliminate certain parts of the paratext. For example, Balzac's intertitles are still a subject of debate among editors.[23] The question of where to place the prefaces to the individual novels of *La Comédie humaine* is still undecided. The 1965 Pléiade edition contains the prefaces in the last volume, while the new edition compiled by Pierre-Georges Castex retains the prefaces with each novel.

Authors' decisions concerning paratext reflect their attitude toward their readers and their work. It is in the diffuse zone between medium and text that it is possible to view the author, implied author, reader, and implied reader as they are seen by the writer. Like a prism that reveals a spectrum of color when light shines through it, paratextual decisions refract the text's light, separating real author from real reader and their fictional projections.[24] It is in the preface that the real author may choose to communicate with the real reader outside of the confines of the text. The authenticity of the preface indicates the degree of openness the author chooses to reveal to the reader. If the preface is authorial and authentic, then the author speaks seriously. When the preface appears to be allographic yet betrays certain authorial intrusions, it becomes what Genette has called pseudo-allographic (172). If the author refuses to leave the mimetic mode and speaks as a fictional character, he enters the realm of the fictive author (175). In all of these hypothetical cases, he is playing a game of "hide and seek." Since the narrator is another character in the novel behind whom the author hides while telling the story to an implied reader, and the implied author may be very different from the real author, the choice of speaker for the preface determines the rhetoric used and reveals something of the writer's attitude toward the reader, understanding of fiction, and view of the distance between reality and the work of art.[25] It is clear from Balzac's use of paratext that he had little confidence in the public's ability to discern real from fiction, and that for him, the line of demarcation between them was tenuous.

Notes

1Gérard Genette, *Seuils* 2.

2In *Seuils* Genette endorses a specific definition of subtitle, an alternate title stated within the title, *Madame Bovary, moeurs de province*, for example (56).

3". . . il vaudrait mieux réserver ce terme à la situation . . . des ensembles à plusieurs volumes dont chacun porte un titre séparé. C'est en particulier celle des séries romanesques du type Rougon-Macquart, *Recherche, Hommes de bonne volonté*, etc. *la Comédie humaine*, de rassemblement ultérieur et d'unité plus lâche, faisant encore un cas à part" (Genette, *Seuils* 59).

4See Honoré de Balzac, *Oeuvres de Balzac*, ed. R. Chollet (Lausanne Rencontres, 1958-62); also, A. Béguin et J. A. Ducourneau, eds., *L'Oeuvre de Balzac publiée dans un ordre nouveau* (Paris: Formes et Reflets, 1949-53); also, Honoré de Balzac, *Oeuvres complètes illustrées*, ed. J. A. Ducourneau (Paris: Bibliophiles de l'Originale, 1965-76).

5Honoré de Balzac, "Moralité de la Première Edition," in *La Comédie humaine*, ed. Pierre Georges-Castex. 12 vols. (Paris: Gallimard, 1979) 10: 1351. All subsequent references to the prefaces or text from *La Peau de chagrin* or other works of *La Comédie humaine* will come from this edition.

6Honoré de Balzac, "Note de l'éditeur pour la Quatrième Edition," 10: 1220.

7Michael Tilby, in "A partir d'une allusion à Sterne dans *La Peau de chagrin*," *L'Année Balzacienne* (1985): 247-62, states that some of the allusions to Sterne refer to a work by Griffith lampooning Sterne. Tilby bases this thesis on a reference to Sterne in the 1838 edition of *La Peau de chagrin*, no longer included in subsequent editions. He does not refer to the mysterious reference to *Tristram Shandy* in the epigraph.

8Roger Pierrot mentions this in his "Notices des Tomes I à X," in the *La Comédie humaine* 11 vols. (Paris: Gallimard, 1965) 11: 1057.

9For a definition and discussion of the implied author, the author's projection of himself within the novel, see Wayne Booth, *The Rhetoric of Fiction* (Chicago: U of Chicago P, 1961).

10Philarète Chasles, introduction, *Romans et contes philosophiques*, by Honoré de Balzac, 3 vols. (Paris: Gosselin, 1831) vol. 1. Pierre Citron mentions this as well in the "Notice" to Philarète Chasles' introduction in *La Comédie humaine*, ed. Pierre-Georges Castex, 12 vols. (Paris: Gallimard, 1979) 10: 1185, 1197. See also Chasles, introduction, *Romans et contes philosophiques* 4 vols. (Paris: Gosselin, 1833). vol. 1.

11See Roger Pierrot's note concerning the authenticity of the preface, Félix Davin, introduction, in Balzac's *Etudes philosophiques*, *La Comédie humaine*, ed. Roger Pierrot, 11 vols. (Paris: Gallimard, 1965) 11: 1098.

12David Bellos, introduction, *Balzac Criticism in France, 1850-1900: The Making of a Reputation* (Oxford: Clarendon P, 1976) 1-17, states that except for the praise and acclaim he received for *La Peau de chagrin*, Balzac was under fierce personal attack from the critics during the 1830s and 40s.

13Honoré de Balzac, "Avant-propos," *La Comédie humaine*, ed. Pierre-Georges Castex, 12 vols. (Paris: Gallimard, 1976) 1: 19.

14Bellos, introduction 5-6. See also Christopher Prendergast, *Balzac:*

Fiction and Melodrama (New York: Holmes and Meier, 1978) 28.

[15]Roger Pierrot lists these journals and uses this quotation in his "Notices," 11: 1056.

[16]Roger Pierrot mentions this article in his "Notices," 11: 1056.

[17]Honoré de Balzac, *Contes philosophiques*, "Avis du Libraire-Editeur sur cette publication," 10: 1198.

[18]For a detailed definition of this example of modern peritextual publicity see *Seuils*, 98-108. The following probably suffices as a short analysis: "Prière d'insérer se rapporte, me semble-t-il, a une pratique antérieure, et plutôt caractéristique du XIXe siècle, où ce genre de textes était adressé, non pas exactement à 'la critique,' et non pas sous forme d' 'encart,' mais à la presse en général (aux directeurs de journaux), sous forme de communiqué destiné à annoncer la parution de l'ouvrage" (99).

[19]Honoré de Balzac, "Catalogue de *La Comédie humaine* " 1: cxxiii-cxxv.

[20]See Honoré de Balzac, *Lettres à Madame Hanska*, ed. Roger Pierrot, 4 vols. (Paris: Les Bibliophiles de l'Originale, 1967-68). See also Honoré de Balzac, "Lettres sur la littérature," in *Oeuvres complètes de Honoré de Balzac*, 40 vols. (Paris: Conard, 1940) 40: 271-329.

[21]Honoré de Balzac, "A Charles de Montalembert," avant le 23 août 1831, in *Correspondance*, ed. Roger Pierrot, 5 vols. (Paris: Garnier, 1960-69) 1: 567.

[22]Jacques Derrida, "Living On: Border Lines." in Bloom et al., *Deconstruction and Criticism* (New York: Seabury, 1979) 97.

[23]In *Seuils* Genette notes the following about recent paratextual decisions concerning *La Comédie humaine*: "L'edition collective de *la Comédie*

humaine, publiée chez Furne à partir de 1842, supprime systématiquement la division en chapitres et, du même coup bien sûr, les intertitres originaux (282-83). In a note Genette remarks that the Pléiade edition of *La Comédie humaine* eliminated the intertitles, whereas the Garnier edition retained them (282-83, note 1).

[24]Since Wayne Booth coined the term "implied author," scholars have become increasingly aware of the various projections of the author and reader in a particular novel. Wayne C. Booth, *The Rhetoric of Fiction* (Chicago: U of Chicago P, 1961).

[25]Wolfgang Iser, *The Implied Reader: Patterns of Communication in Prose Fiction from Bunyon to Beckette* (Baltimore: Johns Hopkins UP, 1974) 102-05.

Chapter Two
The Protean Face: A Paratextual History

Like Proteus, *La Peau de chagrin* has assumed different forms since its publication in August of 1831. The history of the novel's publication from its first edition to its inclusion in *La Comédie humaine* is well documented and provides a firm base for a paratexutal study. Charles de Lovenjoul, in what is perhaps the first paratextual study of the *Comédie humaine*, chronicled how the novels and short stories of the *Etudes philosophiques* were compiled, marketed, and finally shaped into the *Comédie humaine*.[1] William Hobart Royce's *A Balzac Bibliography* and Albert J. George's *Books by Balzac* treat the bibliographical aspect of *La Peau de chagrin's* paratextual history in their cataloguing of Balzac references in literature. Since 1960 *L'Année balzacienne* keeps an annual bibliography of Balzac editions and studies. Later, Graham Falconer has studied the reworking of the text in his article, "Le travail de style dans les révisions de *la Peau de chagrin*," *L'Année balzacienne* (1969): 71-106, concluding that Balzac trimmed its Rabelaisian verboseness with each edition to emphasize the serious side of the novel and to integrate it into the *Comédie humaine*.[2] Although this work concentrates on textual changes, it contains some paratextual information, such as Balzac's changing the title of the first part to *Le Talisman* in the 1838 *Balzac illustré* edition (96). These works, though not focused on the novel's paratextext or its paratextual history, nevertheless constitute a body of paratextual studies.

What follows is a paratextual history of *La Peau de chagrin*. Each of the editions approved by Balzac has a particular paratext: a unique combination of epigraph, title, subtitle, and preface that exists only in one edition. Since it was the first of Balzac's works to bear his real name and his first success under that name, *La Peau de chagrin* occupies a prominent place in the history of *La Comédie humaine*. Every subsequent edition of the novel from the August 1831 to the Furne edition is a picture in a series of images reflecting the different stages of Balzac's art. These editions write a history of the evolution of his aesthetics, and each edition's paratext serves as a frame to each picture in the chronology. A paratextual history would chronicle the changes in the textual frame (paratext) over the years.[3] Furthermore, some editors have made paratextual changes or created new combinations of the works in the *Comédie humaine* with no concern for Balzac's aesthetics. If we continue the analogy of the paratext as a frame, then every change in the paratextual clues of a particular edition are of interest in this history. This study's focus is the frame, the threshold, not the text. Its most important result will be an awareness of new issues that have emerged as the modern reader chooses to consider the work's paratextual frame as an integral part of the fictional work of art.[4]

After Balzac's death, three identifiable paratextual groups of *La Peau de chagrin* editions emerged. The first group includes reprints of the work that appeared during Balzac's lifetime, the so-called classics. Viewed together, these different editions chronicle the artistic changes in Balzac's aesthetics and the changes in his own understanding of his work. Considered in order of their publication, they also write the history of the paratextual evolution of *La Peau de chagrin* from a single novel to an integral part of the *Comédie humaine*. Reprints of *La Peau de chagrin* by editors who take moderate license with Balzac's aesthetic principles comprise the second category of this study. These editors vary the novel's format, but they justify their interpretations by the existence of an analogous work approved by Balzac during his lifetime. A new illustrated version would be a notable example. The third group owes its existence to the tenuous hold that Balzac's categorical principle has on *La Comédie humaine*. This group consists of editions that do not follow Balzac's aesthetic organizational principles, that is to say, editions outside the *Comédie humaine*. Generally, editions that incorporate the *Oeuvres de jeunesse* into a complete works format or those that publish Balzac's works based on thematic or chronological principles fall into this category. Gérard Genette's description of *La Comédie humaine* in *Seuils* points to the special paratextual qualities of Balzac's work.[5] He justifies the existence of unorthodox editions by the weakness of Balzac's organizational principle in the following statement:

> C'est en particulier celle des séries romanesques du type *Rougon-Macquart, Recherche, Hommes de bonne volonté,* etc.—*la Comédie humaine,* de rassemblement ultérieur et d'unité plus lâche, faisant encore un cas à part. En effet, chaque roman nouveau de cet ensemble à venir paraissait séparément, en feuilleton et/ou en volume, et ce mode de présentation s'est maintenu jusqu'à la fin, concurremment à la publication de groupements plus ou moins partiels: *Scènes de la vie privée* (1830), *Romans et Contes philosophiques* (1831), *Etudes de moeurs au XIXe siècle* (1835) (déjà subdivisées en *Scènes de la vie privée, de la vie de province, de la vie parisienne), Etudes philosophiques,* (1835), enfin *la Comédie humaine* (1842), où ces divisions, et quelques autres, se retrouvent dans une construction à plusieurs étages. . . .
> Cette structure n'apparaît évidemment que dans les éditions collectives de *la Comédie humaine,* et les innombrables éditions séparées ne mentionnent souvent même pas l'existence d'un tel ensemble. Il existe d'ailleurs d'autres groupements possibles, même si franchement infidèles aux intentions de l'auteur: par exemple, selon l'ordre chronologique de publication, ou selon l'ordre chronologique de l'action, sans compter la réédition en fac-similé de l'édition Furne de 1842 dans l'exemplaire pourvu par Balzac de corrections manuscrites. Toutes variantes rendues possibles par le fait que l'ordre de *la Comédie humaine,* s'il est assez lâchement thématique (voir les hésitations de l'auteur lui-même), n'est en tout cas pas chronologique.[6]

Text Versus Context: Historicity Versus History

The essential conflict between two paratextual interpretations of the novel can be distilled into text versus context. Each separate edition approved by Balzac represents a snapshot of his mind set, frozen in time. Each changing paratext serves as the frame or lens through which one views the texts, and viewing them together tells a story of evolution, writes a history. After an author's death, history creates a momentum, which in Balzac's case, conflicts with the author's aesthetic principles. Although Balzac never acknowledged his *Oeuvres de jeunesse* and never permitted them to be published with the *Comédie humaine*, editors lost no time before incorporating them into *Oeuvres complètes* editions. As an example, consider the Marescq edition of the 1851-53 *Oeuvres illustrées* and its many reprints. The power of historical momentum is evident in the preponderance of complete works editions published since Balzac's death. This momentum accelerated during the twentieth century with the widespread publication of critical editions. Even OCLC lists Balzac's works under the title of *Oeuvres complètes*, not *La Comédie humaine*. This rendition of the work has destroyed its dimension and perspective in the name of scholarship and "historical context." The historicity of each individual edition has disappeared into the notes and appendices of critical editions.

Every edition approved by Balzac is like the facet on a gemstone, revealing something new about him and his aesthetic. Pierre Barbéris, in his preface to a reprint of the original August 1831 edition to *La Peau de chagrin*, makes the first and most eloquent case for recreating the paratextual history of the novel through reprints of its earlier editions: "On lira pour la première fois depuis près d'un siècle et demi le texte de *la Peau de chagrin* tel que le lurent les lecteurs au mois d'août, 1831 dans les 2 volumes en 8° publiés par Urbain Canel et Charles Gosselin."[7] Barbéris states further that the problem with the majority of the editions of *La Peau de chagrin* is that the definitive edition, published according to Lovenjoul's work on the

Furne corrigé, destroyed the historicity of the novel.[8]

> Il est vrai qu'on ne "travaillait" que sur le texte ultime de *la Peau*, celui que Balzac avait encore corrigé sur un exemplaire personnel de l'édition Furne, et qui, par rapport au texte original, est radicalement transformé. Qui, sauf quelques spécialistes, allaient chercher le vieil exemplaire sur papier à grandes marges de 1831? Les éditions savantes donnaient bien, en note, les versions antérieures, à la dernière revue par l'auteur, ainsi qui lisait ces notes? (ii)

Barbéris is severely critical of the editorial decisions to keep textual variations as notes. "Ainsi en un sens, était mort un livre. Ainsi s'était-il perdu, et toutes les complicités avaient joué, les habitudes éditoriales fournissaient des armes à déhistoriser la littérature" (ii-iii). Later in the preface he writes the following: "*La Peau de chagrin* est la somme de ce Balzac qui masque aujourd'hui le Balzac de *la Comédie humaine* " (vii). To illustrate just how ephemeral the concept is, the publishers of *La Peau de chagrin* ignored Barbéris' words where the paratext was concerned in the very volume that he edited. There is no snake, no line, and no reference to Sterne in the reprint of the first edition of *La Peau de chagrin* by Livre de poche. The idea of reproducing the first edition is simple, yet extending the concept to the paratext was easily lost.

The Eight Editions of *La Peau de chagrin*

Before beginning our paratextual history of *La Peau de chagrin* in the light of the three groups described above, it is important to review the seven different editions of *La Peau de chagrin* that were published during Balzac's lifetime. The first appeared alone, in two volumes, in August of 1831.[9] The preface, written by Balzac, the "Moralité," and the fact that it is unaccompanied, distinguish it as the first edition. (See Chapter I) The second edition, issued in September 1831 had some textual changes, but its paratextual changes are more significant.[10] The "Moralité" was expunged,

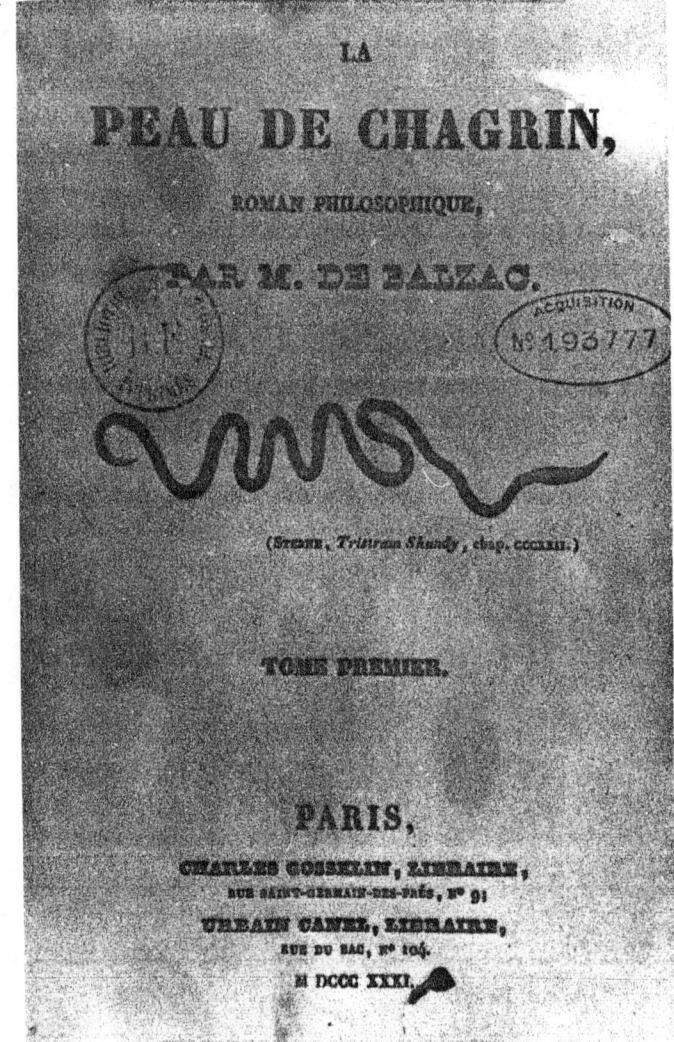

Title Page, First edition
La Peau de chagrin

as well as Balzac's "Préface," replaced with one by Philarète Chasles. Both editions bore the curious epigraph, *Tristram Shandy*, 322, and the dark sinuous line. Since this edition incorporated *La Peau de chagrin* within the *Romans et contes philosophiques*, its paratext changed with a new title and a three-volume format.[11] In 1833, the novel appeared in the same format as the previous edition of the *Romans et contes philosophiques*, except that it grew by one volume.[12] In 1835, the fourth edition was sold as *Les Etudes philosophiques*, Balzac having changed his publisher to Werdet, and substituted the preface by Chasles with a new one by Félix Davin.[13]

In 1838 the fifth edition appeared with lithographs. It was to be called *Les Etudes sociales,* the implication being that more works were to be published under this format.[14] It seems that Balzac planned to incorporate his works into a different organizational structure, but the project was never continued. This edition of *La Peau de chagrin* is like a path the author followed until he found his true way. It is the first and only edition in his *Oeuvres illustrées* series, and it contained no preface. It did, however, contain over 100 exquisite lithographs, many reflecting Dance of Death motifs. Three fourths of the images were made by Ange-Louis Janet and Henri-Charles-Antoine Baron. The principle engraver was Brunellière whose name appears on one of the lithographs.[15] Balzac abandoned his project to publish other novels in such an elaborate form, and the 1838 *Balzac illustré* is the only work of its kind published during his lifetime. Some of the images reappear in later illustrated editions of Balzac's works published after his death or in critical editions of *La Comédie humaine*.

The sixth edition appeared in 1839, published by Charpentier. It was the last printing of *La Peau de chagrin* alone, and its sinuous line is the first to suggest a snake.[16] The Charpentier version has no lithographs. Although the text is identical to that of the 1838 illustrated version, the differing paratexts clearly differentiate the Charpentier edition from others. After the publication of the Charpentier version, *La Peau de chagrin* entered the *Comédie humaine* with the seventh printing of 1845. Sometimes referred to as the Furne edition, it was the first to incorporate Balzac's signed works under the title of *La Comédie humaine*. In addition to the stacked title there are a number of paratextual differences compared to the Charpentier edition. Balzac added a dedication to Félix Savary, an astronomer and mathematician.[17] The first page of text is unusual because it is only three-quarters of a page in length, revealing the epigraph on the page under it and under the new dedication. The Furne snake had no head, but did indicate a mottled color, suggesting scales. Whether this unusual page was a mistake is unclear from Balzac's correspondence.

After Balzac's death, another version of the novel appeared which is difficult to classify. It could be called the eighth edition. Balzac used a copy of the Furne edition to make corrections which Spoelberch de Lovenjoul used when he compiled his version of the *Comédie humaine*.[18] It appeared in 1870 and has been referred to since as the definitive version with Lovenjoul as the editor.[19] Although the textual changes are subtle, the paratextual changes occurring on the first page of *La Peau de chagrin* are significant: to move the epigraph and picture of the wavy line above the "Dédicace" is moved, and the three-quarter page (Lovenjoul A 30) is eliminated. Balzac pasted the partial page to the next page, thereby eliminating this paratextual anomaly (Lovenjoul A 30). For the purposes of this study, the Lovenjoul edition will be referred to as the *Furne corrigé*.

The Balzac illustré

The adjective *illustré*, which appears several times in the history of the novel's publication, invites confusion in recreating the paratextual history of *La Peau de chagrin*. In 1838, Balzac published his famous illustrated edition of *La Peau de chagrin*, now referred to as the *Balzac illustré*. Reproductions of this edition, which are plentiful, would fall into our first paratextual category. During the years 1851-55, the word *illustré* appeared in two titles of Balzac's works: the Houssiaux edition, entitled *Oeuvres complètes illustrée*s and the Marescq edition entitled *Oeuvres illustrées*. The Houssiaux is actually a reprint of the Furne edition and includes illustrations from the latter with some additions. A. J. George describes them in the following manner: " to v. 1 is prefixed Balzac's portrait; to v. 13, 6 ill. were added; to vol. 17 were added the 5 ill. Furne had supplied in 1852; to v. 20 is prefixed an article by George Sand, dated Nohant, Oct. 1853" (63).

The Marescq edition can be included within either the second or third of our paratextual categories: it justifies its inclusion within the former on the existence of the 1838 *Balzac illustré*, within the latter because of its refutation of Balzac's organizational principle. Like other editions of Balzac's works that appeared after 1850, the Marescq et Cie edition of the *Oeuvres illustrées* was a reprint of the Furne's *Comédie humaine* and included his unsigned works.[20] It was supplemented with numerous lithographs by renowned artists: Beaucé, Staal, Meissonier, Bertall, Tony Johannot, Célestin Nanteuil, E. Lampsonius, Henri Monnier, Daumier, and Andrieux. Balzac's old title (surtitle or *surtitre*) of *Etudes philosophiques* appears to have been discarded, and although works from the *Etudes philosophiques* were included in this volume, it did not respect the order established by Balzac in the Furne edition. This volume contained *La Peau de chagrin, El verdugo, Louis Lambert, L'Elixir de longue vie, Massimila Doni, Gambara, L'Enfant Maudit, Les Proscrits, La Femme de trente ans, La Grande Bretèche, Béatrix, La Grenadière, La Vendetta, Une Double Famille*. In parentheses, at the bottom of the last page one may often find the words, "Extraits de *La Comédie humaine.*" From the large thin format, the edition seems to be an ancestor of the magazine. The large size, a bit larger than a large format magazine, includes illustrations and two columns of text on each page.[21] Many of the novel's paratextual elements were eliminated; although the dedication to Félix Savary has been retained, the epigraph and the line have disappeared. To state simply that the edition was reprinted several times, notably by Michel Lévy in 1867 and 1868, does not do justice to the frequency of publication of this version of Balzac's works. In addition to the Marescq version, *La Peau de chagrin* was published in this format by Bureau du Siècle publishers, and later Librairie Nouvelle. Permission to publish Balzac's novels was acquired by the Lévy brothers from Mme Balzac in 1865, when they bought Librairie Nouvelle and its publishing rights.[22] The Bibliothèque nationale catalogue states that the 1854 edition of Bureau du Siècle's *La Peau de chagrin* was reprinted ten times between 1855 and 1866, and OCLC has a listing of an 1879-85 edition by Lévy frères. An 1873 version may be seen at the Bibliothèque nationale, printed by S. Lejay, with no publisher listed.[23]

Title Page, 1838 edition
Balzac illustré, Vol. 1

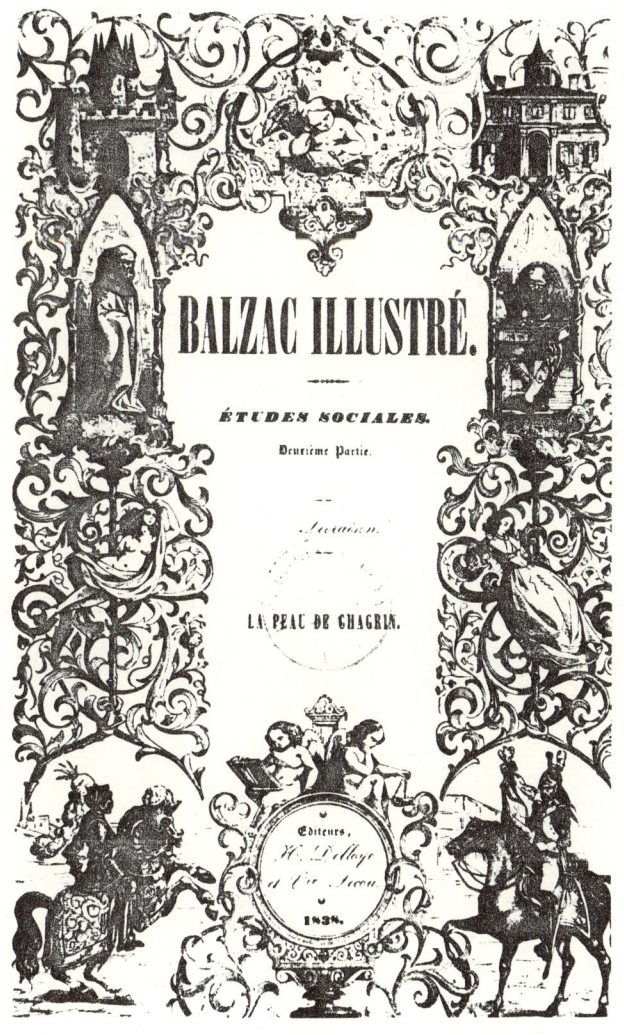

Title Page, 1838 edition
Balzac illustré, Vol. II

First Page, 1851-53 Marescq edition
Oeuvres illustrées

Classifying the Marescq edition is difficult because it belongs simultaneously to two of our categories. Since the *Oeuvres illustrées* included Balzac's unsigned works written before *La Peau de chagrin*, it belongs to the third group because it gives precedence to the complete works' organizational principle rather than Balzac's aesthetic principle. Justifying its existence on Balzac's approval of the *Balzac illustré* (*La Peau de chagrin*, 1838) and some illustrations in the Furne edition of *La Comédie humaine*, the *Oeuvres illustrées* version belongs to the second group as well because it is inspired by one of Balzac's interpretations of his works. Although some of the lithographs are similar to those of the 1838 edition, they are not presented in the same manner, and the magnificent Dance of Death lithographs are not included. This large format edition disappeared at the end of the nineteenth century. The lithographs have survived, however, appearing in various editions of the *Comédie humaine* with little information about the edition they illustrated.

For our paratextual concerns, the difference between the 1838 edition, the Houssiaux, and that of Marescq's *Oeuvres illustrées* is clear. The 1838 version presents a picture of Balzac in metamorphosis, Balzac before *La Comédie humaine*. The new name, *Les Etudes sociales*, suggests an attempt by Balzac to reorganize his works and suggests that he experimented with his own organizational principle. The Houssiaux edition, not really an illustrated version, belongs to our second category of works, justifying its format on the Furne illustrations and the existence of one illustrated edition of Balzac's works. *La Peau de chagrin* from the *Oeuvres illustrées* by Marescq, however, belongs to our third category because it represents a first effort to undermine Balzac's authority by placing both works within the *Oeuvres complètes* format. It is evidence of how powerfully historical-chronological momentum undermines the novelist's authority.

Taking Liberties

The paratextual history of *La Peau de chagrin* is characterized by editors taking liberties, running the gamut from committing minor errors, such as the omission of an epigraph or a dedication, to major ones such as prefixing the 1831 preface to a Furne text. Although all of the editions described in this study fit one or more of the categories proposed in the beginning of this chapter, it is rare that a specific edition would fit exclusively into a particular category. Editors began taking liberties with *La Peau de chagrin* as early as the 1850s with the Marescq and the Houssiaux editions. It is the Houssiaux publishing house that Spoelberch de Lovenjoul criticizes for the metamorphosis of Sterne's black, sinuous epigraph line into a snake.[24] For whatever reason, this interpretation had a strong influence on other publishers of Balzac's works. The tradition of a fully detailed snake continued in the 1874 edition in 21 volumes, a reprint of the seventh edition by Furne, and continues in this century with the 1949-65 Pléiade edition by Gallimard. In the case of Lévy, it published a version of *La Peau de chagrin* in nearly each of our three categories: a complete works edition in 55 volumes (1856-67, first published by Librairie Nouvelle); reprints of the *Oeuvres illustrées* discussed above; a *Comédie humaine* edition in 52 volumes (1891-99, by Calmann-Lévy); and Lovenjoul's definitive edition.

The last version of *La Peau de chagrin* to appear in the nineteenth century was the Rouff edition of 1899. It included no prefaces and was entitled *Les Oeuvres de Honoré de Balzac*. Rouff includes all the paratextual elements of the seventh edition: the epigraph reference to Sterne, the dedication to Savary, and the sinuous line with a detailed snake including scales and a hissing tongue in the tradition of the Houssiaux edition.

In 1900, P. Ollendorf published another edition of Balzac's *Oeuvres complètes illustrées*, different from the one published by Lévy and the Librairie Nouvelle. The 1900 edition bears several subtitles: *Etudes philosophiques* and the description, "roman philosophique." It contains the sinuous line more reminiscent of the first edition of *La Peau de chagrin* with no resemblance to a snake. The lack of preface is significant in that it implies a reprint of the Furne edition, but this edition also lacks the dedication to Savary which would imply an effort to recreate the 1838 illustrated version. The illustrations, however, are new, by Adrien Moreau. It contains the 53 chapter divisions of the first edition and the "Moralité." The appendix includes the preface of the first edition and a note. "La première édition de *La Peau de chagrin* parut en 1831, chez Gosselin et Urbain Canel, en 2 volumes en 8°." The suspension points, used to substitute for Sternean lacunae, were expunged from the first edition. Although Ollendorf's paratext, a curious cannibalization of several earlier editions, may be of some interest to collectors, it does not seem to be faithful to any one edition of *La Peau de chagrin* published during Balzac's lifetime. It does, however, demonstrate an early interest in recreating the first edition of *La Peau de chagrin* for posterity. Appendix D provides a table giving a resume of paratextual information on Balzac editions from 1901 until 1939.

In 1901, the Flammarion edition of *La Peau de chagrin* appeared in paperback. Although it contains the text of the definitive edition, it includes no title to indicate that it is part of the *La Comédie humaine*. Published in 2 volumes, the work contains no preface, introduction, or study. Also missing are the epigraph, the sinuous line or snake, and the dedication. The text contains no illustrations except on the covers of each volume.[25] This work precedes a number of paperback editions of *La Peau de chagrin*, all demonstrating a similar lack of regard for paratextual elements.

In 1903, *La Peau de chagrin* appeared as part of the series entitled "Collection abrégée de ses meilleurs romans populaires" published by the Librairie Populaire. It contained no paratextual elements whatsoever: no dedication, epigraph, or subtitles. The inscription on the ass's skin, which was supposed to be in Sanskrit in later editions, is only in French. This is the only paratextual clue that the work is meant to pass as an earlier edition of *La Peau de chagrin*. Another curiosity is the omission of the novel's conclusion. This strange combination of errors makes the Librairie populaire edition unlike any preceding it, and consequently puts it not only in category II, but also in III because the number of paratextual errors challenges Balzac's authority.

The Larousse editions of *La Peau de chagrin* appeared during the early years of the twentieth century: 1909, 1910, 1912, 1921, and 1925, not as part of the *Comédie humaine* or the *Etudes philosophiques*, but as standalone editions. They appear to be reprints of the definitive edition since they contain no preface. (As noted earlier, all prefaces to the individual works of *La Comédie humaine* were expunged in favor of a general preface to *La Comédie humaine*.) There are no prefaces or references to the

Larousse publishing house. Inscribed are the words, "Je sème à tout vent," the slogan for the company. On the first page with text there appears an elaborate bar at the top of the page with Balzac's name, but the text contains no pictures. Missing from all editions are the epigraph *Tristram Shandy* CCCXXII, and the mysterious line. Editorial paratext here clearly invades the author's domain, obscuring the authorial paratext in these works.26

One of the first to respect the paratext is the 1923 edition by G. Grès et Cie. This work is a reprint of the definitive edition and includes the dedication to Savary on an otherwise blank page. Another page contains the reference to Sterne, *Tristram Shandy*, CCCXXII, representing the snake with a flickering tongue and elaborate detail. The choice to place each element on a separate page, and the elaborate snake, depart from what Balzac specified for his editions of the *Comédie humaine*, both in the Furne and *Furne corrigé* editions (Lovenjoul A 30). On the first page of text of *La Peau de chagrin* are the titles and subtitles: *Etudes philosophiques*, *La Peau de chagrin*, the sinuous line suggesting scales (but with no head), the reference to Sterne, and finally the dedication, in that order. There are no prefaces, no author's notes, no "Moralité" nor any lithographs other than a decoration at the top of the page of each chapter. The following note was found at the end of this edition, clarifying its status as a definitive edition.

> La présente publication a été établie sur l'édition dite définitive de *La Comédie humaine* publiée de 1869 à 1876, à laquelle le vicomte Spoelberch de Lovenjoul donna ses soins. Le volume qui contient *La Peau de chagrin* est le quinzième de la série; il porte la marque de Michel Lévy et la date de 1870. Son texte offrant quelques légères difficultés avec celui de 1845, le dernier, on le sait, qui fut revu par l'auteur avant sa mort, nous avons cru utile d'en relever les variantes. On les trouvera ci-après. Nous devons, toutefois, prévenir le lecteur qu'à plusieurs reprises, et dans la première partie de l'ouvrage, nous avons adopté de très légères corrections inédites faites par Balzac sur un exemplaire de l'édition de 1845,

conservé à Chantilly. (Now at the Bibliothèque de l'Institut de France in Paris.)[27]

In 1927 the first of this century's great Balzac editions appeared, the Conard edition of the *Etudes philosophiques*. It contained illustrations by Charles Huard, with comments and notes by Marcel Bouteron and Henri Longnon. Although the title page lacks some of the traditional paratext (the epigraph and the line), the copious documentation of the paratextual elements as they appeared and evolved during Balzac's lifetime compensates for this omission. Most of the documentation comes from Lovenjoul's article, "*Les Etudes philosophiques.*" This version is listed as one of the principle editions of the *Comédie humaine* published during the twentieth century.[28] It is still used today in critical studies. Martin Kanes, in his work, *Balzac's Comedy of Words*, states his preference for this edition for the following reason: "I make no apologies for my long standing affection for the Conard edition, with its creamy paper, its generous margins, its marvelous engravings."[29] The Conard edition of Balzac's *Oeuvres complètes* was completed in 1940.

Shortly after the Conard edition of *La Peau de chagrin* appeared, Jules Tallandier published another in 1928, curiously cannibalized.[30] The frontispiece, which represents the title page of the 1838 edition, would lead one to believe that this was another reprint of that version. However, it fails to faithfully represent the 1838 paratext because the epigraph reference to Sterne, *Tristram Shandy*, 322, is missing. The text contains the lithographs that appeared in the 1838 edition, but in different order, on a separate page, and two to a page. There is no reference to the fact that they are reprinted from the 1838 edition. That these images are not in correct order is distracting and creates a further distortion of the paratextual history of the novel. The Tallandier edition is a reprint of the 1838 edition, but an inaccurate one indeed and demonstrates the publisher's lack of concern for the novel's paratext and its paratextual history.

The 1930s saw the publication of many fine critical editions, the first by Garnier frères edition of *La Peau de chagrin*, with Maurice Allem's critical comments and notes.[31] The Garnier edition of *La Peau de chagrin*, with an introduction and notes by Maurice Allem, contained the dedication to Savary, and the sinuous line in the form of a snake with a flickering tongue, paying close attention to the paratextual elements. It also included a few of the lithographs from the 1838 edition at the beginning of the volume. The snake and the lack of prefaces from earlier editions suggest that it is a reproduction of a later version, most likely the 1870 Lévy definitive edition. The 1838 lithographs confuse the issue, however. Further confusion is created by placing these lithographs at the beginning of the text, something that was never practiced, thereby creating a historically inaccurate rendition. This work is not a reproduction of any one particular orginal edition; rather, a mixture of paratextual elements from several versions.[32] Later, a Gallimard edition of the *Comédie humaine* appeared with text, comments and notes by Marcel Bouteron.[33] In 1936 Henri Béziat published *La Peau de chagrin*. This time, the collection title identified the editor's intention: to highlight the great writers of the past,"Collection des écrivains illustrés."[34] This work contained a lithograph for the cover, a title page, but no illustrations, prefaces, or "Moralité." There was no attempt to reproduce the *Comédie humaine*. Béziat's version was, instead, a tribute to the work, its author and its popularity through the years.

In 1942, Editions Corbeil published *La Peau de chagrin* in two volumes. It is a veritable paratextual void, containing no epigraph reference, line, nor dedication, in many respects a throw-back to the Flammarion and Larousse editions of the beginning of the century.[35] In 1943, La Nouvelle France published an edition that is also interesting for its paratextual lack. Like its 1942 counterpart, it demonstrates no paratextual elements; no epigraph, dedication, nor prefaces. It does, however, contain illustrations by Paul Cappatti who continues the "Danse macabre" tradition with an illustration of a skeleton, a fact which strongly suggests a familiarity with the 1838 *illustré* edition of *La Peau de chagrin*.[36] (See appendix D for a table of editions from 1940-1950.)

In 1945 two editions of *La Peau de chagrin* were published by Panthéon and Gasmier publishers. The Gasmier contained illustrations by de Beuville. Both of these editions omit the epigraph with the snake, the reference to *Tristram Shandy*, and the prefaces. Both retain the dedication, a signal that they are based on the Furne edition.

Four more editions of *La Peau de chagrin* appeared in 1946, by the following publishers: Gibert, Vie réelle, Ratier, and Martel. The first two are of significant paratextual interest because they contain several errors. In the Gibert edition there are two: the dedication to Savary is above the epigraph, indicating the paratext of the 7th edition; and there is a misprint of the *Tristram Shandy* chapter number in the epigraph, referring to *Tristram Shandy*, CCLXXXIII, instead of 322 as Balzac had intended. The Vie réelle edition contains the same paratextual elements and the erroneous reference to *Tristram Shandy*, chapter CCLXXXIII instead of 322. It contains no preface or "Moralité." The edition by Ratier shows the same lack of paratextual elements as the earlier twentieth century editions: no epigraph, no reference to *Tristram Shandy*, 322, no snake, no dedication, nor any prefaces. It has one illustration depicting a Dance of Death scene with a skeleton and an hour glass. It is, however, the Martel edition that demonstrates the most interesting paratextual variations of the works published in 1946. It contains the "Avant-propos," a title page with a date, no epigraph, no snake, and no dedication. It does contain illustrations by Joseph Hémard. What is most interesting is that it is a precursor of the *Balzac publié dans un ordre nouveau*. A statement made by the editors in the preface meant to serve as justification for their decision to change the order of *La Comédie humaine* foreshadows Genette's own statment in *Seuils* regarding the tenuous hold of Balzac's organization a principle on *La Comédie humaine*. (See note 4.)

> Pour la première fois, les romans de Balzac seront présentées dans un ordre qui n'est pas l'ordre traditionnellement adopté et sous les divisions différentes des divisions habituelles, *Scènes de la Vie Privée, de la Vie de la Province, de la Vie Parisienne, de la Vie Militaire, de la Vie de Campagne*. Nous nous sentons dans l'obligation de défendre cette formule, dans ce qu'elle a d'apparemment sacrilège et de la justifier dans ce qu'elle a de nouveau. *La Comédie humaine* n'est pas, comme on pourrait le croire, une oeuvre majestueusement conçue une fois pour toutes, avec toutes ses divisions et toutes

ses perspectives, dans lesquelles sont venues se ranger successivement et à leur date des romans prévus d'avance.37

In 1947 there were two editions of *La Peau de chagrin*: one by Rasmussen and the other by Vautrain. The Rasmussen, like the paperback editions from the beginning of the twentieth century, contains no paratextual elements. The Vautrain contains the black wavy line, but omits the chapter number. It also retains the title *Roman philosophique*. A weak imitation of the 1838 edition, the cover is a copy of an illustration from the 1838 *Balzac illustré*.

In 1948, editions Gründ published *La Peau de chagrin* with the dedication first and the epigraph line below, indicating the Furne paratext. Sterne, *Tristram Shandy*, CCLXXIII replaces Balzac's own 322. There are a few black and white illustrations by Deslignères.

In 1950, Editions du Dauphin published a paperback version of *La Peau de chagrin* with the dedication first, followed by the epigraph. This time the epigraph line was a snake with a hissing tongue, and the volume contained no preface or "Moralité," thereby reproducing the inauthentic Houssiaux paratext. In 1951, Calmann-Lévy published yet another a reprint of the earlier edition containing the erroneous Houssiaux paratext. (Appendix D gives a paratextual overview of editions published from 1951 through 1970.) In 1952, an unusual edition of *La Peau de chagrin* appeared, published by Albert Guillot. It contained a strange paratextual blend of several editions. Published as the centenary edition of Balzac's illustrated works (Edition du centenaire des oeuvres complètes illustrées de Balzac), this work has illustrations by Raoul Serres. It is clearly part of an *Oeuvres complètes* edition and therefore part of the *Comédie humaine*. It bears the stacked title, *Etudes philosophiques*. However, it also contains the preface and the "Moralité" to the first edition. It does not, however, contain the epigraph nor the sentence, "Pauline riait et ses yeux étaient secs," which indicates an 1831 edition. It has the paratext of an early edition and the text of a later one and therefore is not a valid version of any particular edition published during Balzac's lifetime, being paratextually inaccurate. Although it contains the "Moralité" and the preface typical of the first edition, it does not contain the epigraph or the epigraph line to complete the authentic paratext. It belongs to the third category because it appeared on the centenial of the publication of Balzac's unsigned works in the *Oeuvres illustrées*.

It is during the 1950s that the great editions of Balzac's complete works were published. The Club des libraires de France published Balzac's 1838 edition of *La Peau de chagrin,* containing a preface by Béguin in which some of the paratextual problems in *La Peau de chagrin* are noted:

> Pour *La Peau de chagrin*, il se posait un problème de texte. Comme beaucoup de romans de Balzac, celui-ci a été considérablement remanié lors de ses éditions successives. On eut pu décider, comme on le fait communément, de redonner la dernière version établie par l'auteur, c'est-à-dire le texte de l'exemplaire de 1845 annoté par Balzac en vue d'une édition définitive de *La Comédie humaine*. On pouvait aussi préférer la version originale telle qu'elle était lorsqu'elle conquit à Balzac ses premiers admirateurs.

The work is a faithful reproduction of the 1838 edition, including the lithographs. It contains a reproduction of the cover of the 1838 edition in beautiful paper and includes the epigraph with the wavy line. The dedication, appearing only in the Furne edition, is appropriately absent. The editor affirms in the preface that a paratextual item sets this edition apart from the others.

> Il suffit de feuilleter la présente édition pour comprendre qu'il s'agit là d'un des chefs d'oeuvre de l'illustration romantique. Tant par la qualité des dessins que par l'excellence de la gravure, cette *Peau de chagrin* de 1838 surpasse tous les *Balzac illustrés* qui virent jamais le jour.[38]

The only difference between this edition and the original is that the lithographs appear at the end of the volume, enlarged and in a fold-out format. The implication in this preface is that *La Peau de chagrin* is a special work, because it represents the early stages of *La Comédie humaine*. In the preface Béguin refers to it as the "cellule-mère de *la Comédie humaine*." Because of its unusual position in the chronology of the writing of the *Comédie humaine*, every stage of its development marks the shifts and turns in Balzac's thought and conception of his works.

The 1950s saw another great edition of Balzac's works, the Club de l'Honnête homme edition, started in 1956 and completed in 1963. *La Peau de chagrin* appeared in the *Etudes philosophiques* as Volume 1 of this series, published in 1956. Published jointly by the Société des études balzaciennes and the Club de l'Honnête homme in 28 volumes, it appeared later in 24 volumes by the Club de l'Honnête homme alone. Since the work is an edition it collected Balzac's early prefaces and includes some of the lithographs of the 1838 edition, as well as its frontispiece. Offering as much information as possible, it is nevertheless confusing in its rendition of the paratext because the sinuous line resembles the earliest lines of the 1831 edition, while the 1838 lithographs recall the later edition. Although this edition's paratexts are faithful to neither the 1831 nor the 1838 edition, it is one of the more frequently cited editions of Balzac's works. (Bilodeau, in his work *Balzac et le Jeu des Mots* lists this edition of Balzac in his bibliography.[39]) Since this is a complete works edition, the Furne edition or the *Furne corrigé* should prevail. Illustrations from the 1838 edition do not belong in it except in an appendix or a critical introduction. In 1959, *La Peau de chagrin* appeared as the fourth volume of *La Comédie humaine* by Editions Rencontre. Instead of reproducing the text in the typical way, the editors opted to document the paratextual history of the novel on the reverse of the title page. The editors included the dedication to M. Savary and the epigraph with the sinuous line. This time, as in the original Furne edition, the snake is mottled in color, merely suggesting the reptile. It looks more like the line in the Charpentier edition than that of the Furne edition. What is important, however, is that there was an attempt to reproduce the paratextual elements with great care.

The 1950s saw a second work edited by Béguin et de Jean A. Ducourneau that challenged Balzac's organization of *La Comédie humaine*. *La Peau de chagrin* appeared in Volume 7 of the Club Français du livre de l'art edition of the *Oeuvres complètes publiées dans un ordre nouveau*. This later became the Club français du livre edition, published by Formes et reflets, containing sixteen volumes. The illustrations are mostly provided from the old Marescq, later Bureau du siècle and Lévy, editions of the *Oeuvres illustrées* published from Balzac's death until the 1870s. The illustrators listed are: Daumier, Bertall, Johannot, Monnier, Meissonier, Staal, Gavarin, Doré and Lampsonius, all from the Marescq edition. The division of this work into volumes is based on historical themes in the *Comédie humaine* rather than Balzac's divisions. *La Peau de chagrin* appears in the volume entitled *La Monarchie de Juillet* accompanied by *Le Curé de Village* and *Gambara*. The old prefaces are no longer included, but there is a new critical introduction by Michel Carrouges. Paratextual items include a title page with a sinuous line and the reference to *Tristram Shandy*. The line is clearly not a snake, however, indicating a choice to return to the first edition, pre-*Comédie humaine* paratext. There is one blank page which contains nothing except the dedication to Savary, a departure from Balzac's normal procedure. In 1955, Classiques Garnier reprinted the earlier 1933 edition of *La Peau de chagrin* with Maurice Allem's commentary.

The 1960s were characterized by an increased number and disparate quality of *La Peau de chagrin* renditions. The 1962 Le Monde en 10/18 edition of *La Peau de chagrin*, for example, has no dedication to Savary, no epigraph reference to Sterne's *Tristram Shandy*, nor preface. There is no "Moralité" nor is there an appendix with past prefaces or the "Avant-propos" to the *Comédie humaine*. Its complete inattention to paratext is similar to the Larousse and Flammarion editions of the early twentieth century. In 1966, Livre de Poche published *La Peau de chagrin* as a classical definitive edition, but its 1972 and 1984 editions are reprints of the text of 1831. In 1967 Garnier continued its commitment to republish Maurice Allem's edition of *La Peau de chagrin* separately from the *Comédie humaine*, maintaining a separate page for the title and epigraph, but placing the dedication at the back of the volume. In 1967 an interesting *La Peau de chagrin* edition which closely respected paratext was published by the Bibliophiles de l'Originale.[40] It documents Balzac's corrections to the 1845 Furne edition by including its text with Balzac's handwritten corrections. This could be considered merely another version of Lovenjoul's 1870 definitive edition, but I believe that the inclusion of the corrections represents a significantly different interpretation of Balzac's *Comédie humaine*, an interpretation based in part on paratext. The handwritten corrections draw attention to the paratextual differences between the 1845 Furne and its successor, the 1870 definitive edition, and highlights differences that otherwise would have gone unnoticed (e.g., the placement of the epigraph above the dedication in the Furne edition and Balzac's subsequent correction in the *Furne corrigé*). This edition also contains selected reproductions of some of the illustrations from both the 1838 and 1855 illustrated editions. Although it is understandable that editors wanted to include the beautiful illustrations from both editions, the practice results in an unfaithful paratextual rendition of a version which otherwise paid scrupulous attention to paratextual details. The following notice appears at the end of the volume. "Reproduit en fac-similé l'édition Furne de 1845 d'après l'exemplaire de Balzac, corrigé et annoté de sa main, conservé à Chantilly" (Now at the Bibliothèque de l'Institut). Genette discusses the treatment of the book's cover and spine in *Seuils*, and touches on the outside of the book as part of the paratext. The Bibliophiles de l'Originale edition is the only one to have meticulously observed paratextual documentation by including the binding. On describing the binding for the correction of the Furne edition the editors note: "La reliure identique à celle de l'exemplaire personnel de Balzac a été exécutée dans les ateliers d'André Piel, relieur à Paris." As far as I am able to determine, this is the only volume that made an attempt to reproduce the binding preferred by Balzac.

In 1968 the Club de l'Honnête homme republished *La Peau de chagrin* as part of *La Comédie humaine*.[41] In 1969 another edition of *La Peau de chagrin* appeared whose illustrations are credited to Jean Retailleau. They are not copies of the 1838 edition (although the last page of the volume indicates that Retailleau has seen the 1838 edition), because the lithograph on that page contains a Dance of Death theme. The 1969 edition of *La Peau de chagrin* by Editions G.P. indicates little paratextual awareness and contains neither prefaces nor "Moralité." The illustrations by Jean Retailleau suggest familiarity with the 1838 edition because the last page contains a

Dance of Death scene.[42] The 1960s also saw a Roland Chollet edition of *La Peau de chagrin* in his *Oeuvres complètes*, published by the Cercle du Bibliophile (1965-67) in 24 volumes, *La Peau de chagrin* being Volume 4. This appears to be another edition of Chollet's Editions Rencontres version of Balzac's works. Editions du Seuil published an edition of *La Peau de chagrin* in *La Comédie humaine* with a presentation and notes by Pierre Citron in 7 volumes, of which *La Peau de chagrin* was Volume 6.

The 1970s saw some innovations in publications of *La Peau de chagrin*. Garnier-Flammarion (in 1971) and Gallimard (in 1974) republished their standard editions. (See the Table, Appendix D.) Le Cercle du Bibliophile republished Chollet's *La Comédie humaine* in 37 volumes. The Club français du livre continued to publish an edition of *La Comédie humaine*. A stand-alone version of *La Peau de chagrin illustré* was published by the Société encyclopédique française in 1970. This work, a reprint of the 1838 edition and the Livre de poche reprint of the first edition, clearly indicate a renewed interest in documenting the paratextual history of the novel. The 1970s ushered in a period of keener editorial interest in paratext. In 1972 Livre de Poche republished the original August 1831 edition of *La Peau de chagrin* with a preface by Pierre Barbéris. Although this version claims to be a reprint of the 1831 edition, there is no other original paratextual accompaniment: no epigraph, no sinuous line representing the snake, although it does contain the "Moralité" of the first edition. The title indicates "Texte de l'édition originale 1831,"[43] apparently implying that the paratextual elements should be of lesser importance than the text of the original edition.

In 1973 Michel de L'Ormeraie published a rare version of the 1838 illustrated edition of *La Peau de chagrin*, which itself is a reproduction of an original alternate version published by Houdaille and Company. The editor spared no efforts to reproduce the original lithographs. As in the 1838 edition, the title page contains both the sinuous line and a reference to Sterne, and the cover looks exactly like that of the 1838 edition. Since this predates the seventh edition, there is no reference to Professor Savary. On the title page with the Dance of Death scene from the 1838 cover, the skeleton, plainly visible on the latter, is absent.[44] Talvart and Place state that a small number of the 1838 editions were published by Houdaille and Company which omits the skeleton on the title page.[45]

The Editions Rencontres edition of *La Peau de chagrin* during the 1970's was published in Geneva by the Edito-Service diffusion, Guilde du disque, 1978-79. Based on similar introductions and volume numbers (*La Peau de chagrin* is Volume 4 of the 37 volume edition), it is safe to say that the Guilde du Disque version is a later edition of the Editions Rencontres. Included in volume four of this edition are the following other works: *Jésus Christ en Flandre, Le Chef d'oeuvre inconnu, Le Réquisitionnaire, L'Auberge rouge, Les Proscrits, Maître Cornélius, Le Message, Madame Firmiani*. A note in the preface explains the editor's reason for including *La Peau de chagrin* with *Le Message* and *Madame Firmiani*, a departure from Balzac's wishes and editorial modification of the paratext.

> Les deux récits par lesquels se termine le présent volume, *Le Message* et *Madame Firmiani*, parurent six mois après *La Peau de chagrin*. Ils appartiennent à une série d'études de femmes . . . il nous convient de ne pas les dissocier.[46]

This edition, identifiable by the illustrations from the *Oeuvres complètes illustrées*, also bears a note on the back of the frontispiece. "Illustrations reproduites de la première édition illustrée des oeuvres complètes de Balzac réalisée en 1852 à Paris, par les Editions Marescq et Cie" (Frontispiece). Considering the liberties that the editor takes in rearranging the works, it could be categorized as a thematic reorganization of the *Comédie humaine*, part of the third group, like the editions Martel and the *Ordre nouveau* versions. This edition fails to include the picture on the first page of the Marescq version, and like the Marescq, omits the epigraph reference and line. There is, however, a reference to *Tristram Shandy* and Sterne at the end of the volume.

The 1980s have seen the preeminence of Gallimard's Pléiade editions of Balzac's *Comédie humaine*, with a new critical edition started in 1976 and concluded in 1981. In 1982 another annotated edition of *La Peau de chagrin* appeared, presented and annotated by Madeleine Ambrière Fargeaud and directed by Pierre-Georges Castex. This work contains the sinuous line, but it is the darker line of earlier editions, with the dedication to Savary from the *Comédie humaine*, a paratextual inconsistency. *La Peau de chagrin* appeared alone under that title in the August 1831, the 1838 *Balzac illustré*, and Charpentier editions, and each time without the dedication. In the others, Balzac had superimposed another title, *Romans et contes philosophiques* or *Etudes philosophiques*. The Savary dedication occurred in *La Peau de chagrin* only when it was incorporated into *La Comédie humaine*. The Ambrière Fargeaud edition chronicles the paratextual history of the novel in notes while supplying the reader with a sample of diverse paratextual elements from every version of the novel without differentiating among them. The edition includes pictures of the frontispiece of the Furne edition, the title page of the original August 1831 edition, and the 1838 title page. Unfortunately, the paratextual hodgepodge is not faithful to any particular edition, and though it is a fine chronicle of the historical paratext of the novel, the concept of paratextuality is neglected in reproducing too much information with little or no selectivity. The selection of title pages, however, provides some paratextual history.[47]

As late as the 1980s an occasional edition still appears with paratextual errors. One lesser known critical edition mixes paratextual accoutrements from two different editions. It includes the preface and chapter divisions of the first edition with the text of a later version, as we can verify by the absence of the sentence, "Pauline riait et ses yeux étaient secs." Errors like these prove the fragility of Balzac's authority over the paratext.

The paratextual history of *La Peau de chagrin*, in addition to revealing many things about the novel and the novelist's authority, also reveals much about the nineteenth and twentieth century attitudes concerning paratext. During Balzac's lifetime, his works' paratext and text were treated with equal care because of the author's active participation in the publishing process. After his death, liberties were taken with paratext and interpretations were boldly proposed with little desire to understand or reflect the author's intent. Consider the liberal interpretation of the Houssiaux edition, criticized by Lovenjoul and the *Oeuvres illustrées* by Marescq. In the early twentieth century we witness a total disregard for paratext as illustrated in the Flammarion and Larousse editions. During the third quarter of this century, we have seen a renewed interest in documenting the text and paratext of *La Peau de chagrin* concomitant to Gérard Genette's research. The reprints of the 1831 and 1838 editions, which attempt to copy their models with as much accuracy as possible, demonstrate and validate the new awareness of paratext's role in the historicity of the literary work by yielding to Balzac's authority over the paratext. The changing face of *La Peau de chagrin* continued its metamorphoses after Balzac's death. The most interesting, and perhaps the most reprinted edition, was the 1838 *Balzac illustré*. Through the years, there appears to have been more interest in it than in any other edition. A precedent for all the illustrated editions that followed Balzac's death, its numerous reprints prove its integrity as a valid alternative to the *Comédie humaine*. Renewed efforts during the last twenty years to duplicate the 1838 and 1831 original editions validate these other versions of the novel. The former's influence is indeed pervasive, since lithographs from the work reappear in reprints from the Furne edition to the present.

If we continue our analogy of paratext as the text's frame, perceiving and interpreting it is the first step that the reader takes when he suspends disbelief and enters the fictional world of the novel.[48] Perhaps the paratext is that part of the text's frame that provides the signals to the reader as to how and under what conditions he is to suspend disbelief. It is a spatial and artistic extension of the novelist's authority.

La Peau de chagrin is an ideal subject for this study because its paratext changed frequently during Balzac's lifetime. He enhanced its historical significance as his first signed novel by changing it to adopt whatever shape he wished it to assume as he added novels to the *Comédie humaine*. Since *La Peau de chagrin* appeared at the beginning of Balzac's career under his own name, and continued to change until it was incorporated into the Furne edition of *La Comédie humaine*, it chronicles these protean shifts and changes in the corpus of Balzac's works. Just as Proteus, when caught while making one of these changes, is forced to yield great truths about the future, *La Peau de chagrin*, when it is examined during its many metamorphoses, reveals great truths about Balzac and the nineteenth century novel.

There are more important conclusions to be drawn from this history than the obvious one, that the novel has several valid formats ranging from thematic to chronological.[49]

The paratextual history of *La Peau de chagrin* teaches valuable lessons concerning the meaning of time, history and textual boundaries.[50] It is a parable in which mimetic time struggles with history, and editorial authority challenges that of the novelist. In the post-Kantian era in which spatial movement implies time change, editorial changes in paratextual space move the text from the mimetic to the chronological time frame of History. In *La Comédie humaine*, Balzac eschews chronology to paint what he considers to be true History. When editors change the paratext, they challenge his authority over mimetic time and equate History with chronology.[51]

Since the editorial domain encompasses and dominates all other authority, Balzac's mimetic time and history are swept away by the editorial power of critical editions. In these editions, confusion of chronology with history destroys historicity. Through faithful reprints such as the Livre de Poche first edition, numerous reprints of the 1838 edition, and the Bibliophiles de l'Originale version, the historicity of the text may revive mimetic time and reinstate Balzac's particular vision of History.

In a larger sense the conflicting approach to the paratext is a microcosm of a larger debate on textual boundaries. Exactly where does the work of art end and reality begin? Ignoring paratext implies that the work of art starts with the first line of text only and that its frame is not part of the tableau. Faithful reproductions of the paratext imply that textual boundaries are blurred and affirm that the medium and frame are an integral part of all works of art.

Notes

¹The title of the article is "*Etudes philosophiques* de Honoré de Balzac (Edition Werdet), "*La Revue d'Histoire littéraire de la France* 14 (1907). This article examines the contract between Balzac and the Werdet publishers and treats many paratextual aspects of the *Etudes philosophiques*. Lovenjoul describes his thesis in the following words: "De toutes les bibliographies d'écrivains du XIXe siècle, la plus difficile à établir tout à fait exacte est sans contredire celle de Honoré de Balzac. Et, parmi ses innombrables volumes, ceux dont jusqu'ici l'état civil échappa le plus complètement peut-être aux indications minutieusement précises, ce sont ses *Etudes philosophiques*, ou du moins leur principale réunion avant l'apparition de *la Comédie humaine*, c'est-à-dire l'édition in dix-huit de ces *Etudes*" (393).

²Falconer states the following concerning these corrections: "Toujours est-il qu'à chaque réédition, on voit disparaître en quantité variable des jeux de mots ou de typographie, des noms et des adjectifs exotiques, des boutades et des paradoxes, bref tout un côté 'romantique flamboyant' du texte primitif" (73).

³I use this word advisedly, since the word frame is almost a generic one in narratology for spatial variation within the text.

⁴Carol Sherman, in one of the first articles on paratextuality, "The Deferral of Authority in *La Religieuse*," *Postscript: Publication of the Philological Society of the Carolinas*, 2 (1985), defines this debate as "the conflict between 'art as monolith' and 'anything made is art' " (58).

⁵In *Seuils* Gérard Genette places *La Comédie humaine* in a category by itself because of its loose unifying principle. He describes the subtitles

(what he calls "surtitres") in a statement to be cited later. (note 6) To support his contention, Genette cites the following editions: R. Chollet, ed., *Oeuvres de Balzac,* 37 vols. (Lausanne: Rencontres, 1958-62); A. Béguin and J. A. Ducourneau, eds., *l'Oeuvre de Balzac publiée dans un ordre nouveau,* 16 vols. (Paris: Formes et Reflets, 1949-55) [1949-53] and J. A. Ducourneau, ed., *Oeuvres complètes illustrées,* 25 vols. (Paris: Bibliophiles de l'Originale, 1965-76). (*Seuils* 59, note 1.)

6Gérard Genette, *Seuils* 59-60.

7Pierre Barbéris, "préface," *La Peau de chagrin* by Honoré de Balzac (1831; Paris: Livre de Poche, 1972) v.

8By "déhistoriser" Barbéris means to eliminate the chronological history of the novel by hiding the variations in notes. He was far removed from Julien Greimas' concepts of "histoire événementielle" and "histoire fondamentale." See Algirdas Julien Greimas, "Sur l'histoire événementielle et l'histoire fondamentale," in *Geschichte—Ereignis und Erzählung,* eds. R. Koselleck und W.D. Stempel, *Poetik und Hermeneutik,* 5 (München, 1973) 139-53; See the analysis of these concepts in Manfred Naumann's article "L'événement littéraire et l'histoire littéraire," in *Proceedings of the Xth Congress of the International Comparative Literature Association,* Anna Balakian and James Wilhelm, eds. (New York: Garland P, 1982) 27-33.

9Honoré de Balzac, *La Peau de chagrin,* 2 vols. (Paris: Gosselin et Canel, 1831).

10Honoré de Balzac, *Romans et contes philosophiques,* 3 vols. (Paris: Gosselin, 1831). *La Peau de chagrin* occupied only the first two volumes. Graham Falconer 77-80, has documented the stylistic changes in the second edition.

11Genette would call this a "surtitre."

12Honoré de Balzac, *Romans et contes philosophiques,* 4 vols. (Paris: Gosselin, 1833). Lovenjoul, in *Histoire des Oeuvres de Honoré de Balzac,* gives an inventory of the works contained in this edition: Vols. 1 and 2 contained the "Préface," the "Moralité" and *La Peau de chagrin* ; Vol. 3 contained *Sarrasine, La Comédie du diable, L'Enfant Maudit* (première partie), *El Verdugo,* et *Etude de femme*; Vol. 4 contained *L'Elixir de longue vie, Les Proscrits, Le Chef-d'oeuvre inconnu* (*Gillette*), *Le Réquisitionnaire, Les Deux Rêves* (*Le Petit Souper*), *Jésus Christ en Flandre, L'Eglise.*

13See Honoré de Balzac, *Etudes philosophiques,* 5 vols. (Paris: Werdet, 1835-1837). The "Préface" and the "Moralité" were expunged from this edition in favor of an "Etude" by Felix Davin. It was advertised to include 30 volumes, but only 20 appeared. Lovenjoul *Histoire des Oeuvres de Honoré de Balzac,* 163-64, note 1.

14Honoré de Balzac, *Balzac illustré, Etudes sociales, La Peau de chagrin* (Paris: Delloye et Lecou, 1838).

15See Hector Talvart and Joseph Place, *Bibliographie des Auteurs Modernes de langue française,* 22 vols. (Paris: Editions de la Chronique des lettres françaises, 1928) 1: 149.

16Honoré de Balzac, *La Peau de chagrin* (Paris: Charpentier, 1839).

17Honoré de Balzac, *La Peau de chagrin* in *La Comédie humaine,* 17 vols. (Paris: Furne, 1845) vol. 14. This is where *La Peau de chagrin* entered *La Comédie humaine* for the first time.

18See Honoré de Balzac, *La Comédie humaine,* 26 vols. (1869-76; Paris: Levy, 1924). It was reduced to 24 volumes in 1924.

19Balzac's corrected copy of the Furne edition is in the Lovenjoul collection at the Bibliothèque de l'Institut in Paris. Lovenjoul ms. A 30.

[20]Honoré de Balzac, *La Peau de chagrin* in *Oeuvres illustrées* de Balzac, 10 vols. (Paris: Marescq et Cie, 1852) vol. 5.

[21]The Bibliography of the Gallimard edition of the *Comédie humaine* refers to this edition. It deserves more attention because of its interesting format. See the bibliography in *La Comédie humaine*, 11 vols. (Paris: Gallimard, 1965) 11: 1121.

[22]See Mauricette Berne and Jean-Yves Mollier, *Une Aventure d'éditeurs au XIXe Siècle* (Paris: Bibliothèque nationale, 1986) 10.

[23]Honoré de Balzac, *La Peau de chagrin* in *Oeuvres de Balzac illustrées* (Paris: S. Lejay, 1873). OCLC has a listing for this work published by Lévy during the years 1879-85. The work was alternately referred to as *La Peau de chagrin* or *Etudes philosophiques*.

[24]See Spoelberch de Lovenjoul's "*Les Etudes philosophiques* de Honoré de Balzac," 393-441. See also, Honoré de Balzac, *Oeuvres complètes*, 20 vols. (Paris: Houssiaux, 1853-55) vol. 14.

[25]Honoré de Balzac, *La Peau de chagrin* 2 vols. (Paris: Flammarion, 1901).

[26]Honoré de Balzac, *La Peau de chagrin* (1909; Paris: Larousse, 1930).

[27]Honoré de Balzac, *La Peau de chagrin* (Paris: Crès et Cie, 1923).

[28]Honoré de Balzac, *Oeuvres Complètes,* 40 vols. (Paris: Conard, 1912-40) vol. 27.

[29]Martin Kanes, *Balzac's Comedy of Words* (Princeton: Princeton UP, 1975) 11.

30Honoré de Balzac, *La Peau de chagrin* (Paris: Jules Tallandier, 1928).

31Honoré de Balzac, *La Peau de chagrin,* ed. Maurice Allem (Paris: Garnier, 1965).

32Honoré de Balzac, *La Peau de chagrin,* ed. Maurice Allem (Paris: Garnier, 1967).

33Honoré de Balzac, *La Peau de chagrin, La Comédie humaine,* ed. Marcel Bouteron, 10 vols. (Paris: Gallimard, 1937) vol. 9.

34Honoré de Balzac, *La Peau de chagrin* (Paris: Henri Béziat, 1936).

35Honoré de Balzac, *La Peau de chagrin* (Paris: Corbeil, 1942).

36Honoré de Balzac, *La Peau de chagrin* (Paris: La Nouvelle France, 1943).

37Georges Eudes, "préface," *Louis Lambert, La Peau de chagrin* (Paris: Martel, 1946)1: iii-iv.

38"Préface", *La Peau de chagrin* (Paris: Club des libraires de France, 1956).

39François Bilodeau, *Balzac et le Jeu des Mots* (Montréal: Presses de l'Université de Montréal, 1971).

40Honoré de Balzac, *La Peau de chagrin , Oeuvres complètes illustrées,* 25 vols. (Paris: Bibliophiles de l'Originale, 1967) vol. 14.

41Honoré de Balzac, *La Peau de chagrin. La Comédie humaine,* 24 vols. (Paris: Club de l'Honnête homme, 1968-71) vol. 18. This was published in 1956-63 by Le Prat in 28 volumes.

42Honoré de Balzac, *La Peau de chagrin* (Paris: G.P. 1969).

43Honoré de Balzac, *La Peau de chagrin* (1831; Paris: Livre de Poche, 1984).

44Honoré de Balzac, *La Peau de chagrin* (1838; Paris: Club des Libraires de France, 1973).

45Hector Talvart and Joseph Place, *Bibliographie des auteurs modernes de langue française,* 22 vols. (Paris: Editions de la Chronique des lettres françaises , 1928) 1: 149.

46Raymond Chollet, Préface, *Oeuvres de Balzac,* 37 vols. (Genève: Editions Rencontre, 1978-79) 4: 11-32; 32, note 1.

47Honoré de Balzac, *La Peau de chagrin*, ed. Madeleine Ambrière Fargeaud (Paris: Imprimerie Nationale, 1982).

48In *Dynamics of Literary Response* (New York: Oxford UP, 1968), in a comment on A.R. Gurney Jr.'s *The Rape of Bunny Stuntz*, Norman Holland says the following concerning the line of demarcation between reality and the work of art: "Literary or artistic experience comes to us marked off from the rest of our experiences in reality. We frame the picture, house it in a museum, surround it with 'Do not Touch' signs. Poems and cartoons are printed in such a way that we immediately recognize them as different and separate. Plays happen in special places--I remember one theater where you had to cross water (a moat) to enter that half-magic world. Short stories and novels are usually labeled as such--certainly a sentence or two tells us we are dealing with fiction, not truth" (70). Paratext as frame of the text provides similar signals concerning *La Peau de chagrin*.

49Genette mentions this (59, note 1).

50Carol Sherman, in the process of making several points about authority in "The Deferral of Textual Authority in *La Religieuse*" 59, states that talk of "textual identity, textual boundaries, coherence, and unity " are part of an "art as monolith" argument in a debate against the proponents of "anything made is art." In many respects this is a pioneer work on paratextuality. For a study devoted to one aspect of paratextuality, prefaces from the Middle Ages to the present, see Catherine Jones West, "La Mise en Jeu de l'autorité dans la Préface de Roman" diss. U of North Carolina, 1989.

[51]Carol Sherman writes the following concerning the editor's domain in "Changing Spaces," in *Diderot: Digression and Dispersion: a Bicentennial tribute*, eds. Jack Undank and Herbert Josephs (Lexington: French Forum, 1984): "the passage to an editor's domain . . . projects a new frame encompassing and dominating retrospectively the authority of all the others" (221).

Chapter Three
Balzac's *Tristram Shandy*, 322: Sterne and *La Peau de chagrin*

"C'est la seule épigraphe de *La Comédie humaine* où subsistent à la fois critique et mystification."[1]

Laurence Sterne rode the wave of Anglomania in France from the beginning of the eighteenth into the beginning of the nineteenth century.[2] His popularity is evident from the number of editions published of *A Sentimental Journey*, the most popular of Sterne's works during this period.[3] Francis Brown Barton analyses Sterne's success as follows:

> La manière sternesque de sentir et d'écrire eut beaucoup d'imitateurs et fut adaptée aux divers genres littéraires: poésie, roman, satire, pièces de théâtre. On peut citer, parmi les écrivains qui sentirent l'influence de Sterne, les noms illustres de Diderot, Xavier de Maistre, Charles Nodier, Victor Hugo, Théophile Gautier. (Barton 11)

If Dr. Barton had continued her research on Sterne's influence on French writers during the nineteenth century, Balzac's name certainly would have joined the illustrious list. Although all annotated editions of *La Peau de chagrin* mention Sterne's influence on Balzac, the last ten years have seen relatively few studies on the subject. Of these the most notable are Sandra Soares Donnelly's dissertation, "Balzac and Sterne," and Michael Tilby's excellent article, "A partir d'une allusion à Sterne dans *La Peau de chagrin.*"[4]

Fernand Lotte lists four references to Sterne in *La Peau de chagrin*,[5] one of which is a reference to one of Balzac's favorite painters, Gerard Dow. "L'inconnu suivit son conducteur et parvint à une quatrième galerie où successivement passèrent dans ses yeux fatigués plusieurs tableaux un Gérard Dow qui ressemblait à une page de Sterne . . ." (10: 73-74). Dow's painting *Le Peseur d'or* has been suggested as the model for the "antiquaire" in *La Peau de chagrin*,[6] and the following passage offers conclusive evidence of this assumption. "Son large front ridé, ses joues blêmes et creuses, la rigueur implacable de ses petits yeux verts dénués de cils et de sourcils, pouvaient faire croire à l'inconnu que le *Peseur d'Or* de Gérard Dow était sorti de son cadre" (10: 78). The description of Planchette contains another reference to Sterne that directs the reader to Sterne's views on sex and celibacy.

> Ce bonhomme ressemblait à Sancho Pança racontant à Don Quichotte l'histoire des chèvres, il s'amusait à compter des animaux et les numéroter. Arrivé sur le bord de la tombe, il connaissait à peine une petite fraction des incommensurables nombres du grand troupeau jeté par Dieu à travers l'océan des mondes, dans un but ignoré. Raphaël était content. "Je vais tenir mon âne en bride," s'écriait-il. Sterne avait dit avant lui: "Ménageons notre âne, si nous voulons vivre vieux." (10: 242)

In *Tristram Shandy*, there is a particular meaning for the lowly ass. Walter Shandy used the word to refer to sexual desire. The following passage from the French translation of *Tristram Shandy* bears the title, "L'Ane et le califourchon."

> De tout ce que pouvait dire mon père, si quelque chose était capable de désoler mon oncle Tobie (surtout pendant la durée de ses amours), c'était l'usage continuel et perfide que faisait mon père d'une expression qu'il employait tous ces moyens

pour empêcher son âne de régimber; voulant dire, pour réprimer l'aiguillon de la chair.

Mon père était enchanté de cette expression, non pas seulement à cause de son laconisme, mais parce qu'elle ravalait les désirs et les appétits de la partie de nous-mêmes la plus grossière.[7]

Sterne's original version of the passage is almost the same.

If anything in this world, which my father said, could have provoked my uncle Toby, during the time he was in love, it was the perverse use my father was always making of an expression of Hilarion the hermit; who, in speaking of his abstinence, his watchings, flagellations, and their instrumental parts of his religion—would say—tho' with more facetiousness than became a hermit—"That they were the means he used, to make his ass (meaning his body) leave off kicking."

It pleased my father well; it was not only a laconic way of expressing—but of libelling, at the same time, the desires and appetites of the lower part of us. . . . [8]

The vitalist philosophy implied in this chapter, that phenomena are partly controlled by mechanical forces and that they are in some measure self-determining, is certainly replayed in the story of Raphaël's life, shortened with every desire that he expresses. Although Lotte's "Index" and studies on foreign influences have been of great value to Balzac scholars, recent criticism and research reveal that the question of Balzac's references to Sterne is more complex than had been thought.

Presence, Absence, and Imposture

When absence is conspicuous it becomes presence. In *Tristram Shandy*

Sterne uses a series of asterisks to indicate a lacuna in the text: sometimes as a substitute for dialogue, sometimes to suggest that a scatological passage should replace the lacuna. At times Sterne goes so far as to indicate a chapter number with no text, such as Chapters XVII and XIX of Volume IX of the James A. Work edition of *Tristram Shandy*. In the August 1831 edition of *La Peau de chagrin*, Balzac also introduces a lacuna into the text. Instead of using asterisks as Sterne does, he uses suspension points in the manner of his translator, Frenais.

Enfin, ne pouvant bientôt plus former de sons, il mordit Pauline.
....
....
....
....
....9

The use of these typographical devices to convey lacunae in the text is eliminated in subsequent editions such as the *Etudes philosophiques*, and Balzac's correspondence suggests no apparent reason for the elimination of the Sterne-like experiments.

One of the references to Sterne, recently proven to be false, is particularly interesting. Lotte's "Index des personnes réelles et des allusions littéraires" refers to the following passage as one of the four references to Sterne in *La Peau de chagrin* (41).

> Devant ce laconisme parisien, les drames, les romans, tout pâlit, même ce vieux frontispiece: *Les lamentations du glorieux roi de Kaërnavan, mis en prison par ses enfants* ; dernier fragment d'un livre perdu, dont la seule lecture faisait pleurer ce Sterne, qui lui-même délaissait sa femme et ses enfants. (10: 65)

In his article, "A partir d'une allusion à Sterne dans *La Peau de chagrin*," Michael Tilby reveals that this reference is not to Sterne at all, but to

Les Mémoires de Sterne, an apocryphal work by Richard Griffith which was included in the translation of Sterne's *Oeuvres complètes*, published in 1818.[10] According to Tilby, who documents the success of the hoax, Balzac was but one of many who failed to question the authenticity of *Les Mémoires de Sterne*, along with Nodier, Janin, Philarète Chasles, Poe, even Goethe.[11] Critics who accepted the bogus work as authentic Sterne include A. Hédouin, *Sterne inédit Le Koran. Oeuvres posthumes complètes* (Paris: Librairie nouvelle, 1853); A. Prioult, *Balzac avant La Comédie humaine* (Paris: Courville, 1936); R. Chollet, "Une heure de ma vie, ou Lord R'Hoone à la découverte de Balzac," *L'Année balzacienne* (1968); and René Guise's notes in the 1976-81 Pléiade edition of the *Comédie humaine* (Tilby 251). Tilby concludes that although there is no question of Sterne's influence on Balzac, Balzac's idea of Sterne was based, in part at least, on an unauthentic work.

In this study, we shall not venture beyond the "threshold" of *La Peau de chagrin*, focusing on two paratextual items which occur together: the epigraph which includes the reference to Sterne's *Tristram Shandy*, CCCXXII; and the sinuous line that some editors have interpreted as a snake.[12] From the wealth of Sternean references in *La Peau de chagrin* we shall select only one, the epigraph reference to Sterne. A study of the epigraph will permit us to do what might be considered daring in comparatist studies: establish the precise source edition of *Tristram Shandy* that Balzac used when he wrote *La Peau de chagrin*. This is more than René Guise hoped for in 1970 when he wrote "Balzac et l'étranger" for *L'Année balzacienne*, urging Balzac scholars to attempt more studies of foreign sources to the *Comédie humaine* and to think more in terms of "emprunt possible" rather than "source" (12-14).

Snake or Stick?

The epigraph is the first reference to Sterne listed in Lotte's "Index des Personnes réelles et des allusions littéraires de *La Comédie humaine* " (41). The last thing seen by the reader before entering the world of *La Peau de chagrin* is Sterne's name with Chapter 322 of *Tristram Shandy* in Roman numerals next to the title. Above the epigraph lay the mysterious sinuous line, suggesting a serpent.[13] In *Tristram Shandy* the line is more vertical than horizontal, and dark with no details. In the August 1831 edition of *La Peau de chagrin*, the sinuous epigraph line is also dark, and similar in shape to the one in *Tristram Shandy*, the only difference being that the line is more horizontal than vertical. An examination of the epigraph lines of each of the editions of *La Peau de chagrin* published in Paris during Balzac's lifetime reveals that the epigraph line in the Charpentier edition of 1839 suggests a snake and is no longer completely black. While its mottled color implies the texture of snake scales, the line has no head or other details that would suggest a snake. In his article, "*Les Etudes philosophiques* de Honoré de Balzac," Charles de Lovenjoul reproduced the epigraph line of the editions published during Balzac's lifetime (408-09). His reproduction of the Charpentier epigraph reveals the same mottled coloration visible in the original, thereby discounting any argument that the 1839 epigraph line was mottled because of uneven fading with age.

Sterne's name in the right-hand corner of the August 1831 edition and the reference to chapter 322 of Sterne's *Tristram Shandy* have provided a mystery that Balzac scholars have avoided or failed to notice. The most obvious anomaly concerning the reference to Chapter 322 is that there is no Chapter 322 in *Tristram Shandy*. The chapter containing the sinuous line occurs instead in Volume IX, Chapter IV of Sterne's novel. If continuous chapter numbers were used, the number would be 282. The episode to which the epigraph refers relates a discussion among corporal Trim, uncle Toby, and Tristram's father, about the merits of marriage and celibacy. At the end of the discussion, Trim uses his baton to sketch a line in the air.

> Monsieur connaît, répliqua le caporal, les malheurs de Tom; mais ceci n'a aucun rapport, sinon que le pauvre Tom n'avait pas épousé la veuve; ou si Dieu eût permis qu'après leur mariage ils n'eussent mis dans leurs saucisses que de la chair de porc, le malheureux n'aurait pas été enlevé dans son lit et traîné à l'inquisition.—C'est une épouvantable chose que l'inquisition, ajouta le caporal; quand une fois un pauvre

homme y est renfermé, monsieur sait bien que c'est pour sa vie.

(Toby says)—Et qu'y a-t-il d'aussi doux que la liberté? Rien au monde, Trim.

Tant qu'un homme est libre, s'écria le caporal. En même temps il fit avec son bâton, le moulinet par dessus sa tête à peu près de cette manière.14

Your honor, replied the Corporal, knows of Tom's misfortunes; but this affair has nothing to do with them any further than this, that if *Tom* had not married the widow—or had it pleased God after their marriage, that they had but put pork into their sausages, the honest soul had never been taken out of his warm bed, and dragg'd to the inquisition—'Tis a cursed place—added the Corporal, shaking his head,—when once a poor creature is in, he is in, an' please your honour, for ever.

'Tis very true; said my uncle *Toby* looking gravely at Mrs. *Wadman's* house, as he spoke. Nothing, continued the Corporal, can be so sad as confinement for life—or so sweet, an' please your honour, as liberty.
Nothing, Trim—said my uncle *Toby*, musing—Whilst a man is free—cried the Corporal, giving a flourish with his stick thus—
(At this point the sinuous line appears.)
A thousand of my father's most subtle syllogisms could not have said more for celibacy.15

The sinuous line in *Tristram Shandy* is the motion of corporal Trim's baton, the significance of which is never completely explained. The implication of the episode, taken as a whole, is that man is a prisoner of his sexual desires and that celibacy is liberating. The chapter has nothing whatsoever to do with snakes. In his study of the evolution of the epigraph line in *"Les Etudes philosophiques* de Honoré de Balzac," Charles Spoelberch de Lovenjoul claims that the editor of the 1853-55 Houssiaux edition turned the line into an elaborately detailed snake because he thought it had something to do with the talisman (408-09). Some editors have interpreted the line as a snake after reading allusions made by Félix Davin in his "Introduction" to the *Etudes philosophiques*.

> L'effet produit par le désir, la passion, sur le capital des forces humaines, n'y est-il pas magnifiquement accusé? De là cette morale que peignait si énergiquement le caporal Trim, par le moulinet qu'il trace en l'air avec son bâton et dont M. de Balzac a fait une épigraphe si mal comprise par la plupart des lecteurs. Peu de personnes ont vu qu'après un tel arrêt porté sur notre organisation il n'y avait d'autres ressources, pour la généralité des hommes, que de se laisser aller à l'allure *serpentine* de la vie, aux ondulations bizarres de la destinée.[16]

Because Félix Davin only represented what Balzac approved for publication and was considered Balzac's "porte parole," it is appropriate to posit two fundamental assumptions: that this was also Balzac's interpretation; and (since the preface's date is 1834, preceding the publication of the Charpentier edition of 1839) that the editor of the Houssiaux edition read the preface to the *Etudes philosophiques*, examined the Charpentier edition closely, then transformed the line according to Davin's "Introduction." This is but one facet of the mysterious epigraph to *La Peau de chagrin*.

The Critical Reaction: Inconsistency and Indifference

Critics have debated sporadically and halfheartedly which French translation of Sterne's works inspired Balzac's *Comédie humaine*. The majority do concur in one respect: that Balzac made an error and that he should not have called the epigraph that he wrote *Tristram Shandy*, 322, but 312. This is puzzling because the correct reference should be to Book IX, Chapter IV, which is the correct chapter number listed in the English editions. Although this assertion appears in many critical editions, chapter numbers are never cited to support the contention.

On the identification of the correct source edition of *Tristram Shandy*, the critics contradict each other, and in some cases, themselves. The inconsistencies, too flaccid to be called controversies, slide along almost imperceptibly. A. Prioult believed that Balzac used the six-volume 1818 edition as his source.[17] René Guise proposed the 1825 edition of Sterne in his notes on the *Physiologie du Mariage,* and then hedged his bets by citing the 1818 edition elsewhere in the same volume of the *Comédie humaine*.[18] Sandra Suares Donnelly claimed that Balzac used the 1803 edition of Sterne's complete works (29-31). Michael Tilby opts for the 1818 edition in four volumes. It was Tilby's contention that the verification of the correct source of Sterne's complete works could be traced through a bogus work included in the 1818 edition. The work in question is entitled *Les Mémoires de Sterne* by Richard Griffith. Tilby also attached importance to the fact that the author of the *Mémoires de Sterne* was Griffet de la Baume. Tilby is closer to the truth than his predecessors, but he made some errors in arriving at his conclusion.

One can conclude that until now, the salient issue concerning the epigraph has been Balzac's error in citing chapter 322 of *Tristram Shandy* and the history of the evolution of the sinuous line, treated by Lovenjoul in his article, "*Les Etudes philosophiques*." Another reason for the apparent lack of interest in the Sterne epigraph is that *A Sentimental Journey*, the most popular of Sterne's works that influenced Balzac, appeared in so many translations that it would have been difficult for critics to identify the correct source edition (Martin, Mylne, and Frautschi 143). None of these editions has revealed why several critics have concurred in the contention that Balzac meant Chapter 312 instead of 322.

The Search for *Tristram Shandy*, 322

It is surprising that the critics have not considered the obvious in explaining the mystery of *Tristram Shandy*, 322, i.e., that Balzac did not make an error in his epigraph. It seems reasonable to assume that he would have corrected the chapter number in subsequent editions had an error been made. Further evidence that the chapter number is correct is found in Lovenjoul's *Histoire des Oeuvres de Balzac*, where it is specifically mentioned in a promotional article by Balzac, signed with the pseudonym Alexandre de B. (167-8). In the same volume, we find that Charles de Bernard also referred to Chapter 322 of *Tristram Shandy* in an article on *La Peau de chagrin* in *La Gazette de La Franche-Comté*, 13 août 1831 (Spoelberch de Lovenjoul 354). With numerous opportunities to correct the chapter reference, neither Balzac nor Charles de Bernard saw fit to do so. The existence of two promotional articles is strong evidence that Balzac saw an edition in French of *Tristram Shandy* with the chapter including the sinuous line numbered 322.

A survey of the French translations of Sterne in the late eighteenth and early nineteenth centuries reveals part of the answer to the mystery of *Tristram Shandy*, 322. According to Martin, Mylne, and Frautschi, the first half of the novel was translated in two volumes by Joseph-Pierre Frenais in 1776 (203). His translation did not receive favorable reviews from his contemporaries, primarily because Frenais was not faithful to Sterne's original work. He inserted his own literary views into his unfinished translation, an action which inspired outrage and ridicule among his contemporaries (Barton 12). Nine years later, the marquis Charles-François de Bonnay published his own translation of the last half of *Tristram Shandy*, entitled *Suite de la Vie et des Opinions de Tristram Shandy*. Together, they became *La Vie et les Opinions de Tristram Shandy,* 4 vols. (York and Paris: Ruault, Volland; 1776-1785). In 1785 Griffet de la Baume completed another French version, entitled *Suite et fin de la vie et des opinions de Tristram Shandy, suivies de mélanges, lettres, pensées, bons-mots, et mémoires, traduits de l'anglais de Sterne par M.D.L.B*. The Frenais translation and the Griffet de la Baume version together became *La Vie et les Opinions de Tristram Shandy,* 4 vols. (Paris: Bibliothèque de la Rue Richelieu, 1776-1785). Although Griffet de la Baume's translation was more accurate, it was de Bonnay's version of the last half of *Tristram Shandy* that was most often published to complete Frenais' first half of Sterne's work. This translation is frequently cited when critics discuss French versions of Sterne.

Another edition of Sterne's *Oeuvres complètes* appeared in 1803, described by Quérard as "incorrect."[19] It contained the following works by Sterne: *Les Opinions de Tristram Shandy*; *Le Voyage sentimental*, *Les lettres de Sterne à Eliza*; *Seize Sermons*; *Lettres de l'auteur*; and *Pensées et des Anecdotes*. This 1803 edition also contains the bogus *Mémoires de Sterne*, a work which Tilby implies did not appear until the 1818 edition of Sterne's works.[20] Conclusive proof that Balzac could not have used the 1803 edition when he wrote *La Peau de chagrin* is in the epigraph. There is no chapter 322 or 312 in any of the six volumes. Clearly Frenais and de Bonnay changed the numbering and placement of the chapters and added their own titles, as chapter numbers begin anew in each separate volume.

In 1818, Ledoux and Tenré published two different versions of *Les Oeuvres complètes de Sterne*: a second edition of the complete works in six volumes, with the de Bonnay conclusion to *Tristram Shandy*; and an edition in four volumes with the Griffet de la Baume translation of the last half of the novel. Prioult believed that the six-volume edition was the one used by Balzac, basing his contention on the accessibility of this edition to the author.[21] Prioult did not consider the epigraph when he made his claim. Chapter 322 of the 1818 four-volume edition contains the sinuous line and the debate between Toby and Trim concerning celibacy. Because no other preceding edition of *Tristram Shandy* contains the sinuous line in chapter 322, it appears that the 1818 four-volume edition is the first possible source for *La Peau de chagrin*, strongly suggesting that Balzac was not in error when he made the reference to *Tristram Shandy*, 322.

The last edition of Sterne that predates *La Peau de chagrin* is the *Oeuvres de Sterne*, published by Salmon in 1825. Here, the famous chapter 322 also contains the sinuous line. Indeed, as Michael Tilby indicated in "A partir d'une allusion à Sterne dans *La Peau de chagrin*," René Guise cites this edition in his notes on the *Physiologie de mariage*.

Identification of the correct source of *Tristram Shandy* depends ultimately upon the criteria applied to analyse the numerous French editions of Laurence Sterne's works. Information uncovered by previous scholars provides important criteria that, when compiled and applied to the identification of the correct edition, reveal the answers to the questions surrounding *Tristram Shandy*, 322.

The first criterion to be applied is primairily chronological; *Tristram Shandy* must be part of a complete works edition published before Balzac's youthful works refer to Sterne. All partial editions of *Tristram Shandy*, then, may be eliminated from consideration because the wealth of Sternean references in *La Comédie humaine* implies that Balzac used an edition of Sterne's complete works (Donnelly 16). This eliminates all versions appearing before 1800. Since Balzac's early writings show Sterne's influence, the latest date for a plausible source is between 1820 and 1822. The plethora of references to Sterne in Balzac's unsigned works proves that the 1825 edition appeared too late to influence Balzac. Therefore, using chronological criteria, we have eliminated the editions of 1785 and 1825.

An additional criterion which serves to narrow the possible French sources is the requirement that the edition contain *Les Mémoires de Sterne*, the spurious work written by Richard Griffith. Michael Tilby has studied the passage in *La Peau de chagrin* that refers to the *Mémoires de Sterne* and posits that Balzac used the 1818 four-volume edition of Sterne's complete works. Although he is correct, Tilby implies that the *Mémoires de Sterne* are in some way a satisfactory criterion by which to determine Balzac's French source of Sterne's works. He also states that Griffet de la Baume was the translator of the *Mémoires de Sterne*, the implication being that this work proves that the 1818 four-volume edition of Sterne's complete works was the correct French source for Balzac's translation of Sterne. Griffet de la Baume was most likely the translator of the *Mémoires de Sterne* because this work is listed in Griffet de la Baume's translation of the last half of *Tristram Shandy*, published in London in 1785 (Martin, Mylne and Frautschi 283). The spurious work, however, is not a good criterion alone to determine the correct source edition because the *Mémoires de Sterne* appeared in four other editions of Sterne's complete works. Nevertheless, if the *Mémoires de Sterne* and the chronological criteria are applied together toward the identification of the correct source, the following editions appear as possible sources of Sterne: 1803, Bastien; 1818, Ledoux et Tenré in four volumes; 1818, Ledoux and Tenré in six volumes. It is only when the epigraph reference to *Tristram Shandy*, 322 is included in the criteria that the correct edition becomes apparent. There is only one edition that meets all the above criteria and at the same time contains chapter 322 with the sinuous line and the discussion on celibacy, that of 1818 in four volumes.

One possible explanation for the consensus among the critics, that Balzac erroneously cited *Tristram Shandy*, 322, instead of 312, is that the corresponding chapter in the 1818 edition in six volumes is numbered 112 of the third volume.[22] Critics who saw only the four-volume edition of Sterne's *Complete Works* would logically conclude that this chapter was number 312 in the edition and that Balzac had misread the number. In view of the availability of the six-volume edition and the rarity of the four-volume edition, such an error is understandable.

Identification of the correct French edition of Sterne makes one thing clear: it does not suffice to say that Sterne influenced Balzac. The assimilation process was far more complicated than would appear. French translations of Sterne inspired Balzac and simultaneously acted as screens to conceal the real Sterne from Balzac. The first part of *Tristram Shandy* is a poor translation. Sandra Donnelly devotes a chapter of her dissertation to Frenais' rendition of *Tristram Shandy*, which she calls a "distortion" of Sterne's style (66). She ascribes this "distortion" to the inadequate translator's "cuts, additions, inflated prose, and exaggerations of Sterne's stylistic idiosyncrasies" (66). For example, many of Sterne's typographical devices were missing in the Frenais translation. In the first part of *Tristram Shandy*, Frenais substituted suspension points for what in Sterne's work were asterisks, thus falsifying Sterne's use of these devices (Donnelly 61). It is the translator's typographic device that Balzac imitated in the first edition of 1831, not Sterne's: he used suspension points in the manner of Frenais. Griffet de la Baume's translation, on the other hand, was more faithful to Sterne, and introduced Balzac to the more subtle aspects of Sterne's style. It is more accurate to state that the discovery of Balzac's *Tristram Shandy*, 322 reveals the three "Sternes" who inspired Balzac: Frenais' caricature of Sterne in the first half of *Tristram Shandy*, Griffet de la Baume's more faithful rendition of Sterne in the last half of the translation, and the real Sterne behind the translator's screen.

Readers and critics often look beyond the paratext into the text for the answers to their questions, never stopping on the novel's "threshold" to receive what guidance the author and editors provide to ensure a proper reading. Yet, it is only from the Genettean "threshold" of *La Peau de chagrin* that we may clearly see the sources for what lies within the text. Identifying the correct edition that Balzac used while he was composing the first novels to be included in the *Comédie humaine* is important to historians of literature because it provides important information about Balzac's interpretation of Sterne. Balzac's idea of Sterne was distorted by Frenais' poor translation and his inclusion of bogus works. His conception of the last part of *Tristram Shandy,* on the other hand, was closer to the real Sterne, primarily because Griffet de la Baume was more literary and took fewer liberties with his translation. Every author, when inspired by another, assimilates what has been read by a process of selection and rejection, and as we have seen, knowing precisely which of Sterne's editions was used by Balzac helps us to understand how the French novelist grafted Sterne's works onto *La Comédie humaine.*

Notes

[1] Lucienne Frappier-Mazur, "Parodie, imitation et circularité: les épigraphes dans les romans de Balzac," *Le Roman de Balzac: recherches critiques, méthodes, lectures,* eds. Roland Le Huenen and Paul Perron (Montreal: Didier, 1980) 85.

[2] Francis Brown Barton, *Etude sur l'influence de Laurence Sterne en France au dix-huitième siècle* (Paris: Hachette, 1911) 3.

[3] A. Martin. V. G. Mylne, R. Frautschi, *Bibliographie du genre romanesque français 1751-1800* (London: Mansell, 1977) 143.

[4] See Sandra Soares Donnelly, "Balzac and Sterne," diss., U of Florida, 1974 (Ann Arbor: UMI, 1989) 34:7227A. See also Tilby 247-62. In his article Tilby studies one of several references to Sterne in *La Peau de chagrin* establishing that it is inspired by *Les Mémoires de Sterne*, a bogus work penned by Richard Griffith. See also Raïssa Reznik's note, "Sur l'épigraphe de *La Peau de chagrin*," *L'Année balzacienne* (1972): 373-75. For earlier works that treat Sterne's influence on Balzac, see the following: Fernand Baldensberger, *Orientations étrangères chez Honoré de Balzac* (Paris: Champion, 1927); Pierre Barbéris, *Aux Sources de Balzac: les romans de jeunesse* (Paris: Bibliophiles de l'Originale, 1965); Pierre Barrière, *Honoré de Balzac, les romans de jeunesse* (Paris: Hachette, 1928).

[5] Fernand Lotte, "Index des Personnes réelles et des allusions littéraires," *La Comédie humaine*, ed. Roger Pierrot, 11 vols. (Paris: Gallimard, 1965) 11: 41. See also a similar "Index" in Honoré de Balzac, *La Comédie humaine*, ed. Pierre-Georges Castex, 12 vols. (Paris: Gallimard, 1981) vol. 12.

[6] See Madeleine Ambrière Fargeaud's introduction to *La Peau de chagrin*

(Paris: Imprimerie National, 1982) 341. She says that this painting served as a model for the hero of *Gobseck* as well.

[7]Laurent Sterne, *Oeuvres complètes*, 4 vols. (Paris: Ledoux et Tenré, 1818) 2: 445-46. The other editions of Sterne's complete works cited in this study are the following: Laurent Sterne, *Oeuvres complètes*, 4 vols. (Paris: Bastien, 1803); *Oeuvres complètes*, 6 vols. (Paris: Ledoux et Tenré, 1818); *Oeuvres de Sterne*, 4 vols. (Paris: Salmon, 1825).

[8]Laurence Sterne, *Tristram Shandy*, ed. James A. Work (New York: Odessy, 1940) 583-84. All English references to *Tristram Shandy* are from this edition.

[9]Honoré de Balzac, *La Peau de chagrin*, 2 vols. (Paris: Gosselin and Canel, 1831) 2: 346. The other old edition cited in this chapter is *La Peau de chagrin* (Paris: Charpentier, 1839).

[10]Laurent Sterne, *Oeuvres complètes*, trans. Josephe-Pierre Frenais and Griffet de la Baume, 4 vols. (Paris: Ledoux et Tenré, 1818). Tilby 247-62.

[11]Tilby, 253. In his bibliography, Wilbur L.Cross in *The Life and Times of Laurence Sterne* (New Haven: Yale UP, 1929), states that even Goethe was taken in by Griffith's forgery in his entry concerning the 1773 edition of Sterne's *Letters from Yorick to Eliza*. Cross 606.

[12]*Tristram Shandy's* chapter CCCXXII is written as a roman numeral in the novel's epigraph, and most subsequent editions refer to the chapter number in this manner. The arabic numeration appears in Balzac's promotional article reproduced in *La Caricature*, 11 août 1831 printed in Charles Spoelberch de Lovenjoul's in *Histoire des Oeuvres de Honoré de Balzac* (1888; Genève: Slatkine, 1968) 167-68. I will hereafter refer to the chapter number in arabic numerals for the sake of convenience.

[13]Charles de Lovenjoul traces the evolution of this dark line from the first

edition published in August of 1831 to the 1853-55 Houssiaux edition in which the sinuous line appears as a finely detailed snake replete with scales and serpent's head. Although all editors of *La Peau de chagrin* pay attention to the epigraph, Lovenjoul's article is the first and best one on paratextuality in Balzac's works. See Charles Spoelberch de Lovenjoul, "*Etudes philosophiques* de Honoré de Balzac" 408-09.

14Laurent Sterne, *Les Oeuvres complètes de Sterne*, trans. Joseph-Pierre Frenais and Griffet de la Baume, 4 vols. (Paris: Ledoux et Tenré, 1818) 2: 474.

15Laurence Sterne, *Tristram Shandy*, ed. James A. Work, 603-04.

16See Davin's introduction to the *Etudes philosophiques*, *La Comédie humaine*, ed. Pierre-Georges Castex, 12 vols. (Paris: Gallimard, 1979) 10:1213. The English translation that follows is mine. "The effect produced by desire and passion on the most essential of human drives, is it not magnificently accused: From this we have this moral that Corporal Trim painted so energetically by the 'moulinet' that he traced in the air with his baton and of which M. de Balzac made an epigraph so little understood by the majority of readers. Few people have seen that after such a halt effected upon our persons there is no other recourse, for the majority of people, than to allow themselves to follow the serpentine direction of life, the bizarre undulations of destiny." Chasles makes a similar reference.

17A. Prioult 230.

18Michael Tilby 248 note 4, documents the confusion surrounding the edition, especially René Guise's identifying two source editions. Although Tilby is right when he states that the 1818 edition of Sterne's works in four volumes is the correct source for Balzac's works, his proof is inconclusive. See also Honoré de Balzac, *La Comédie humaine*, ed. Pierre-Georges Castex, 12 vols. (Paris: Pléiade, 1980) 11: 1779; 1815-16. The notes are by René Guise.

[19]Josephe Marie Quérard, *La France littéraire, ou Dictionnaire bibliographique,* 12 vols. (Paris: Firmin Didot, 1827-64) 9: 265.

[20]The passage from the *Mémoires de Sterne* that Tilby cites in his article may also be found in *Oeuvres complètes de Laurent Sterne,* 6 vols. (Paris: Bastien, 1803), 1: xlvi. See the chapter entitled "Sur La Mélancolie." Fluchère clearly states in his bibliography that Frenais translated the *Mémoires de Sterne* instead of Griffet de la Baume, as Tilby contends. See also Henri Fluchère, *Laurence Sterne, de l'homme à l'oeuvre: biographie critique et essai d'interprétation de "Tristram Shandy."* (Paris: Gallimard, 1961) 662.

[21]Prioult 230.

[22]Laurent Sterne, *Oeuvres complètes*. trans. Josephe-Pierre Frenais and Charles de Bonnay, 6 vols. (Paris: Ledoux and Tenré, 1818) 3: 254-56.

Chapter Four
Four Prefaces: A Dialogue on Novelistic Technique

"Il est périlleux de se fier aux préfaces de *la Comédie humaine*."[1]

Prefaces have received more attention than all other forms of paratext. Works like Benveniste's separating discourse from narration (*discours* from *récit*), mark an important beginning in paratextual studies: that of separating the preface from the text.[2] Benveniste's definition of discourse includes the present tense, the proper deictics implying the present, and the first person, which for him connotes by necessity an interchangeable second person. Ann Banfield continues the discussion by asserting that, contrary to Benveniste, not all first person discourse implies a second person.[3] It is Henri Mitterand, however, who first asserts that all prefaces are discourse according to Benveniste's definition. "Il est assez facile de montrer que la préface porte tous les traits du discours, c'est-à-dire, selon la définition de Benveniste. . . ."[4] Since the preface is discourse and the story is narration, Mitterand points out that a common error in studying prefaces is to fail to separate the "I" of the preface from the "I" of the narration. "Elles confondent deux figures qu'il faut distinguer, sous le même visage, si l'on veut éviter les contresens: la figure du préfacier, et la figure du romancier" (33). This double image of the preface writer and the author is the most likely reason for the unreliability of prefaces in general and in Balzac's prefaces in particular. In her dissertation Catherine West comes to the conclusion that most prefaces highlight the text's insufficiencies.[5] As the epigraph to this chapter implies, Wurmser expressed his doubts on the reliability of

Balzac's prefaces.

> Ecrites à posteriori et à des fins publicitaires, elles ont la prétention de souligner l'idée profonde qu'aurait développée l'auteur, un fameux philosophe à les en croire. Elles semblent, le plus souvent, rédigées par un scribe trop hâtif pour apprécier le véritable mérite du roman. (290)

Although Wurmser warns us not to rely on them, *La Peau de chagrin's* four prefaces reveal much about how Balzac reacted to his critics, conceived his aesthetics, and defined his work. The four prefaces examined here include Balzac's first preface to *La Peau de chagrin*, that of Philarète Chasles to the *Romans et contes philosophiques*, Félix Davin's "Introduction" to the *Etudes philosophiques*, and finally, Balzac's "Avant-propos" to the *Comédie humaine*. Considered together, they constitute a dialogue on literary technique, with an opening statement by Balzac, a response by Chasles, a masked response by Balzac in Félix Davin's name, and a last word by Balzac. Although Balzac replaced his first preface within a month, it reveals many of his theories about novelistic technique. As we know, Philarète Chasles' preface for the *Romans et contes philosophiques* replaced Balzac's one month later.[6] Although Chasles and Balzac had been friends since 1825, the former accorded Balzac not unqualified praise but constructive criticism in his article on *La Peau de chagrin* and in his preface.[7] On the other hand, Félix Davin's subsequent "Introduction" to the *Etudes philosophiques* contained no criticism at all of Balzac. As noted in an earlier chapter, there is substantial evidence that Balzac rewrote Davin's prefaces to suit his own ends.[8] In this case, Davin willingly provided Balzac a mask through which he responded to Chasles for the purpose of clarifying his aesthetic. The fourth preface, the "Avant-propos," by Balzac, provides a final picture of Balzac's critical views in 1842.

The dialogue among "préfaciers" is characterized by masking and camouflage that oscillates between the subtext's author and the author of the preface. It is not in Balzac's stated preface to *La Peau de chagrin* that we may glimpse the beginnings of his aesthetics, but in the hidden preface contained within it where absences and contradictions communicate his first real treatise on novelistic technique. The aesthetic that emerges is a paradoxical one, the basic tenet of which is an antithetical interpretation of fantasy and reality. In later versions the masking continues, shifting emphasis from the preface itself to the identity of its author. It is only in Balzac's last preface that the mask is lifted and the most important tenet of his aesthetic is revealed: the choice of simultaneity over chronology as an organizing principle for *La Comédie humaine*.

Balzac's Hidden Preface

Balzac's preface to *La Peau de chagrin* is unique, not just because it holds the record for the shortest-lived preface, but because it is in fact two prefaces in one. On the printed page, one reads a defense of Balzac's earlier novel, *La Physiologie du mariage*, together with some comments on novelistic technique. Between the lines of this preface, a hidden message may be read in which Balzac reveals his paradoxical aesthetic. On the surface, Balzac's major points are the following. (a) He claims authorship of *La Physiologie du mariage*, considered a *succès de scandale* by his contemporaries. He attempts to clarify that which separates an author from the subject of his works (10: 47). He proposes Rabelais and Brillat-Savarin as examples. "Les auteurs tragiques les plus sombres n'ont-ils pas été généralement des gens fort doux et de moeurs patriarcales?" (10: 48) Balzac believes that readers confuse the narrator, implied author, and author when they create a picture of the author in their mind. Because of that concern, he reveals himself as young and proper, not as the lascivious narrator of *La Physiologie du mariage*. Readers, according to Balzac, crystalize the picture of the author that they create. "Involontairement, ils dessinent, dans leur pensée, une figure, bâtissent un homme, le supposent jeune ou vieux, grand ou petit, aimable ou méchant" (10: 48). (b) He presents his definition of literary genius, a powerful mind that can operate either to recreate events and states in the imagination or to transport himself anywhere through space and time (10: 53). "Les hommes ont-ils le pouvoir de faire venir l'univers dans leur cerveau, ou leur cerveau est-il un talisman avec lequel ils abolissent les lois du temps et de l'espace?" (10: 53). He describes this special power among philosophical writers as a kind of second sight, which permits them to see the truth in all situations or to transport them "where they want to be" (10: 52). Balzac asserts that some men may be able to express their thoughts, but not act on them. According to him, writers have an uncanny ability to see everything and create every experience in their imagination. "Beaucoup d'hommes distingués sont doués du talent d'observer, sans posséder celui de donner une forme vivante à leurs pensées. . . " (10: 52). (c) Balzac reveals that he has a kind of Rousseauesque view of history; he does not believe in progress. He reveals his frustration with a public that demands an image of society more beautiful than its reality. "Le monde nous demande de belles peintures? où en seraient les types?" (10: 55) In a direct attack on the July revolution, Balzac declares that his only weapon against the evils of society are irony and satire, suggesting that history does not bring progress. "Nous ne pouvons aujourd'hui que nous moquer" (10: 55). He discloses that his view of history was one of the reasons why he wrote *La Physiologie du mariage*.

> *La Physiologie du mariage* était une tentative faite pour retourner à la littérature fine, vive, railleuse et gaie du dix-huitième siècle, où les auteurs ne se tenaient pas toujours droits et raides, ou, sans discuter à tout propos la poésie, la morale et le drame, il s'y faisait du drame, de la poésie et des ouvrages de vigoureuse morale. L'auteur de ce livre cherche à favoriser la réaction littéraire que préparent certains bons esprits ennuyés de notre vandalisme actuel, et fatigués de voir amonceler tant de pierres sans qu'aucun monument surgisse. (10: 54)

On the surface, this preface appears to be entirely devoted to *La Physiologie du mariage*. An apologia for *La Physiologie*, it could be a preface to a later edition of the novel. *La Peau de chagrin* is not named and is only alluded to in the last paragraph.

Nicole Mozet and Pierre Barbéris have referred to deeper meanings in

Balzac's preface to *La Peau de chagrin*. In her article, "La Préface de l'édition originale: Une Poétique de Transgression," Mozet writes that Balzac's first preface is of great critical interest because it does not "dissociate the problems of reading and writing."[9] Interested in the ambiguous autobiographical elements of the preface and the text, Barbéris examines the mixture of autobiography and fantasy in *La Peau de chagrin*.[10] These references to a deeper meaning in Balzac's first preface suggest that there must be another preface hidden beneath the words of the concrete one. The aesthetic in this hidden preface can answer the questions posed by Mozet and Barbéris. Balzac appears not to dissociate reading and writing because he sees his work as a necessary combination of fantasy and reality. The fusion of the problems of reading and writing result from his paradoxical aesthetic. Its precise meaning is difficult to grasp because its operative principle is paradoxical: the fusion of the fantastic and the realistic. His view is that he is not a writer of fiction, but a chronicler of something more "real" than history. Balzac does not refer to himself as a novelist or to his novels as "fiction;" rather, his novels are "books," "works," or "scenes" (Mozet 13). Two important literary techniques depend upon this paradoxical aesthetic: paratextual time and the separation of autobiography and fiction.[11]

Time is perhaps the most interesting element in the August 1831 preface underlined by the intriguingly short life of the preface itself. In *La Dissémination*, Jacques Derrida ponders the curious temporality of the preface.

> Une préface, je rappellerai, annoncerait ici une théorie et une pratique générales de la déconstruction, cette stratégie sans laquelle il n'y aurait que velléité empiriste et fragmentaire de critique, confirmation non équivoque de la métaphysique. Elle énoncerait au futur (vous allez lire ici) le sens ou le contenu conceptuels (ici cette étrange stratégie sans finalité, cette défaillance organisatrice du *telos* ou de *l'eschaton* qui réinscrit, l'économie restreinte dans l'économie générale de ce qui aurait *déjà* été *écrit*. Donc assez *lu* pour pouvoir être rassemblé en sa teneur sémantique et d'avance proposé. Pour

> l'avant-propos, reformant un vouloir-dire après le coup, le texte est un écrit—un passé—que, dans une fausse apparence de présent, un auteur caché et tout puissant, en pleine maîtrise de son produit, présente au lecteur comme son avenir . . . Le pré de la préface rend présent l'avenir, le représente, le rapproche, l'aspire et en le devançant le met devant. Il le réduit à la forme de la présence manifeste. (13)

If the "pré" of the preface unites a false present with a false future, Balzac has created an interesting variation in this preface to *La Peau de chagrin*. According to Derrida, all authors create a false present, an illusion of the present, in which the text enjoys an illusory future created by the preface's pretense of present. If this be true, *La Peau de chagrin* is the future for its preface, but it is also the future perfect of the *Physiologie du mariage*. Balzac is creating a simultaneity in this preface, in which the surface looks to the past, and the hidden preface creates a false present and a false future for the novel. If, as Derrida states, we say "you are going to read here" for most novels, in this particular preface the author is stating, "in *La Physiologie du mariage* you will have read. . . ." He has, in effect, created two different paratextual times that work simultaneously for the two novels, a point of considerable significance because it reveals that Balzac was already thinking in terms of a synchronic system rather than a diachronic one, in effect subverting the chronological unifying system through the creation of two contradictory time frames.

The curious simultaneity of paratextual time introduces and frames the paradox of fantasy versus autobiography, the blurred boundary between the "I" of the preface and the "I" of Raphaël's confession. The use of the autobiographical in *La Peau de chagrin* diffuses the line between the first person of the preface and that of Raphaël's confession. How do we separate the "I" of the autobiographical account during the orgy that recalls details of Balzac's life from that of Balzac the preface writer when he confesses publicly that he is the author of *La Physiologie du mariage*? Balzac erases these boundaries of the "I" of the preface and the "I" of Raphaël's confession in the orgy by using metalanguage in both confessions, referring to himself in the preface as a poor "héros de préface," (10: 50) and during the orgy having Emile tell Raphaël, "Oh! de grâce, épargne-moi ta préface" (10: 120).

Many critics suggest that the vicious personal attacks on Balzac by his contemporaries explain his insistence on putting distance between Balzac the author and narrator of *La Physiologie du mariage*. Few mention that the protests were probably an effort to emphasize the real autobiography in *La Peau de chagrin*, not that of the lascivious depraved Raphaël, but that of the studious meek Raphaël of the Hôtel St. Quentin. They read the wrong elements as autobiographical and gloss over the important information necessary to comprehend *La Peau de chagrin*, focusing only on the immorality of *La Physiologie du mariage's* implied author. The 1831 preface conveys dual messages. The surface preface defends *La Physiologie du mariage* and hides a second preface that points toward *La Peau de chagrin*, creating the aesthetic paradox through a double mix: autobiography with fantasy and the paratextual future with the future perfect.

Chasles' Preface: Incomprehension and Correction.

One month after the appearance of the novel, Balzac's preface became obsolete, replaced with one by Philarète Chasles in which part of Balzac's remained embedded. The irony is that Chasles' praise and criticism are based on his perception of only a part of Balzac's paradoxical aesthetic. Unable to read the sub-preface, he treats *La Peau de chagrin* as fiction and examines Balzac's preface on the basis of the surface claims referring to *La Physiologie du mariage*. Chasles commends Balzac on several points, in particular on his analysis of how an author conceives a work of art. Further, Chasles agrees with Balzac's evaluation of the physiological process of the creation of a work of art. In fact, he reproduces this part in his own preface thereby implying his approval. "L'auteur explique avec autant de sagacité que de finesse, le procédé physiologique qui préside à la création d'une oeuvre d'art..." (10: 1192).

Chasles also approves Balzac's moralistic stance, elaborating on the comparison to Rabelais. Chasles finds Rabelais and Balzac similar in that they both perceive and attack the basic immorality of their century: Rabelais, the religious thought, Balzac, "égoïsme" (10: 1188). Chasles believes that Balzac's style is in the epic tradition of Rabelais because it renders a complete picture of contemporary society through the gallery of social types he created (10: 1189).

While Balzac ignores any differences between himself and Rabelais, Chasles also touches on these. He makes the point that Rabelais would not have written in the same style had he lived in the nineteenth century. His comments suggest that he finds Balzac's inclusion of the "Moralité" which appeared at the end of the first edition somewhat pretentious. His efforts to distinguish between the two authors implies a correction of Balzac by Chasles, and what could be described as a lesson for Balzac. Chasles says that Rabelais could not have written as he did had he lived in a different time. "Certes Rabelais s'il n'eût pas vécu au commencement du seizième siècle, tout à la fin de ce qu'on appelle Moyen Age, n'eût rien écrit de pareil" (10: 1189). Balzac and Rabelais differ because of the social differences of the times in which they wrote. "L'ère de Rabelais a expiré" (10: 1189). Chasles declares that Rabelais' day is gone because in the nineteenth century the faults that will require the writer's talents are analytical sensualism and egoisme, an egoism resulting from a blasé, indifferent, and difficult time (10: 1187-88). Chasles believes that the underlying reason for this is misanthropy. "Ce fonds misanthropique, qu'une verve de gaieté et une fécondité d'invention incontestables raniment et font étincler, vous le retrouvez..." (10: 1188). He emphasizes that both men are, above all, novelists, writers of fiction. Chasles' basic premise throughout this preface is that both authors' social criticism amuses the public. Balzac is a story-teller, "Un conteur, un amuseur de gens qui prend pour base la criminalité secrète, le marasme et l'ennui de son époque..." (10: 1187). He emphasizes the fictional aspect of Balzac's novel, never alluding to the reality depicted by him, specifically referring to Balzac as a raconteur. "Voici un conteur, qui arrive à l'époque la plus analytique de l'ère moderne, toute fondée sur l'analyse..." (10: 1186). He makes numerous references to the contes. Chasles compares Balzac's *La Peau de chagrin* to an Arabic tale. "Ce livre a tout l'intérêt d'un conte arabe..." (10: 1191). Like most works of fantasy, the work appeals greatly to imagination: "lisez *La Peau de chagrin*, vous en avez pour trois nuits d'images éclantantes et terribles qui soulèveront les rideaux de votre alcôve pour peu que nature vous ait doué d'imagination..." (10: 1191-92).

The greatest difference between Chasles and Balzac is centered on their divergent vision of what is meant by literary technique. Chasles acknowledges the fictionality of the work and the author's role as a creator of fiction. Balzac never allows that he writes fiction, and in his preface, the word "narrator" never appears, yet Chasles often uses the term in the second preface. He calls Balzac's defense of his personal morality unnecessary. A survey of the vocabulary used by both men is revealing. In Balzac's preface the words "roman," "romancier," " fiction" (novel, novel writer, fiction), do not appear. Balzac uses such words as: "auteur," "écrivain," "héros de préface" (author, writer, preface hero), while Chasles prefers the terms "conteur," "narrateur," "récit," "amuseur de gens"(story-teller, narrator, account, amuser of the public). Chasles is critical of Balzac's evaluation of his readers' sophistication, noting that the latter's efforts to convince the reader of the difference between Balzac, the person and narrator in his novel, were unnecessary. Chasles also is critical of Balzac. He correctly criticizes Balzac's naïveté for believing that the public had marked him as an impudent cynic and suggests for Balzac a more traditional definition of the novel. The novel is fiction above all else.

> Mais l'auteur.... avait tort de croire que *la Physiologie du mariage*, oeuvre d'ironie et d'analyse, eût marqué son front d'un sceau de cynisme et d'impudence: on ne confond plus les fantaisies de l'art avec le caractère de l'artiste.... (10: 1192)

Chasles chides Balzac for believing that the public might confuse the narrator of a novel with the author and defends the sophistication of the contemporary reader. These two prefaces constitute an attempt at critical exchange on the aesthetics of the novel: Balzac posits in his surface and hidden preface, a new aesthetic based on a paradoxical definition of fiction, while

Chasles, failing to read the sub-preface, holds to the tenets of traditional literary technique.

Félix Davin: Mask and Defense

Davin's introduction to the *Etudes philosophiques* replaced Chasles' preface in 1835. Because of the overwhelming evidence that Balzac rewrote it to suit himself, it can be considered his response to Chasles. There is not the sense of criticism or independence of spirit exhibited in this preface as is evident in that written by Chasles. Rather, Davin seems to serve as Balzac's mask, functioning in this preface merely as a variation on the pseudonyms that Balzac used when he planted complimentary pre-publication reviews and articles in journals of the time.

Davin's introduction contains many laudatory remarks about Chasles, but some of his comments imply a correction of the latter's work. Davin criticizes him for two errors: (1) Chasles' claim that Balzac's work is fiction, and (2) his inability to see the larger implications of Balzac's work, namely that Balzac is a philosopher and historian rather than a mere writer of fiction. At the outset Davin compliments Chasles on his preface. "Le critique ingénieux qui nous a devancé dans l'appréciation de cet ouvrage, et à l'originalité, à la profondeur duquel nous rendons d'ailleurs une justice entière. . . " (10: 1201). But, as we can see, the last half of the sentence implies that Chasles was naïve in his analysis, and that he failed to comprehend the deeper meaning of Balzac's preface. Davin attempts to express more openly the tenets that exist beneath the surface of the August 1831 preface to *La Peau de chagrin*.

> . . . (Chasles) a cru lui-même sur parole l'humble étiquette que M. Balzac avait sur le voeu d'un libraire, primitivement attachée à ses oeuvres, et s'était borné à examiner en lui le talent du conteur sous toutes ses faces et avec toutes ses qualités sans doute, mais en le réduisant nécessairement à d'étroites proportions. (10: 1201)

Davin states that Chasles was wrong in considering Balzac's work in the light of an aesthetics that accepted only the fictionality of the work.

After correcting Chasles, Davin tries to find some areas of agreement. They agree that critics of the period had proved unable to comprehend Balzac's work and identify this point as the common thread that runs through both prefaces. Chasles cites his own article from *Le Messager* in that regard. "Je jure que le plus habile critique de 1800 à 1820 ne se ferait pas une idée nette sur un pareil ouvrage. Il briserait sa toise, il jetterait son compas" (10: 1190). Chasles' attack seems to center around the critics' desire to analyze too closely, to create forced analogies. To him the reader or critic is so wedded to the concept that Balzac's work is a representation of reality, that he cannot suspend disbelief and accept the fictionality of the work. Davin's criticism of the reader, however, seems to focus on his inability to understand the philosophical qualities of Balzac's art. "Or, les critiques n'ont pas vu que *La Peau de chagrin* est un arrêt physiologique, définitif, porté par la science moderne, sur la vie humaine. . . " (10: 1213). In other words, the critics have not seen that the work is an abstraction of individual social types, that *La Peau de chagrin* is similar to a *conte philosophique*.

Although Davin flatters Chasles, he still categorizes him among those who do not understand Balzac because he failed to understand the real import of *La Peau de chagrin*. Davin goes so far as to say that Balzac's philosphy as it manifested itself in his early work was beyond the comprehension of most critics (10: 1202-03). This theme continues throughout the introduction to the *Etudes philosophiques*. He takes issue with the criticism that Balzac's work is less important because he sometimes works in minor genres such as contes and novelle.

> Quelques critiques n'ayant pas l'échelle de proportion ou n'étudiant pas les divers travaux de l'auteur d'aussi près que nous peut-être, qui avons suivi avec amour toutes les phases de son talent, ont critiqué le peu d'étendue des sujets, les appelant ici des *contes*, là des *nouvelles*, et presque partout les amoindrissant. (10: 1206)

According to Davin, the critics have not understood the scientific and analytical qualities of the novel, nor have the readers understood the moral of the novel expressed in the epigraph, "une épigraphe si mal comprise par la plupart des lecteurs..." (10: 1213).

In Davin's preface, the emphasis returns to the same concerns as those expressed in the August 1831 preface, distress over personal attacks on the character of the author. Like Balzac who was worried that the public would judge him by *La Physiologie du mariage*, Davin frets about the critics' personal attacks on his mentor. This worry is apparently justified because Bellos states that some of the critics were libelous in their attacks (Bellos 1). Davin states that the only autobiographical elements in the novel are references to Balzac's studious past when his father forced him to live in penury.[12] Perhaps Davin's insistence on the critics' confusing the author's life and works proves that Chasles was naïve and that Balzac was right.[13] Davin refers to the tendency among Balzac's critics to attack him on personal grounds.

> Mieux informé que ne l'ont été certains critiques empressés déjà d'attaquer M. de Balzac par le côté biographique, et qui l'ont peint fort inexactement, nous avons eu des renseignments sur la partie la plus studieuse et la plus inconnue de sa vie, sur son moment le plus poétique. Ce fut aux jours d'une misère infligée par la volonté paternelle, alors opposée à la vocation du poète, et qui nous ont valu le beau récit de Raphaël dans *La Peau de chagrin*, ce fut pendant les années 1818, 1819 et 1820 que M. de Balzac, réfugié dans un grenier près de la Bibliothèque de l'Arsenal, travailla sans relâche à comparer, analyser, résumer les oeuvres que les philosophes et les médecins de l'Antiquité.... (10: 1202-03)

Is this an effort to correct Chasles and to reveal the combination of autobiography and fantasy hidden beneath the surface preface that is a result of

Balzac's paradoxical aesthetics?

In order to underline the truth and reality of Balzac's enterprise, Davin likens Balzac to an architect and each conte to an important architectural detail (10: 1206-07), again contradicting Chasles by insisting that Balzac's works are representations of reality. Davin compares Balzac sometimes to an architect, sometimes to a painter, implying that the *Etudes philosophiques* were a building or a work of art (10: 1209).

> Quel architecte n'a ses trous de boulins à combler, son dernier grattage à faire.... Cette partie du monument (les individualités), la plus vaste, la plus ardente, multiple en ses combinaisons, devait occuper principalement la jeunesse de l'auteur. Pour pouvoir aborder de si diverses peintures, ne faut-il pas avoir encore quelques facultés exorbitantes, des idées qui débordent, une féconde chaleur de coeur? Ces choses accomplies, l'auteur n'aura-t-il pas fait sur des proportions gigantesques une sorte de *speculum mundi*? (10: 1209)

The metaphor of the edifice continues throughout Davin's preface. "Dans les premières assises de cette construction sont pressées et foulées les individualités typisées; dans la seconde se dressent des types individualisés" (10:1210). He describes Balzac's work as a "monde écrit" (10: 1210). Elsewhere, he compares the corpus of Balzac's work to a "cathédral" (10: 1217).

> Et n'est-ce point ici le lieu de remarquer qu'un des traits distinctifs de M. de Balzac est d'avoir, le premier, ramené le roman moderne à la vérité, à la peinture des infortunes réelles, tandis que de toutes parts on n'exploitait que des bizarreries et des exceptions, émouvantes sans doute à la manière des topiques, mais qui ne touchaient point et laissaient peu de souvenirs dans l'âme. (10: 1207)

Continuing his rejection of the traditional interpretation of the novels as fiction, Davin affirms that Balzac is really more a historian than a raconteur. This is a clear difference between Chasles, Balzac, and Davin. "Le roman . . . doit être en effet l'histoire des moeurs. . . . Sous ce rapport, M. de Balzac est un historien qui restera" (10: 1207-08). Davin believes that Balzac's project was so complicated that the author himself could not have conceived it at the outset. "L'auteur lui-même avait-il embrassé d'un coup d'oeil l'étendue du canevas qu'il remplit chaque jour? Nous ne le pensons pas" (10: 1201). According to Davin, if Balzac had understood the vast undertaking before him, he would never have begun it. It is one of the biggest undertakings anyone has conceived: " il s'agit ici d'une des plus immenses entreprises qu'un seul homme ait osé concevoir . . . " (10: 1217).

Davin indicates that literature gives us few examples of the elaboration of a single idea that starts out in a few stories and ends up being the basis of a philosophy (10: 1201). (He describes Balzac's analyses as "ces hautes vues philosphiques" [10: 1217].) The emphasis of the preface writer on the philosophical conception of the work is significant in that it avoids discussion of novelistic technique, even calling the work scientific. "De ces premières études a donc surgi une oeuvre scientifique dont nous aurions volontiers développé le but . . . " (10: 1203). It is a vast work, perhaps too difficult for the author to control. "Sous peine d'affaissement, l'auteur ne pouvait suivre, comme un ouvrier qui taille son bloc de granit, une ligne tracée au cordeau" (10: 1202). Davin blames the seeming lack of continuity of the work on the exigencies of public taste and commercial necessities. "La mode, au-devant de laquelle courent les libraires, exigeait des livres à toute force; peu leur importait le sens des oeuvres qu'ils publiaient" (10: 1202). It is in this area that the difference between Balzac and Chasles becomes clear. Chasles did not comprehend Balzac's philosophy and his premise that thought is the cause of man's destruction.

> Pour nous, il est évident que M. de Balzac considère la pensée comme la cause la plus vive de la désorganisation de l'homme, conséquemment de la société. Il croit que toutes les idées, conséquemmment tous les sentiments, sont des dissolvants plus ou moins actifs. . . . il croit que la pensée,

> augmentée de la force passagère que lui prête la passion. . .
> devient nécessairement pour l'homme un poison, un
> poignard. (10: 1210)

Davin quotes Chasles, but takes considerable liberties with Chasles' text.

> "Assurément," dit M. Ph. Ch., il n'est pas de donnée plus tragique. A mesure que l'homme se civilise, il se suicide. Le désordre et le ravage portés par l'intelligence dans l'homme, considéré comme individu et comme être social, telle est l'idée que M. de Balzac a jetée dans ses oeuvres. (10: 1211)

Although Davin quotes Chasles and confirms his contention that *la pensée* is the tragic weakness of man, the passages cited really say completely different things.[14] Although they both state that *la pensée* is the cause of man's tragic end, their interpretation of the word *pensée* is entirely different. For Chasles, it means intelligence. "Ce ne sont plus les ravages de la pensée idéaliste, mais ceux du sensualisme analytique que le romancier philosophe peut retracer aujourd'hui" (10: 1211). Chasles is referring to intellectual thought only in this passage as questioning and analyzing. He accuses those who want to know everything about the talisman of *La Peau de chagrin* of unwillingness to suspend disbelief upon entering Balzac's fictional world. *La pensée* for Balzac is a specific emotional activity resulting from the demands of expressing subconscious mental activity. In *La Peau de chagrin* the previous owner, the antique dealer, conserves his energy through purely intellectual activity, "le savoir" versus "le vouloir." He substitutes intellectual activity, i. e., *pensée*, for desire and energy in order to prolong his life. Balzac and Chasles are having a *dialogue des sourds* in this preface. They are in complete opposition, Chasles demonstrating no comprehension of Balzac's philosophy and aesthetics, and Davin using Chasles' statements to support his own assertions.

> Donc, après avoir poétiquement formulé, dans *La Peau de chagrin*, le système de l'homme, considéré comme

> organisation, et en avoir dégagé cet axiome: "la vie décroît en raison directe de la puissance des désirs ou de disssipation des idées," l'auteur prend cet axiome comme un cicérone prend la torche pour vous introduire dans les souterrains de Rome, il vous dit: "Suivez-moi!" (10: 1213)

Balzac's concepts of *idée* and *pensée* are also expounded upon in Davin's preface, clarifying what Chasles seemed incapable of understanding. According to Davin, Balzac proves that *idée* exaggerates instinct, which combined with the forces of society, is destructive. *Idée* is the verbalization of the subconscious (Kanes 246). "Il s'élance , montre l'idée exagérant l'instinct, arrivant à la passion, et qui, incessamment placée sous le corps des influences sociales, devient désorganisatrice" (10: 1213). In speaking of *Le Réquisitionnaire* he describes the heroine as being destroyed by her maternal instincts, using the word *idée* to indicate the expression of subconscious maternal feelings.

> Dans *Le Réquisitionnaire*, c'est une mère tuée par la violence du sentiment maternel. Voilà donc la femme considérée sous ses trois faces sociales, comme amante, comme épouse, comme mère, et devenant, sous ses trois aspects, vicitime de *l'idée*. (10: 1213)

Philarète Chasles is cited in this discussion of *idée*. "Là, cite encore M. Ph. Ch., le parricide est ordonné par une famille et au nom d'une chimère sociale, le parricide pour sauver un titre!" (10: 1213) Chasles never implies a comprehension of *idée* and *pensée* in his preface. Davin uses this sentence to support his own conclusions, grafting it to his preface without regard to its context. He claims that the idea of dynasty makes the hero of *El Verdugo* kill his father. "Dans *El Verdugo*, c'est *l'idée* de dynastie mettant une hache dans la main d'un fils, lui faisant commettre tous les crimes en un siècle" (10: 1213). He uses the word *pensée* to indicate that thought can kill the thinker. "*Louis Lambert* est la plus pénétrante et la plus admirable démonstration de l'axiome fondamental des *Etudes philosophiques*. N'est-ce pas *la pensée tuant le penseur* ?" (10: 1215) Davin quotes Chasles' analysis of Balzac's philosophical criticisms behind the irony in his work (10: 1216). He announces that other works would illustrate the author's philosophy and calls Balzac the greatest genius of this time.

> Ces hautes vues philosophiques seront complétées par plusieurs autres *études* en germe dans la pensée de l'auteur, mais que son inépuisable verve aura peut-être fait éclore avant que nous ayons achevé nous-même ces pages arides où nous disséquons péniblement le génie le plus chaud, le plus vivace, le plus fécond de notre époque. (10: 1217)

To recapitulate, Chasles focuses on Balzac's work as fiction and Balzac's talent as a raconteur whereas Davin sees it as an accurate view of reality. Unable to perceive Balzac's hidden preface under the August 1831 preface, Chasles does not acknowledge Balzac as a great philosopher, nor does he consider Balzac's philosophy. Davin, on the other hand, accepting the aesthetics of the hidden preface, never alludes to Balzac as an author of fiction. He makes no references to the narrator or the fictionality of the work. Behind Davin's mask, Balzac is free to reveal his hidden preface in order to correct what he considers Chasles' lack of vision. When the "I" of Balzac's preface is autobiographical, he buries a sub-preface beneath the surface, but when he takes on the mask of the preface's author, he unmasks his hidden preface.

Balzac's Last Word: History, Philosophy and Truth

In 1842, Balzac announced the incorporation of all his signed works into the *Comédie humaine*. For this enterprise, his "Avant-propos" could be described as the last word in his dialogue with Chasles. Balzac continues to deny the fictionality of his works and reasserts his status as a recorder of society's history. For Balzac, society was the historian; he called himself the secretary (1: 7). It is interesting to note that Benveniste uses the term "histoire" to refer to narration and "historien" to refer to the writer (142-43). Banfield points out the ambiguity of Benveniste's term, but does not connect it to Balzac (142-43).

To emphasize his point, Balzac evokes the talent of Walter Scott, a writer of historical fiction, enjoying significant prestige. Balzac never used the word *romancier* in this preface nor does he refer to Scott in those terms. He calls Scott a "trouveur" (sic) *trouvère* (1: 10). He speaks of himself as a "writer" and evokes the great philosophers: "Machiavel, Hobbes, Bossuet, Leibnitz, Kant, Montesquieu sont la science que les hommes d'Etat appliquent" (1: 12). In this preface also, we continue to read Balzac's reluctance to refer to himself as a novelist, referring to himself instead as author, writer, or philosopher. His preferences are "écrivain," "auteur," or "moraliste" (1: 10). He seems to be teaching a lesson on the writer's mission. "Un écrivain doit. . . se regarder comme un instituteur des hommes . . ." (1: 12). Referring to his works as a painting of society, he claims to be anything but a novelist. His aversion to the word fiction is apparent by its absence.

> En lisant attentivement le tableau de la Société, moulée, pour ainsi dire, sur le vif avec tout son bien et tout son mal, il en résulte cet enseignement que si la pensée, ou la passion, qui comprend la pensée et le sentiment, est l'élément social, elle en est aussi l'élément social, elle en est aussi l'élément destructeur. (1: 12)

Balzac cites *Louis Lambert* to support his contention which would indicate that he considers *Louis Lambert* the philosophical treatise on his aesthetics (1: 13). He gently corrects the critics by saying that they did not know his work's goal. "Comme la critique ignorait le plan général, je lui pardonnnais . . ." (1: 15). Balzac's view of his art is completely representative because he describes his work as a copy of society.

> En copiant toute la Société, la saisissant dans l'immensité de ses agitations, il arrive, il devait arriver que telle composition offrait plus de mal que de bien, que telle partie de la fresque

représentait un groupe coupable, et la critique de crier à l'immoralité, sans faire observer la moralité de telle autre partie destinée à former un contraste parfait. (1: 14-15)

Balzac alleges that he did better work than the historian. "J'ai mieux fait que l'historien, je suis plus libre" (1: 15). He insists on calling his work a history. "Dans ces six livres sont classées toutes les *Etudes de moeurs* qui forment l'histoire générale de la Société . . ." (1: 18). Balzac seems more interested in expressing his philosophical view than his aesthetics. He attempts to clarify his views on progress and the sciences, specifically electricity and animal magnetism (1: 16-17). He believes that he gives as much attention to the causes and principles of facts, daily secrets and individual acts as the historians give to the public life of nations: "j'accorde aux faits constants, quotidiens, secrets ou patents, aux actes de la vie individuelle, à leurs causes et à leurs principes autant d'importance que jusqu'alors des historiens en ont attaché aux événements de la vie publique des nations" (1: 17). He says that the internal struggles of his characters are as important as any great battle that a historian would describe.

> La bataille inconnue qui se livre dans une vallée de l'Indre entre Madame de Mortsauf et la passion est peut-être aussi grande que la plus illustre des batailles inconnues: *Le Lys dans la Vallée*. Dans celle-ci, la gloire d'un conquérant est en jeu; dans l'autre, il s'agit du ciel. (1: 17)

He also insists that each work explains his philosophy. "Ces six livres répondent d'ailleurs à des idées générales. Chacun d'eux a son sens, sa signification, et formule une époque de la vie humaine" (1: 18). He vows that he has completed a tableau of society. "Cette vaste peinture de la société finie et achevée ne fallait-il pas la montrer dans son état le plus violent, se portant hors de chez elle, soit pour la défense, soit pour la conquête?" (1: 19) The truth in this work exists in the larger immaterial principles: "Dans ce livre, se trouvent les plus purs caractères et l'application des grands principes d'ordre de politique, de moralité" (1: 19). He mentions that *La Peau de chagrin* connects *Etudes de moeurs* and the *Etudes philosophiques* by an "anneau de fantaisie" in which life is painted in conflict with desire (1: 19). It is interesting to note that although Balzac protests that his painting is a true picture of his times, he places his work in the tradition of Perrault and Rabelais.[15]

The four prefaces reveal much about Balzac's view of his own art, his disagreement with Chasles, and his relations with other contemporary critics. They also prove that although Balzac's conception of what he wanted to convey came more clearly into focus, his view toward fiction and refusal to discuss narrative technique changed little during his career. Balzac, a recalcitrant student, remains impervious to Chasles' admonishments and lessons on novelistic technique. For Balzac, technique was unimportant because he was a painter and sculptor, not a novelist. He was a philosopher, a moralist in the tradition of Molière and Rabelais.

Balzac appears to see the novel as a vehicle to convey more truth than history. His refusal to acknowledge the fictionality of his works is an interesting comment on the novel of the nineteenth century, and perhaps one of the reasons for the disdain of the critics of his time. It is not that Balzac did not accept the fictionality of his work; he was much too sophisticated not to understand it. He felt however, that what was paramount was the reality that he was conveying to the public. His aesthetic could not accept fictionality because his work conveyed so much truth about man in society. Balzac reveals his paradoxical aesthetic in the "Avant-propos" when he maintains that *La Peau de chagrin* holds everything in *La Comédie humaine* together by the "anneau de fantaisie." We have all the elements: philosophy, history, science, reality, autobiography, and fantasy. All of these are the necessary ingredients of what Balzac and his critics refer to as the world of *La Comédie humaine*, which reflect his philosophy: his views on science, the flow of energy, and the survival of the human animal in the Darwinian jungle of Parisian and French society. The truth he conveys is the painting of his times, its conflicting forces, and the laws of his universe. This is why he is so interested in the public view of his persona as the author. Fiction is one layer of significance similar to the laughter in Rabelais' work. Rabelais compared his work to boxes decorated with sileni whose grotesque, amusing exterior belied a precious interior. For Balzac, fiction was the false exterior and the philosophy and history behind his works was the precious essence. What characterizes his interpretation of the novelistic universe is a new concept of history that is not diachronic, but synchronic. For Balzac, events, culture, and society are suspended in one dimension. This concept is hidden beneath the preface, where paratextual time implies a simultaneity. Referring to two novels at once, Balzac's first preface creates two paratextual time systems. Davin's introduction to the *Etudes philosophiques,* a preface for several works at the same time, creates simultaneity of paratextual time and unmasks the aesthetic of the hidden preface. The "Avant-propos" achieves a similar simultaneity by combining all of Balzac's works, finally accomplishing the goal that Balzac attempted in the hidden preface of August 1831. Simultaneity of paratextual time spills onto the narration with the use of the present tense and the first person within the novel, erasing the boundaries between discourse and narrative.

Balzac's contes are full of disguise, and *trompe l'oeil.* In *La Fille aux yeux d'or,* Paquita, who appears to be the mistress of the Marquis, is in reality his wife's lover, the protagonist's sister. In *Sarrasine,* la Zambinella, who appears to be a woman, is in reality a castrated man. This same element of masking and camouflage exists in the prefaces to *La Peau de chagrin.* A more exigeant Balzac than most critics would admit, requires his readers to search. They must find the masked preface, then the narrative hidden by discourse, and finally the preface author and his paradoxical aesthetic before they enter the world of *La Comédie humaine.*

Notes

[1] André Wurmser, *La Comédie inhumaine* (Paris: Gallimard, 1965) 290.

[2] Emile Benveniste, *Problèmes de linguistique générale* (Paris: Gallimard, 1966). See also Käte Hamburger, *The Logic of Literature*, trans. Marilynn I. Rose (Bloomington: Indiana UP, 1973).

[3] Ann Banfield, *Unspeakable Sentences: Narration and Representation in the Language of Fiction* (Boston: Routledge & Kegan Paul, 1982).

[4] Henri Mitterand, *Le Discours du roman* (Paris: PUF, 1980) 23.

[5] Catherine Jones West, "La Mise en Jeu de l'autorité dans la préface de roman." diss. U of North Carolina. 1989, 2.

[6] That Saint Beuve did everything he could to discredit Balzac is well-known. For more on Balzac's critical reception among his contemporaries see David Bellos 78. Apparently Balzac received some harsh criticism because critics confused the man with his works.

[7] In a comment on Chasles' review of *La Peau de chagrin* in *Le Voleur,* Pierre Barbéris, in "L'Accueil de la critique aux premières grandes oeuvres de Balzac (1831-1832)," *Année balzacienne* (1968): 166, says the following concerning Chasles' article which was reproduced in part in his preface to the *Romans et contes philosophiques*: "Chasles était certes 'camarade' avec Balzac depuis 1825, mais sa fulminante analyse, elle-même à valeur de témoignage sur le mal du siècle, relève quand même, évidemment, de tout autre chose que la complaisance."

[8] Roger Pierrot believes that Balzac took liberties in correcting Davin's

introductions. See Roger Pierrot, ed., *La Comédie humaine,* by Honoré de Balzac, 11 vols. (Paris: Gallimard, 1965) 11: 1098. See also Balzac's *Lettres à Mme Hanska,* ed. Roger Pierrot, 4 vols. (Paris: Bibliophiles de l'Original, 1967-68) one in particular dated January 4, 1835: "Vous devinerez facilement que l'Introduction m'a autant coûté qu'à M. Davin, car il a fallu le serinetter et le recorriger jusqu'à ce qu'il eût exprimé convenablement ma pensée...." (1: 293).

9Nicole Mozet, "La Préface de l'édition originale: Une Poétique de transgression," *Balzac et "La Peau de chagrin,"* ed. Claude Duchet (Paris: CDU and SEDES, 1979) 12.

10Pierre Barbéris, "Autobiographie: Pourquoi? Comment?" 25-42. Balzac enjoyed working with contradictions. Per Nykrog, *La Pensée de Balzac dans "la Comédie humaine"* (Copenhague: Munksgaard, 1965) states the following: "Le parti pris de Balzac est de suivre son exemple, d'être toujours 'entre la toise du savant et le vertige du fou.' Car si les deux attitudes sont en principe inconciliables, on peut fort bien osciller entre elles, tirant profit des deux" (28). In *Fiction et Diction* (Paris: Seuil, 1991) Gérard Genette devotes a chapter to the line of demarcation between fiction and reality. See "Récit fictionnel, récit factuel," (65-93). He affirms that paratext gives more important clues as to the fictionality of the work than the text (89).

11See Pierre Barbéris' article above, 25-42.

12Bernard Weinberg, *French Realism: The Critical Reaction, 1830-70:* (Chicago: U of Chicago Libraries, 1937) See also Michael Raimond, "Balzac vu par les romanciers français de Zola à Proust," an unpublished thesis 1966. La Sorbonne Library, 1966.

13In his praise of Charles de Bernard's article on *La Peau de chagrin* in *La Gazette de Franche-Comté* Pierre Barbéris makes the following statement in his article, "L'Accueil de la Critique aux premières grandes oeuvres de

Balzac (1831-1832)," concerning the many provincial articles on Balzac's work: "Il faut lire, relire, cet article de Charles de Bernard après avoir lu, relu, les articles puant de suffisance des bourgeois des *Débats*, du *Constitutionnel*, de *La Quotidienne*." (166). See Spoelberch de Lovenjoul, *Histoire des oeuvres de Balzac* 357.

[14]For more on Balzac's philosophy see Per Nykrog, *La Pensée de Balzac, dans "la Comédie humaine."* In *Balzac's Comedy of Words,* Martin Kanes describes the two terms as *pensée* equaling the flow of psychic energy and *idée* being the specific "concretization of that energy in our encounter with reality" (68).

[15]Mozet 17.

Part Two
Crossing the Threshold

Chapter Five
Foedora, Job, and the Lazarus Grid: Naming and Narrating
La Peau de chagrin

The epigraph and the many references to Sterne in *La Peau de chagrin* suggest that if there is some Sterne on the surface of *La Peau de chagrin*, there must be more Sterne beneath that surface. It is perhaps Sterne's influence on how Balzac conceived the characters in his early poetry that determines the process by which he planned for his readers to make their way through *La Peau de chagrin,* and perhaps through the other works of the *Comédie humaine*.[1] These early character patterns and their persistent reappearance in the *Comédie humaine* reveal much about how Balzac created and developed his gallery of players.

In a report on Balzac the young student, a school administrator, M. Mareschal-Duplessis, related Balzac's unsuccessful attempts to write poetry, and how he was ridiculed by his schoolmates who taunted him with one of his more unfortunate lines: "O Inca, ô roi infortuné et malheureux!"[2] Although poetry was not Balzac's forte, there are some pieces from his early literary efforts to be found in the Lovenjoul collection and in Lovenjoul's work, *Histoire des oeuvres de Honoré de Balzac*.[3] Some of Balzac's "poems" are complete, and others are simply sketches without the romantic conventions of rhyme and versification.[4] Balzac's works, "Le Livre de Job" and "Foedora," serve two functions: they act as blueprints for the construction of Balzac's characters, and they provide a crucible in which the essential elements of his characters' relationships become crystallized as Balzac reproduces them for entry in the *Comédie humaine*. These two poems were first drafts for the characters that were later to come to life in *La Peau de chagrin*. They are rarely mentioned with regard to *La Peau de chagrin*, because their link with the novel is not readily observable. The poem entitled "Foedora," the most obvious source of the famous "femme sans coeur" of the same name in *La Peau de chagrin*, is mentioned occasionally by Balzac's critics, and "Le Livre de Job" is never mentioned as a source for Balzac's novels.[5] We will examine these two poems and Sterne's sermons to see how they enter into the complex and contradictory process of "naming" and "narrating" the end of which is the reading of the novel.[6]

Naming the Text

In *S/Z* Roland Barthes describes as "naming" the subjectivity that the reader brings to the text, the selective remembering and forgetting in which he or she engages.

> Lire, c'est trouver des sens, et trouver des sens, c'est les nommer; mais ces sens nommés sont emportés vers d'autres noms; les noms s'appellent, se rassemblent et leur groupement veut de nouveau se faire nommer: je nomme, je dénomme, je renomme: ainsi passe le texte: c'est une nomination en devenir, une approximation inlassable, un travail métonymique.[7]

In an effort to advance quickly through the text, the reader takes a series of leaps and fills in gaps in the text by "naming" and categorizing conventionalized character types or plot situations. In *Morphology of the Folktale*, Vladimir Propp established categories of "spheres of action," such as "villain, hero, sought-for-person."[8] A. J. Greimas has established a series of names for characters that fulfill specific functions in a work of fiction: "subject, object, sender, receiver, helper and opponent."[9] Eco calls this process "overcoding." He believes that the "plot laws" introduced by Propp were an abductive proposal that brought to light the existence of an overcoded language. According to Eco, once society recognizes these laws, they become a "subcode."[10] The reader fills in the narrative space or "gaps" between these names, creating the novel in his or her mind (McCarthy 99). The characters from Balzac's early poetry provide important clues about naming the text, and the naming process creates a novelistic momentum, a desire to complete itself. In order to require the reader to hold a stereotyped reading in abeyance in favor of an original interpretation, an obstruction is necessary. This necessary obstruction creates an opposing force that interferes with the naming of the text. In *La Peau de chagrin*, this necessary obstruction is the "Lazarus Grid."[11]

Foedora

Sterne alludes to two kinds of obsession in *Tristram Shandy*. The first is the hobby-horse, the *dada*, a generic term used to refer to all types of obsession. The second variety of obsession is the passion that Uncle Toby feels toward the widow Wadman. According to Sterne this passion must be fought because only celibacy conserves strength. In *La Peau de chagrin*, Raphael loves Foedora, "la femme sans coeur," pursues her, spends his last "sous" to go to see her, while her only response is to reject him. In "Rereading femininity," Shoshana Felman discusses the various ways the proper names in *La Fille aux yeux d'or* echo the French word for "gold" (Felman, "Rereading Femininity" 35-39). When pronounced, the name Foedora recreates the French words *fée* and *or*, meaning fairy and gold.

Foedora is one of the first characters of *La Comédie humaine* and is also one of the first characters to appear in Balzac's poetry, written during his youthful attempts at that genre. She is the heroine of Balzac's poem of the same name.[12] An examination of the excerpts of "Foedora," contained in the Lovenjoul collection, reveals that there are two poems entitled "Foedora." Claude Serval, in "Une énigme Balzacienne," cites a prose rendition in paragraph form.[13] Louis Arrigon, in his work, *Les Débuts littéraires de Balzac*, reproduces excerpts of "Foedora" in verse.[14] Which is the real Foedora? Evidently, the answer is "both," but arriving at this answer is more complicated than would appear.

Of the two documents in the Lovenjoul collection entitled "Foedora," one is written in Balzac's hand, a collection of approximately twenty pages, some written on the backs of envelopes (Lovenjoul A 83). It is a combination of verse and prose description. Thierry Bodin in his article, "Balzac poète," described it as not very good verse and, in some places, as just plain bad.[15] It is very difficult to read because it is in the form of a rough draft and contains many variants over which Balzac appeared to be hesitating.

A second file, A 168, contains Baron Spoelberch de Lovenjoul's edition of the poem. It is he who separated the scrawling into two separate columns with verse on the left side and prose description on the right. He made some deletions and rearranged part of the text. He also eliminated the variants that Balzac had listed, basing his decisions on Balzac's own marginal notes. Lovenjoul's copy shows enough variation from the file written in Balzac's hand to suggest that there were more pages to the file at one time, perhaps in such poor condition that they did not survive. The structure of the text in Serval is so similar to the Lovenjoul file that it is apparent that he transcribed that version of "Foedora." The existence of the two poems entitled "Foedora" leads to several questions. Has a portion of the text been lost? Did Lovenjoul make liberal editorial decisions about the poem? He refers to the prose narrative in the poem as "plan." Did Lovenjoul add this himself? Although these questions many never be answered, the critic should keep the two "Foedoras" in mind when examining the poem. Since the Lovenjoul file is clearer and more organized, all references will be to that file, A 168.

Reboussin states that Foedora stood for "high society, vain, egoistic, hostile to sensitive men."[16] In "The Swirl; Eroticism in Balzac and Flaubert," Kenneth Rivers maintains that the "luscious women" and "the precious accessories of gold, silver, and marble" were almost interchangeable.[17] Since a beautiful woman is a sign of wealth, Foedora's "gold" sparkles, charms, and attracts many men. She marks the first link in a lengthy signifying chain. The man who possesses a beautiful rich woman assumes her fortune and her social status. Thus, the chain lengthens; woman stands for riches, and social acceptance. It is obvious that Foedora in *La Peau de chagrin* is a sign for love and sexual desire. It is ironic perhaps that she also signifies objects that have little to do with love. Love and sexuality are merely the currency in an exchange for money and social position. These basic themes appear in the poem "Foedora" and reappear in *La Peau de chagrin*. The character of Foedora remained the symbol of high society throughout the following novels of *La Comédie humaine*: *Sarrasine*, *Le Contrat de mariage*, and *Le Père Goriot*. She was deleted from these works in subsequent corrections of *La Comédie humaine* in favor of society women from Balzac's later novels.[18]

"Sparkle, shimmer, and disorder" are the hallmarks of Balzacian desire (Rivers 140). Light accompanies the descriptions of both the Foedora of the poem and the novel. In the poem, Foedora appears in the morning light amid dew-drops. Balzac describes her "white arms" as she waltzes on the prairie. She is a sprite, a muse.[19] Her snow-white arms, the luster of her legs ("le poli de ses flancs") foretell the play of light seen later in the voyeur scene of *La Peau de chagrin* in which Raphaël watches her undress in her boudoir. Upon disrobing, Foedora projects bright light.

> Je la contemplai curieusement au moment où le dernier voile s'enleva. Elle avait un corsage de vierge qui m'éblouit; à travers sa chemise et à la lueur des bougies, son corps blanc et rose étincela comme une statue d'argent qui brille sous son enveloppe de gaze. (10: 184)

The Foedora of the poem, like that of *La Peau de chagrin*, is rich, beautiful, a countess, and a virgin. "Elle est veuve, comtesse, riche, jeune, belle, bienfaisante, douce, et son mari étant mort avant de franchir le lit nuptial, l'avait laissée vierge. . . " (Lovenjoul A 168 f°153; Appendix B, "Plan," 215).

In the poem Foedora is devoted to her lover, Georges. In *La Peau de chagrin*, however, she is cold and distant. When surrounded by men, she favors no individual. When Raphaël declares his love, Foedora decides never to see him again. She exclaims: "Non, je ne vous aime pas; vous êtes un homme, cela suffit" (10: 189). Later she scoffs at Raphaël's love: "Tous les hommes nous disent plus au moins bien ces phrases classiques. . ." (10:

189). An interesting echo of the poem is the exchange between Foedora and her maid in *La Peau de chagrin*. She refers to one of her entourage who appears to be in love with her. For a moment the couple of Georges and Foedora from the poem are resurrected in *La Peau de chagrin*, only to be destroyed by the Foedora of the novel. She says that she will send Georges away because he is in love. "Georges est amoureux . . . je le renverrai" (10: 183). Although the Foedora of each poem has a different attitude toward love, both the loving Foedora of the poem and the aloof Foedora of the novel are celibate.

In addition to possessing riches, social success, and celibacy, both the Foedora of the poem and that of the novel demonstrate another attribute of Balzac's ideal woman; they are foreign. The foreign woman was often depicted in Balzac's works.[20] For him, Russia represented high society, an association which apparently springs from the large number of Russian aristocrats in Paris in the 1830s (Fortassier 389). Foedora from the poem is Russian whereas the Foedora of the novel is half Russian. Rastignac describes her in the following manner:

> Ne pas connaître Foedora! Une femme à marier qui possède près de quatre-vingt mille livres de rentes, qui ne veut de personne ou de qui personne ne veut! Espèce de problème féminin, une Parisienne à moitié Russe, une Russe à moitié Parisienne! (10: 145-46)

The same ingredients of love, desire, and alienation appear in the two works, but their proportions change, and they are allotted to two different characters. Love is expressed in terms of alienation and finally death in both the poem and the novel, thus expanding the signifying chain from riches and social standing to death. Alienation exists in both of these poems and in the relationships that both Foedoras have with their suitors. In the poem "Foedora," it is the lover, Georges, apparently tortured by his shameful profession, who becomes distant from Foedora. When she tries to kiss him, he turns away from her. "Quand elle y déposait furtivement un baiser, Georges plissait son front, lui jetait un regard qui l'épouvantait et lui disait : Tu en auras peut-être regret un jour. . ." (Lovenjoul A 168 f°157; Appendix B, "Plan," 219). When a minor character, L'Anglaise, (who perhaps reminds readers of Lady Dudly from *Le Lys dans la vallée*) is attracted to Georges and tries to question him, Georges frightens her: "mais un regard de Georges la glaça de terreur" (Lovenjoul A 168 f°155; Appendix B, "Plan," 218). In *La Peau de chagrin* alienation is the result of every romantic encounter that Raphaël experiences. Foedora rejects him after he declares his love. Although he knows that Pauline loves him, Raphaël never confides his troubles to her when the skin continues to shrink. Indeed, the relationship Raphaël-Pauline is similar to that of Foedora-Georges in the poem, "Foedora." The lover is alienated because of a secret the other will not share. The same emotions are in both works, only the combination and allocation among the characters differ. That Foedora signifies wealth and social success is particularly interesting because she ultimately rejects Raphaël. The signifying chain of Foedora-wealth-social success must include another signified, alienation.

In the poem Balzac makes the following allusion to death indicating that Georges would have died for Foedora. "Georges avait un amour immense. Foedora l'aurait envoyé mourir, si elle avait pu le vouloir" (Lovenjoul A 168 f°157; Appendix B, "Plan," 219). In *La Peau de chagrin*, Raphaël tells Foedora that he loves her: "O je voudrais pouvoir signer mon amour de tout mon sang" (10: 189). In the poem, L'Anglaise sees the letter M in Foedora's hand, a symbol for "La Mort," signifying death (Lovenjoul A 168 f°155; Appendix B, "Plan," 218). This foreshadowing of death occurs in *La Peau de chagrin* when Pauline predicts that Raphaël would have a rich wife who would ultimately cause his death. "Vous épouserez une femme riche! dit-elle, mais elle vous donnera bien du chagrin. Ah! Dieu! elle vous tuera" (10: 177). At the end of the novel, Pauline realizes that her prediction has been fulfilled: "Il est à moi, je l'ai tué, ne l'avais-je pas prédit?" (10: 292) Similarly, the shocking end to the poem "Foedora" is that Georges is an executioner, and the discovery of this tragic fact kills everyone. Foedora sees her lover as executioner holding a bloody head. "Elle voit la main chérie qu'elle couvrait de baisers. . . / Cette main tenait une tête sanglante, et la montrait au peuple" (Lovenjoul A 168 f°158; Appendix

B, "Plan," 220). These beautiful women with the same name are signs of love and desire. However, they only begin a signifying chain that leads each partner and the reader through riches, social position, and ultimately to death. Death is the ultimate signifier for the golden fairy, Foedora.

Job

The name Job is another signifier which runs parallel to that of Foedora. Both enable readers to "name" the text by filling gaps, selecting information, according to assumptions they make at the outset. According to Fernand Lotte, there are eight different references to Job in *La Comédie humaine*: *Honorine II, Les Illusions Perdues, Béatrice, Les Secrets de la Princesse de Cadignan, L'Envers de l'histoire contemporaine, Le Lys dans la vallée.* [21] Although Job's name does not appear in *La Peau de chagrin*, Raphaël is a signifier for Job. Like Job, he experienced the loss of health and riches, and like Job, the loss of his wealth caused society to shun him. Raphaël has all the characteristics of Job, but in inverted proportions. Job is the Biblical incarnation of the successful man who has lost everything. Thus, the signifying chain emerges with Raphaël at one end and Job, the Biblical character, at the other. Job is the symbol of the wealthy man favored by God; Raphaël is the poor man who sold his soul to the devil. The most likely source for the signifier Job is Sterne's sermons, in which Job is referred to several times. If we assume that Balzac used the 1818 four-volume edition of Sterne's complete works, we know which of Sterne's sermons Balzac had read.[22]

In his sermon entitled "On the character of Shimei," Sterne relates the story of Job to emphasize society's major failing, that it often shuns, rather than helps, the man who has lost his material possessions. This is the human weakness Sterne highlights when he cites the episode of Job's comforters:

> "That a man, who always wept for him who was in trouble;
> —who never saw any perish for want of clothing;—who never suffered the stranger to lodge in the street, but opened

his door to the traveler;—that a man of so good a character, (sic)—"that he never caused the eyes of the widow to fail,—or had eaten his morsel by himself alone, and the fatherless had not eaten thereof;"—that such a man, the moment he fell into poverty, should have occasion to cry out for quarter,—Have mercy on me; O my friends! for the hand of God has touched me.—"This fellow, we know not whence he is,"—was the popular cry....[23]

Un homme qui avait toujours pleuré avec les malheureux, qui n'avait jamais vu périr un misérable sans le secourir, qui n'avait jamais souffert qu'un voyageur logeât dans la rue, mais qui lui avait toujours ouvert sa porte; un homme qui avait tari les larmes dans les yeux de la veuve, et qui, loin de manger seul son pain, le partageait avec le pauvre: et bien! cet homme charitable, au moment où il tombe dans la pauvreté, a besoin de crier partout: Ayez pitié de moi, mes amis; car la main de Dieu m'a touché. . . . Cet homme! nous ne savons d'où il est. Tel est le premier cri du peuple....[24]

Sterne wrote another sermon referring to Job, the French translation of which is entitled "Les Plaintes de Job sur les malheurs de la brièveté de la vie" (4: 71-87). In it, he describes Job as a man who experienced the two extremes of good and bad fortune:

Il avait si long-temps (sic) navigué sur cette mer orageuse, son passage avait été tellement éclairé, tantôt par le soleil, tantôt par les feux de la foudre, qu'il atteignit aux extrémités et du bonheur et de l'infortune. (4: 72)

... Job... had himself waded through such a sea of troubles, and in his passage had encountered many vicissitudes of storms and sunshine, and by turns had felt both the extremes, of all the happiness, and all the wretchedness, that mortal man is heir to. (1: 156)

Raphaël the rich man becomes a signifier of Job, the poor man shunned by society. It is interesting to note that Sterne's Biblical source for the sermon entitled "Les Plaintes de Job" sums up the theme of *La Peau de chagrin*. "Man that is born of a woman, is of few days, and full of trouble;—He cometh forth like a flower, and is cut down; he fleeth also as a shadow, and continueth not" (Job 14.1-2). Evidence that Job was an important character in Balzac's imagination is that the poem "Le Livre de Job" is to be found in the Lovenjoul collection (Lovenjoul A 84 f° 6-8; Appendix C, 223-24). It is a short piece, containing only 40 lines which Charles de Lovenjoul reproduced in his *Histoire des oeuvres de Honoré de Balzac*.[25]

The Job of Balzac's poem is a virtuous man ("un très saint homme"), who enjoyed many sons and material wealth (Lovenjoul A 84 f°8; Appendix C, 223). One line in particular foreshadows the themes of *La Peau de chagrin*. "Aussi, tous les enfants, plongés dans la liesse, / L'un chez l'autre invités et couronnés de fleurs, / En fêtes fortunés consommaient leur jeunesse..." (Lovenjoul A 84 f°8; Appendix C, 224). To imply that pleasure and amusement in fact were of limited duration, Balzac wrote: "Quand le cercle trop court de ces belles journées, / Séparait par la fin leur troupes étonnées, / Soudain de ce repas..." (Lovenjoul A 84 f°8; Appendix C, 224).

The poem ends with Job about to make a sacrifice, pondering the effects of his easy life on his children (Lovenjoul. A 84 f°8; Appendix C, 224). But this image of Job is only the rich man, and it is clear from the fragment that Balzac planned to develop the poem within a Gothic format. Raphaël, then, is a signifier for the man who has lost everything, but by contradiction signifies the man who has everything. Raphaël's lack signifies Job's plenty, and Job's temporary losses signify Raphaël's fate.

The reader's desire to name, to make his or her way through the text, to consume the text, is aided by these two names that have their origins outside *La Peau de chagrin*: Foedora and Job, from Balzac's youthful poetry; and Job from his readings of Sterne. Foedora, the signifier of riches, social success, alienation, and ultimately death is a fixture created within Balzac's aesthetic world which he endows with allegorical qualities.[26] The Job of Balzac's early poetry becomes a "signified," a well-known figure of western culture as well as a fixture of the *Comédie humaine*. Balzac does not have to endow Job with allegorical attributes, for he is already a mythical personage.

The Lazarus Grid

Another process, not contrary to the action of naming, but on a different plane, is the text's desire to tell its own story.[27] This process exists athwart the reader's naming process, subverting a quick assimilation of the text. At every point at which the naming and the narrating intersect, readers must stop and review the information that they have received. The reader must combine old "names" in a different order, to create the novel within his or her own mind.

La Peau de chagrin is a distorted retelling of the Lazarus story from the Bible, the account of the character that Jesus raised from the dead. Indeed, Lazarus is part of the store of western cultural knowledge. Raphaël is a nineteenth century romantic's Lazarus. While Lazarus was the dead man who was restored to life, Raphaël is the living person who has condemned himself to death. Raphaël's story is really that of a suicide; the beginning of the novel is really the end of Raphaël's life. He has lost all and gambled away his last cent. He is described as a dead man in the gambling scene at the beginning of the novel when he contemplates his suicide:

> La morne impassiblilté du suicide donnait à ce front une
> pâleur mate et maladive, un sourire amer dessinait de légers
> plis dans les coins de la bouche, et la physionomie exprimait
> une résignation qui faisait mal à voir. (10: 61)

When he contemplates jumping into the Seine, Raphaël sees the irony in the fact that he is worth more dead than alive. "Mort, il valait cinquante francs, mais vivant il n'était qu'un homme de talent sans protecteurs, sans amis, sans paillasse, sans tambour, un véritable zéro social. . ." (10: 66). Raphaël is dying during the entire novel; his death is merely postponed and then prolonged by his efforts to conserve the shagreen's skin. Throughout the novel Raphaël embodies a paradox; he is a living dead man. This paradox is acceptable to the reader because the story of Lazarus, risen from the dead in Biblical literature, is part of the cultural baggage that one brings to the reading of *La Peau de chagrin*.

In Fernand Lotte's "Index des personnes réelles et des allusions littéraires," there is only one listing under Lazarus; he is described as "Le personnage biblique, réssuscité par le Christ" (11: 1217). References to Lazarus are in the following works of *La Comédie humaine*: *Ursule Mirouet, La Rabouilleuse, Seraphita, Les Martyrs Ignorés*, and *La Muse du département* (11: 1217). It is impossible to say whether Balzac developed his image of Lazarus from the Bible alone or whether he used Sterne as a source. We do know that Balzac read Sterne's sermons because some of them were published in Sterne's *Oeuvres complètes*. One sermon in particular is entitled "Lazare et l'homme riche," Sermon XIII.[28] This Lazarus is not the famous one who is risen from the dead, but his story evokes many of the same themes. Sterne's sermon refers to "Lazarus and the rich man" (Luke 16.20-31). It is the episode in which another Lazarus, the beggar, full of sores, lay at the gate of a rich man. After both men died, it was Lazarus who rose from death while the rich man suffered in hell. After the rich man asked that Lazarus be sent to his house to inform his brothers, so that they might be spared, the Lord responded: "If they hear not Moses and prophets, neither will they be persuaded, though one rose from the dead" (Luke 16.31).

Although Balzac never alludes to Lazarus in *La Peau de chagrin*, he is the ultimate signified with Raphaël as his signifier. Raphaël is the living dead whose direct opposite is the the miracle of Lazarus raised by Jesus. Raphaël is attached to Lazarus on an oppositional semantic axis.[29] This paradoxical combination of life and death is acceptable to the reader because the Lazarus convention is embedded in western culture. Superimposed athwart the reader's naming of Job and Foedora, the myth creates a breakdown in the reader's efficient naming of the text. The encounter of these signifying chains creates a grid with two strategies working simultaneously, the result of which is that the reader's progress through the text is slowed.[30] It is the coincidence of the "Lazarus Grid," and the reader's desire to name the text that determines the way we make our way through *La Peau de chagrin*. The "Lazarus Grid" forces us to stop at stereotypical interpretations, preventing us from naming the text and allowing the narrative to tell its own story, to satisfy its own desire.

Notes

[1]See Mary Susan McCarthy, *Balzac and His Reader: A Study of the Creation of Meaning in "La Comédie humaine"* (Columbia: U of Missouri P, 1982). This work examines Balzac's strategies to create a desired interpretation by his reader. Thierry Bodin believes that Balzac's early poetry shows his talent as an apprentice writer. Thierry Bodin, "Balzac poète," *L'Année balzacienne* (1982): 166.

[2]Charles Spoelberch de Lovenjoul published this letter from M. Mareschal-Duplessis, director of the Collège de Vendôme, to M. Armand Baschet, July 20, 1855, in *Histoire des oeuvres de Balzac* 402.

[3]See the Baron Spoelberch de Lovenjoul collection which has now been moved from Chantilly to the library of the Académie française, quai de Conti, in Paris.)

[4]See Thierry Bodin's article for an excellent analysis of Balzac as a poet. "Balzac poète" 151-66.

[5]Pierre Barbéris, in his preface to the reprint of the 1831 original edition of *La Peau de chagrin*, says that the poem "Foedora" has little to do with *La Peau de chagrin* (xxxvii). For a detailed study of Balzac's early works see L. J. Arrigon, *Les Débuts littéraires de Honoré de Balzac* (Paris: Perrin et Cie., 1924).

[6]This work will not undertake to redo McCarthy's work on Balzac's strategies to influence the reader's interpretation of the *Comédie humaine*. This study examines just one of Balzac's "Map[s] to Guide us" through the *Comédie humaine*. McCarthy's terms, *Balzac and his Reader* 39-72.

⁷Roland Barthes, *S/Z* (Paris: Seuil, 1970) 17-18. In *S/Z* Barthes discusses *La Sarrasine* with respect to five codes that form a network through which the text passes in becoming text: "code herméneutique, proaïrétique, culturel, symbolique et sémiotique." He defines *code* in the following manner: "Le code est une perspective de citations, un mirage de structures; on ne connaît de lui que des départs et des retours; les unités qui en sont issues (celles que l'on inventorie) sont elles-mêmes, toujours, des sorties du texte . . ." (27).

⁸Vladimir Propp, *Morphology of the Folktale*, trans. L. Scott (Bloomington: U of Indiana Research Center, 1958).

⁹A.J. Greimas, *Sémantique structurale* (Paris: Larousse, 1966).

¹⁰Umberto Eco, *A Theory of Semiotics* (Bloomington: Indiana UP, 1976) 134.

¹¹Shoshana Felman uses the term "chains of significance" concerning Balzac in her excellent article, "Rereading Femininity," *Yale French Studies* 62 (1981): 19-44. In this article on Balzac's *La Fille aux yeux d'or* she uses the term in the following statement: "And the triangle is a screen in that it cancels out, precisely, the propriety of its three proper names, setting them in motion, as interchangeable, in a substitutive signifying chain which subverts, along with their propriety, their opposition to one another, subverting, by the same token, the clear-cut polarity, the symmetrical, dual opposition, of male and female, masculine and feminine" (31). This is, however, a Lacanian term. These "chains of significance" include a sign and in some cases a series of signifiers that form an axis of meaning even if the signifiers and signs may contrast. For Lacan, signifier and sign are separated by repression which prevents identification of the true signified. See Jacques Lacan, "L'Insistance de la lettre dans l'inconscient ou la raison depuis Freud," *Ecrits* (Paris: Seuil, 1966). See also Shoshana Felman's chapter, "Jacques Lacan: Folie et Théorie," in *La Folie et la chose littéraire* (Paris: Seuil, 1978) where she says: "interpréter, c'est-à-dire trébucher sur *l'arbitraire* du signe pour en apprendre, précisément, qu'il n'y a pas de

hasard; trébucher sur l'arbitraire du signe pour en apprendre à interpréter, justement, le *non-arbitraire* de la connexion des signifiants" (230). Its translation in "Jacques Lacan: Madness and the Risks of Theory (The uses of Misprision)" in *Writing and Madness*, trans. Martha Noel Evans (Ithaca: Cornell UP, 1985) reads as follows: "To interpret is to stumble on the *arbitrariness* of the sign so as to find out that chance, paradoxically, does not exist; to stumble on the arbitrariness of the sign so as to learn to interpret the *non-arbitrariness* of the connection between the signifiers" (132).

[12]There are two files entitled "Foedora" in the Lovenjoul collection at the Bibliothèque de l'Institut de France; one is in Balzac's handwriting, and the other was copied by Lovenjoul. See Lovenjoul collection, A 168 f°151-59 and A 83. The poem dates from 1823, consisting of approximately 40 lines. See Arrigon, 156-57 for a transcription of part of the poem and an analysis. See also Claude Serval's "Une énigme balzacienne: La Foedora de *la Peau de chagrin*," *Le Bulletin de la Société historique et archéologique des VIIIe et XVIIIe arrondissements de Paris* ns 5 (1925-26): 387-441. Thierry Bodin also transcribes parts of Balzac's "Foedora," choosing to include fragments. I have chosen to follow Serval's and Arrigon's technique of transcribing complete strophes only. See Appendices A-C.

[13]Serval 399-400.

[14]Arrigon 157.

[15]In "Balzac poète," Thierry Bodin describes Balzac as a poet in the following manner: "Balzac, certes, n'est pas un grand poète; à dire vrai, il n'est même pas poète, et ses vers sont souvent fort mauvais. La vraie poésie de Balzac est la poésie du roman. On peut cependant se demander si des exercices parfois laborieux n'ont pas eu leur rôle à jouer dans la formation littéraire de Balzac" (166).

[16]Foedora is "la haute société vaniteuse, égoïste, hostile aux hommes de coeur." Marcel Reboussin, *Balzac et le mythe de Foedora* (Paris: Nizet,

1966) 25.

17Kenneth Rivers, "The Swirl: Eroticism in Balzac and Flaubert," *Eroticism in French Literature*, French Literature Series. 10 (Columbia: U of South Carolina P, 1983) 140.

18Anthony Pugh, *Balzac's Recurring Characters* (Toronto: U of Toronto P, 1974) 18, 77, 96, 300, 341.

19See Balzac's "Dédicace," ("Foedora," Lovenjoul A 168 f°151) "C'est à elle que sera dédié cet essai d'une jeune muse.")

20Rose Fortassier, *Les Mondains de "la Comédie humaine"* (Paris: Klincksieck, 1974) 385-91, analyses the foreigner in Balzac's works.

21Lotte 11: 1209.

22Tilby 248 note 4. See also René Guise's notes to the Gallimard edition (1976-1981) 11: 1779; 916 note 2.

23Laurence Sterne, *The Sermons of Mr. Yorick*, 2 vols. in *The Complete Works and Life of Laurence Sterne*, 6 vols. (New York: The Clonmel Society, 1899) 1: 265-66. All quotation marks are reproduced according to the English translation. All English citations of Sterne's sermons come from this edition.

24Laurent Sterne, *Oeuvres complètes*, 4 vols. (Paris: Ledoux et Tenré, 1818) 4: 96-97. This is from Sterne's Sermon VI entitled, "Le caractère de Semei." All French translations of Sterne will be cited from this edition.

25Spoelberch de Lovenjoul, in *L'Histoire des oeuvres de Honoré de Balzac* 99, states correctly that Balzac's conception of Job was radically different from the Job portrayed in the Bible. In the manuscript, at the end of the poem are the bizarre words: "Ici Balzac s'interrompt—à coup le bonhomme Job l'emmène . . . et il est tenté par les merveilleuses aventures de Mobu-le-Diable" (Lovenjoul A 84 f°8). All translations of Balzac's poems are my own. Arrigon dates this poem 1819, one year after the publication of Sterne's *Oeuvres complètes*.

[26]In the poem "Foedora," the heroine's death becomes an apotheosis in which the characters rise to the heavens to form a constellation. "Mais la plaintive Isis, le couvrant de ses voiles, / Vint emporter leur âme au séjour des étoiles; / En un songe éternel / Et le marin, le soir assis sur le rivage,/ De leurs pieds lumineux reconnaît le passage, / En consultant le ciel." (Lovenjoul A 168 f°159) " But merciful Isis, covering them with her veils, / Came to carry their souls to the heavens; / In an eternal dream. / And the sailor, seated on the shore at evening, / Recognizes their passage from their shining footprints, / While he consults the sky." In the "Epilogue" to *La Peau de chagrin*, Balzac tells his readers that Foedora is the personification of society. "Elle est partout, c'est, si vous voulez, la société" (10: 294). "She is everywhere, she is, if you will, society." In both works, Foedora assumes mythical proportions.

[27]Peter Brooks, "Narrative Desire," *Style* Summer (1984): 312-27. He states the following when speaking of narration in general: "Any narrative plot, in the sense of a significant organization of the life story, necessarily espouses in some form the problematic of the talisman: the realization of the desire for narrative encounters the limits of narrative, that one may tell a life only in terms of its limits or margins. The telling is always *in terms of* the impending end (320). Most of the article treats Raphaël's desire to narrate. He states: "If the motor of narrative is desire, totalizing,building ever-larger units of meaning, the ultimate determinants of meaning lie *at the end*, and narrative desire is ultimately inexorably, desire *for* the end" (319).

[28]In *The Sermons of Mr. Yorick*, it is entitled "The Parable of the Rich Man and Lazarus Considered," Sermon XXIII, 2: 21-39. See also the French translation, 4: 188-203.

29Umberto Eco says of oxymorons: "Provided that the rules not of formal logic but of rhetoric are in play, then [a semantic unit]. . . acquires. . . markers . . . which were previously seen to be antonymically incompatible. Sometimes the incompatibility thus challenged reveals itself in some form of 'wit' (a baroque device, as in *oxymorons*: /a strong weakness/). Sometimes the oppositional axis is really upset and the addressee must ask himself whether it needs to be reorganized" (285).

30Jacques Derrida, *Glas* (Paris: Galilée, 1974) 233. He uses the word "dredge," (*grille*) to refer to the action of examining each work's effect upon the meaning of the text. He believes that each word that is studied with respect to a particular text provides a key or grid that can be moved through the text.

Lithograph, 1838 edition
Balzac illustré

Chapter Six
Dance of Death Tableaux and the Self-Consuming Narrative

Paratextual evidence that death is the subject of *La Peau de chagrin* is apparent as early as the first edition where one may read the following statement in the "Moralité:"

> L'auteur mérite d'être grandement vitupéré pour avoir osé mener un corbillard sans saulce, ni jambons, ni vin, ni paillardise, par les joyeux chemins de maître Alcofribas, le plus terrible des dériseurs, lui, dont l'immortelle satire avait déjà pris, comme dans une serre, l'avenir et le passé de l'homme (10: 1351).

The 1838 edition of *La Peau de chagrin*, republished frequently over the years, contains many examples of nineteenth century engravings, including several Dance of Death lithographs, one of which is the title page depicting Raphaël being dragged away by a skeleton which represents Death. Many of these are Dance of Death lithographs reminiscent of the paintings that decorated the walls of the church of the Holy Innocents in Paris during the Middle Ages.[1] As in the early paintings, the lithographs in *La Peau de chagrin* are not actual dances but tableaux representing death. They teach a moral lesson typical of the Middle Ages: *Memento mori*. All men must die, and death spares no one for economic or social reasons. Lithographs could be considered a form of paratextuality although Genette does not discuss their use as such in *Seuils*. The decision to use lithographs seems to have been more within the purview of the editor who would contract with artists and use illustrations as he saw fit. In Balzac's case illustrations are analogous to diegesis because they demonstrate author-editor collaboration in conveying an approved interpretation to the reader. Derrida states that diegesis is an example of invagination, a folding of the exterior which creates a pocket within the text.[2] Illustrations, though not part of the work, nevertheless provide valuable clues to its interpretation. Since they are not text, they can only be paratextual folds within the text.

Yvonne Bargues-Rollins, in her article "Une 'Danse macabre': Du fantastique au grotesque dans *La Peau de chagrin*, " explores the Dance of Death in that novel.[3] Chronicling the research on the fantastic in *La Peau de chagrin*, she cites Pierre Barbéris' work on movement in Balzac's novel, specifically a point where he refers to "la fête des morts," citing a passage from *La Peau de chagrin*: "les joies provoquées par le jeu vont dansant comme les sorcières de Macbeth."[4] Bargues-Rollins uses the term "tourbillon," meaning whirlpool, to describe what she terms a recurring "dance of desire" in the novel.[5] Confusing the swirl metaphor with the Dance of Death, she seems to accept the term "dance" literally in the expression, which leads to a confusion of two types of tropes and prevents real understanding of rhythm in *La Peau de chagrin*.[6]

Bargues-Rollins' research demonstrates that there is confusion among the critics concerning the Dance of Death and on the larger issue of movement and rhythm in *La Peau de chagrin*. Until now scholars have failed to separate or organize these metaphors and analyze their significance, a necessary task if one is to find the key to understanding tempo within the narration. If the Dance of Death and Bargues-Rollins' whirlpool are viewed with the paratext in mind, separating them becomes less difficult because we are guided in the reading of each trope by different paratextual elements. The lithographs of the 1838 edition and the "Moralité" of the 1831 edition alluded to the Dance of Death, whereas the swirl or whirlpool metaphor is completely different and correlates with the serpentine line of the epigraph.[7] It is the whirlpool metaphor that governs the pace and rhythm of the novel, while the Dance of Death communicates dilation and absence of forward movement.

It is my contention that there is a series of Dance of Death tableaux in *La Peau de chagrin* which do not connote movement in the novel. Just the opposite, they constitute the static part of the work in which Balzac experiments with the linear time scheme typical of the traditional novel. Balzac could not conceive of time in the manner of Proust, but his treatment of it in *La Peau de chagrin* demonstrates that he could stretch linear time to its limits by making it move so slowly that it seems to stand still. The first two-thirds of the novel covers events that happen over hours. Raphaël loses his money, goes to the antique dealer's shop, accepts the talisman, and goes to an orgy where he relates his past to Emile. The flashback allows Balzac to refer to the past, but the time scheme remains linear. The novel's time creeps along against an inert narrative surface.

There has been little study of rhythm in *La Peau de chagrin*, perhaps because we expect few surprises from the conventional novelists. I. A. Richards approves of Sonnenschein's view of rhythm.[8] He provides the following definition:

> Rhythm is that property of sequence of events in time which produces in the mind of an observer the impression of proportion between the durations of the several events of which the sequence is composed.[9]

According to Mieke Bal, there is little study at all of space in narratology.[10] Two important studies of Balzac's use of time and space are François Bilodeau's "Espace et temps romanesques dans *La Peau de chagrin*" and Lucienne Frappier-Mazur's article "Espace et Regard dans *La Comédie humaine*," the most renown is Georges Poulet's work in *La Distance intérieure* and "Espace et temps balzaciens."[11] Frappier-Mazur sees space linked to and suppressed by the "regard," both Balzac's own, and that of his characters (325). She concludes that "round space" indicates the spiritual and the infinite and that closed areas destroy space. Georges Poulet emphasizes that the concept of immenseness goes beyond metaphoric expression (122-93). Pierre Barbéris treats time in his article "Autobiographie

Pourquoi, Comment?" and concludes that Balzac's opening reference to time, "vers la fin d'octobre," proves that he is doing something new: he is using real time as a point of reference for fictional time (31). Martin Kanes writes that the mythical structure of *La Peau de chagrin* is characterized by "dancing and staining."[12] Bilodeau emphasizes the novel's musical construction, noting that the decor and music of the novel create three tableaux similar to those to be found in an opera.

> Par le rôle qu'y jouent les personnages, le décor et la musique, nous avons voulu montrer que la première partie de *La Peau de chagrin* se divise en trois tableaux obéissant aux lois du théâtre et de la musique, c'est-à-dire aux lois de l'Opéra. (53)

Bilodeau focuses on the three most famous scenes of the novel: the gambling house, the antique shop, and the orgy, contending that the musical structure reinforces a circular interpretation of time.

The concept of death is introduced at the very beginning of the novel and is immediately linked to a mysterious dark substratum to the *Comédie humaine*. Peter Brooks alludes to this hidden layer when he interprets references to mud on Rastignac's boots, descriptions of society as a "mudhole," and society's humiliations as "lapping up mud" in *Le Père Goriot*.[13] In *La Peau de chagrin*, this black underlayer sometimes bubbles to the surface of the narration in two forms: as night, and as the waters of the Seine. Most of the scenes in the first two-thirds of the novel occur at night. Raphaël is always leaving buildings or apartments at night or in the waning hours of dusk or early dawn. The Seine seems to lap at Raphaël's feet as he crosses it for the second time on the night that he postpones drowning himself in its waters.

Tension between anal and oral images throughout the novel supports a surface narrative which hides the muddy underlayer to the *Comédie humaine*. The ebb and flow of these competing primal fantasies reinforces the tension between these two sets of images, and, rather than moving the action forward, makes it static. Against the motionless surface, Dance of

Death tableaux represent tears or dilations in which narrative and tableaux disintegrate as they dissolve one into the other, thereby exposing the underlayer of Balzac's world.

Orality Versus Anality

Orality may be represented by a number of symbols that suggest the vaginal opening of the female, or the open sucking mouth of the infant at the breast. Like Freud and other analysts, Erik Erikson locates its origins in infancy when a child is dependant on its mother for its oral needs, creating a trust which leads to "identity." "Basic trust in mutuality is that original 'optimism,' that assumption that 'somebody is there' without which we cannot live."[14] "Identity" begins with the mother because children's views of themselves are linked to their perception of the mother as separate.[15] According to Norman Holland, as a child develops it enters a series of pleasure-giving phases:

> For our purposes, we can enlarge the customary five phases and list seven: oral, anal, urethral, phallic, oedipal, latent (or latency, during which the child renounces his oedipal wishes), and genital (the period of puberty and after).... in normal development, these phases culminate, so that successful mastery of conflict in one is precondition of development in the next. Unresolved conflicts will persist, finding expression in the new idiom of the next stage. It is common, in clinical psychoanalysis, to trace the influence of early issues even to the end of life. As the twig is bent, so grows the tree. (32)

The first identifiable stage in the child's life is the oral stage, occurring during infancy (Holland 34). His life is focused on everything that enters the mouth. For Freud, the important psychological development is that the child starts to see himself as separate from the mother. An infant at the breast does not as yet distinguish his ego from the external world as the source of the sensations flowing in upon him. He gradually learns to do so, in response to various promptings. Holland interprets all symbols of being swallowed up as oral images (35).

> In literature, this earliest phase appears as fantasies of losing the boundaries of self, of being engulfed, overwhelmed, drowned, or devoured, as in Poe's stories of being buried alive. But these fantasies can also be of a benevolent merger or fusion, as when Chaucer's bridegroom gets a "bath of bliss." (35)

Holland states further that fairy tales and blatantly fantastic works play to oral fantasies and often reveal their "oral basis by the presence of an all-powerful, maternal woman" (35). Maternal images in *La Peau de chagrin* are abundant. The water theme, present everywhere within the novel, and the nighttime backdrop emphasize the feeling of being engulfed and devoured.

Symbols of castration can also be considered symbols of orality.[16] The presence of the two very strong women, Pauline and Foedora, is characteristic of the maternal mode. Some might hold that Foedora is not a maternal character, but one should remember that Balzac often saw the mother character as cold and unfeeling. Pauline is maternalistic in her concern for Raphaël, and every time she is with him, his desire for her causes the skin to shrink further. In this character dynamics, Pauline devours Raphaël, her last words being: "Il est à moi, je l'ai tué, ne l'avais-je pas prédit?" (10: 292) All of these are maternal, oral images, and when Pauline claims that he belongs to her, Raphaël is again at one with the mother (30). The maternal themes in the last part of the novel, suggested by Pauline's letters and the smothering maternalness of the Auvergnat peasant woman, are castrating symbols that shore up the surface narration.

As the maternal theme ebbs and the anal images flow in *L'Agonie*, the last third of the novel sees a shift in the oral-anal tension that effectively supports the cover narrative. Anal images are easy to recognize, as Holland reminds us.

> "Anal writing" is very striking, easy to recognize once one has met the type. Images of dirt are the essential clue. The oral fantasies of being engulfed or devoured become, in anal writing, fears of being devoured by what is foul, dirty, or sordid. Realists tend to be anal writers. (40)

For Holland, anal imagery is preoccupied with bodily waste, dirt, and transformations of those images.

> As for imagery, one finds in anal writings a preoccupation with dirt, with smells, particularly those that evoke disgust, and then with their transformations: fog, mist, sweet smells, pure air, light, even, ultimately, *logos*, the word of God. By this mechanism of "displacement upwards," the ear may come to stand for the anus—sounds are common anal images . . . . Anal fantasies tend to stress laws and rules, particularly meticulous, precise, petty behavior, which deals especially with collecting or excessive cleanliness or rituals. Control, either by oneself or by another, is an important theme. (40)

The basis for these fantasies lies in the second phase in childhood, called the anal phase.[17] The child feels pleasure in the act of retention and excretion. "The question of holding onto or giving up this part of his body becomes of paramount importance, both to himself and to his parents" (39). Holland states that the child's attitude toward language develops significantly during this state because language is focused on "commands and decisions concerning defecation" (39). The powerful influence of the anal phase with all its conflicts is due to the child's confusion of defecation and giving birth (39).

> The child is likely to feel that he is being forced to give up a treasured part of himself, perhaps even a living being like himself. He may confuse the process of defecation with that of giving birth, both taking place in about the same covered

and tabooed part of the anatomy. The child's confusion as to whether his excrement is a living thing or not may grow into a confusion between people and objects and tendency to treat people like objects or objects like people (39).

As a result of this phase, the child learns the concepts of disgust, value, neatness, and possession (39). The anal theme appears in the beginning in the form of a trickle with Raphaël's dirty hands in the gambling scene. "Ses mains, jolies comme des mains de femme, étaient d'une douteuse propreté . . . " (10: 62). The chimney sweep who takes Raphaël's last cent has a dirty face. "Un jeune ramoneur dont la figure bouffie était noire, le corps brun de suie, les vêtements déguenillés, tendit la main à cet homme pour lui arracher ses derniers sous" (66). After the orgy, the anal themes flow as Raphaël focuses on retention and control to avoid the shrinking of the skin and his resulting death.

Narrative Surface

Since anal imagery is the property of realistic fiction, and maternal imagery dominates the fantastic genres, the controversy among critics on whether *La Peau de chagrin* is a fantastic or a realistic novel tends to highlight the curious mixture of anality and orality in the novel. The list of critics who contend the preponderance of realism, fantasy, or the simultaneous existence of both in *La Peau de chagrin* is long, meaning that anal, realistic images and oral, fantastic images co-exist in a bizarre and delicate tension. Martin Kanes sees the confusion surrounding the wild ass's skin as due to a general feeling among the critics that the "symbolism of the skin" is "regrettable romanticism."[18] In *Balzac et le mal du siècle* Pierre Barbéris described this combination of fantasy and reality as something that hurt the novel (1:152-56). In "Logic and Language in *La Peau de chagrin*, " Martin Kanes attributes the curious combination of realism and the fantastic in *La Peau de chagrin* to a "fundamental shift in point of view" (245).

Oral images are visible in the darkness of every night scene, every reference to water, and in the female characters of the novel, while anal images of light, flowers, music, and death create the opposing force that suspends the narrative surface. Early in the novel, the oral fantasy appears as Raphaël (in his imagination) throws himself in the Seine, attempting suicide. Drowning is the first of numerous oral images. Raphaël fears that waters could swallow him up, corresponding to the primal male fear of being devoured during the sexual act. He feels the river lapping at his feet and is afraid. The water of the Seine creates mud which forms an opposing primal image, an anal image. It is introduced early in the novel as one of the characters philosophizes about ambition. "L'ambitieux se rêve au faîte du pouvoir, tout en s'aplatissant dans la boue du servilisme" (10: 60). The chimney sweep, covered with sweat and grime, begs Raphaël for money (cited earlier, 10: 66). The gambling house is dirty. "Le parquet est usé, malpropre" (10: 59). Raphaël's hands are dirty despite his elegant appearance (10: 62). The gambling scene and the walk to the antique shop occur in the waning hours of daylight. While there, Raphaël sees night come suddenly. "Pendant un moment encore, les vagues reflets du couchant lui permirent d'apercevoir indistinctement les fantômes par lesquels il était entouré; puis toute cette nature morte s'abolit dans une même teinte noire" (10: 77). The significant commentary on the action follows: "La nuit, l'heure de mourir était subitement venue" (10: 77). Raphaël had postponed his suicide until the nighttime. With the night comes all the childhood dread of the darkness, the empty void into which children fear monsters will carry them, there to be devoured. Night is the time of sleep, an imitation of death. The scenes in the antique shop and orgy take place at night. When Raphaël crosses the bridge over the Seine again with his friends, he sees the river and thinks of his death.

> En ce moment, Raphaël passait avec ses amis sur le Pont des Arts, d'où, sans les écouter, il regardait la Seine dont les eaux mugissantes répétaient les lumières de Paris. Au-dessus de ce fleuve, dans lequel il voulait se précipiter naguère, les prédictions du vieillard étaient accomplies, l'heure de sa mort se trouvait déjà fatalement retardée. (10: 90)

The love affair with Foedora is related in a flashback set against the black backdrop of night in a little room at Taillefer's house. Within the interpolated story, many of the events involving Foedora occur at night, including the party scene at her home, Raphaël's evening out with her, and the powerful voyeur scene where Raphaël hides in Foedora's room.

The bright daylight of the morning after the orgy creates a switch of themes, but the same tension is present: daylight signals a dominant anal image with oral images taking a minor role. After the orgy there are many daylight scenes which complement Raphaël's efforts to control his desire as he wanders from place to place: Aix-les-Bains, Mont d'Or, and Burgundy. In every locale, water plays an important role. In Aix-les-Bains, Le Bourget, the lake of Lamartinian fame, occupies an important part of the landscape. The reason for the trip are the "curing waters" which are recommended by Raphaël's doctors (10: 262-63). Just as the waters of the Seine served as the backdrop to the beginning of Raphaël's story, the presence of Bourget lake is the key to Raphaël's tranquility in his last desperate efforts to grasp at life. "Raphaël ne supportait son fardeau qu'au milieu de ce beau paysage, il y pouvait rester indolent, songeur, et sans désirs" (10: 270). As the waters of the Seine were waiting to swallow up Raphaël, the lake is a reminder that he is being swallowed up—by the desire that makes the skin shrink.

Water is also in the retreat at Mont d'Or. There is a small lake at the bottom of a crater. "Au fond de cette coupe, peut-être l'ancien cratère d'un volcan, se trouvait un étang dont l'eau pure avait l'éclat du diamant" (10: 277). The lake took up so much room compared to the cow path, that it almost denied space for passage. [19]

> Irrégulièrement taillé en dents de loup comme le bas d'une robe, l'étang pouvait avoir trois arpents d'étendue; selon les rapprochements des rochers et de l'eau, la prairie avait un arpent ou deux de largeur; en quelques endroits, à peine restait-il assez de place pour le passage des vaches. (10: 277)

The water, round in the form of "dents de loup" suggests the fantasy of the *vagina dentata*: more importantly, the lake consumes all freedom of movement. It is a female image consistent with other oral images in *La Peau de chagrin* which smother and consume Raphaël's energy. These images run the gamut from the numerous allusions to water, to the overly sollicitous peasant woman whom Raphaël feels is condeming him to death. Her description as she appears before Raphaël is of darkness. "Tout à coup l'Auvergnate elle-même se dressa soudain devant lui comme une ombre dans l'ombre du soir . . ." (10: 284). She pronounces his death sentence by talking about Raphaël's declining health and pitying him (10: 285). When he departs to avoid her mothering, water again plays an important part of the scene. He goes to Burgundy, where two rivers are described: the Allier and the Loire. "Tantôt l'Allier déroulait sur une riche perspective son ruban liquide et brillant . . . la Loire et ses longues nappes diamantées reluisirent au milieu de ses sables dorés" (10: 286).

In the last part of the novel, *L'Agonie*, oral images ebb, and anal images flow (in contrast to the first two-thirds of the novel). Every scene in this part of the novel takes place in brilliant sunlight which is typical of upward displacement (Holland 40). All the scenes in Aix-les-Bains, Mont d'Or, and the little village in Burgundy are bathed in light. Desire for control motivates Raphaël in the last section of the novel as he attempts to prevent the shrinking of the skin and the ebbing of his life's forces. The strict ritual imposed by Raphaël upon his valet Jonathas is designed to control the shrinking of the skin with meticulous attention paid to language. Only Jonathas is permitted in Raphaël's room. Ritual takes over, and Raphaël gets up at seven o'clock every day. Every morning Jonathas must say, "Monsieur le marquis, il faut vous réveiller et vous habiller" (10: 213). His menus are planned in advance. The valet replaces any personal items that wear out, and lays out his master's clothes on the same chair. If the weather is nice, he is supposed to invite his master to go out "Vous devriez sortir, Monsieur?" (10: 214) He has a carriage ready to take him wherever he might want to go. As Jonathas says "M. le marquis n'a rien à souhaiter" (10: 214). In "Logic and Language in *La Peau de chagrin*," Martin Kanes has analyzed the fact that it is the expression of the desire that shrinks the skin, not the desire itself. Ritual prevents involuntary expressions of desire.

> In each case in which the skin is involved in the expression of an *Idée*, the key to its reaction lies in the act of verbalization. At Taillefer's orgy the skin shrinks when Raphaël expresses the desire to be a millionaire, although he has actually been one since the death of his uncle O'Flaharty in 1828. . . . Later, when Raphaël is about to engage in a duel at Aix, he again formulates the desire for his opponent's bullet to misfire. . . . (It costs Raphaël no more to desire the death of his opponent (sic) rather than his being wounded, since the shrinking of the skin is occasioned by the *fact* of verbalization not by its *subject*.) (Kanes 250)

Raphaël learns to his horror that even involuntary interjections are capable of shrinking the skin when he uttered the seemingly meaningless statement to his old professor: "Je souhaite bien vivement que vous réussissiez" (10: 219).

Since the slightest error by Jonathas brings Raphaël nearer to death, meticulous attention to detail is of paramount importance. Raphaël gave Jonathas a book with his duties to memorize, describing the rituals. He must maintain the apartment at the perfect temperature and anticipate Raphaël's every desire: "toutes les portes s'ouvrent d'elles-mêmes par un mécanisme. Pour lors, il peut aller d'un bout à l'autre de sa maison sans trouver une seule porte fermée" (10: 215). Raphaël's effort to control the shrinking is similar to the child's anal fantasies of losing a part of himself in defecation. The scene of Raphaël's and Pauline's love-nest, sunlit and flower-filled, indicates transposed anal imagery, dirt being changed into cleanliness, brilliant sunlight, and flowers. The description of Pauline, surrounded by flowers, is another displaced anal theme. When Raphaël returns from the meeting with the scientists, he finds Pauline described in floral terms: "elle était là, semblable à une rose du Bengale sur un monceau de roses blanches" (10: 253). She invites him to die with her. "Mourir avec toi, demain matin, ensemble, dans un dernier baiser, ce serait un bonheur" (10: 253).

Another example of anal imagery is found in Raphaël's meticulous system of tracking the shrinking of the skin. "Il mit la Peau de chagrin dans le cadre où elle avait été naguère enfermée, et après avoir décrit par une ligne d'encre rouge le contour actuel du talisman, il s'assit dans son fauteuil" (10: 252). The consistency of the skin recalls a stool, alternately described as supple and hard: "mais la souplesse de la Peau quand il la maniait, mais sa dureté lorsque les moyens de destruction mis à la disposition de l'homme étaient dirigés sur elle, l'épouvantaient" (10: 252). Like bodily excretion, the skin is ever-present, and Raphaël can never escape from it. As Holland reminds us, the image of death and the preoccupation with it are anal images (41). The Dance of Death scenes reinforce the anality of the last half of the novel because the Mephistophelian antique dealer, or any image of death, such as a skeleton, is yet another anal theme (Holland 41). Raphaël's trajectory at the end of the novel can best be described in fits and starts, as classic anal images: "procrastination, or moving by fits and starts would suggest that we are dealing with an anal fantasy, as would a concern with precise timing" (Holland 41).

Dehumanization, another anal theme, is apparent in this last third of the novel. Raphaël uses the term "to vegetate." To become dehumanized is exactly what he must do to survive; he must become a vegetable.

> Il me répète souvent qu'il veut vivre comme une vergétation, en vergétant. Et pas plus tard qu'hier, Monsieur Porriquet, il regardait une tulipe, et il disait en s'habillant: "Voilà ma vie. Je vergète, mon pauvre Jonathas"(10: 215).

When he goes to Auvergne where there is exclusively vegetation, Raphaël temporarily halts the dying process. At home, he uses drugs to fall into a dream-like state, thereby killing his active imagination, eliminating his desire, and preventing the shrinking of the talisman.

> Raphaël demeura pendant quelques jours plongé dans le néant de son sommeil factice. Grâce à la puissance matérielle exercée par l'opium sur notre âme immatérielle, cet homme

> d'imagination si puissamment active s'abaissa jusqu'à la hauteur de ces animaux paresseux qui croupissent au sein des forêts, sous la forme d'une dépouille végétale, sans faire un pas pour saisir une proie facile (10: 288-89).

He puts out the light, and the narrator states that daylight will never enter his room again.

> Vers les huit heures du soir, il sortait de son lit: sans avoir une conscience lucide de son existence, il satisfaisait sa faim, puis se recouchait aussitôt. Ses heures froides et ridées ne lui apportaient que de confuses images, des apparences, des clairs-obscurs sur un fond noir. Il s'était enseveli dans un profond silence, dans une négation de mouvement et d'intelligence. (10: 289)

Oral, maternal imagery reaffirms itself as Raphaël chooses to remain in a vegetative state in order to suspend time. He becomes a kind of foetus in the womb as a result of his drugged state and the complete darkness of the room. However, the short scene depicting the party given by Jonathas for Raphaël's distraction is full of anal imagery. In the penetrating light of the room we encounter a detailed luxury and an abundance of flowers, all anal allusions.

> Aussitôt Raphaël, inondé de lumière, fut ébloui, surpris par un spectacle inouï. C'était ses lustres chargés de bougies, les fleurs les plus rares de sa serre artistement disposées, une table étincelante d'argenterie, d'or, de nacre, de porcelaines; un repas royal, fumant, et dont les mets appétissants irritaient les houppes nerveuses du palais. (10: 289)

Light, flowers, Jonathas' intricate planning, and the triumph of death at the end of the novel, all imply anality, and ultimately the triumph of anality over orality. However, oral primal images are predominant in the novel.

Two-thirds of the novel depicts night scenes, and Raphaël finally chooses to maintain a foetal state in his room shutting out the light of day to conserve what life he can salvage for himself. The tension between oral and anal imagery in the novel, rather than propel the novel's action forward, creates tears in the surface narration, allowing us a view of the underlayer of Balzac's world. The answer to questions about direction and force of movement in the novel lies in an understanding of the role of its tableaux. The movement generated by the tearing is not a forward motion, but a dilation.

Tableaux

Suspended at intervals within the narration are five Dance of Death tableaux. Ironically the name "dance" is inappropriate, because these tableaux create pauses in the momentum of the narrative. They are textual recreations of the paintings and lithographs of the Middle Ages and the Renaissance. Their operative principle is the same as that of the lithographs from the 1838 edition: the use of contrast techniques, a mixture of movement and life, and the juxtaposition of the macabre and the hedonistic. These tableaux form a set, a collection, as if they could have been sold together in the antique shop. Each one constitutes a pause in the incredibly slow narrative pace, a spot where the fiction tears, ultimately disintegrating. This process is acheived by the use of language on two different levels. First, Balzac uses a kind of metalanguage, setting apart the scenes he describes as tableaux. Words such as "frame" and "picture" are common markers for these scenes.[20] Next he uses language to suggest an allegorical figure representing death, the antique dealer in the early part of the novel, Raphaël himself at the end of the work.

Death is the dominant theme in the first scene of the novel when Raphaël contemplates suicide. A "Dance of Death" tableau appears again after the orgy as the revelers wake up in the light of morning. The women, beautiful the night before, are distorted and grotesque: "les bouches naguère délicieuses et rouges, maintenant sèches et blanches, portaient les honteux stigmates de l'ivresse" (10: 205-06). They are described as cadaverous in this scene, "cadavéreuses comme des fleurs écrasées dans une rue." (10: 206), and in a figurative manner Balzac places a skeleton in the picture, which also includes a satanic laugh.

> Ce réveil du vice sans vêtements ni fard, ce squelette du mal déguenillé, froid, vide et privé des sophismes de l'esprit ou des enchantements du luxe, épouvanta ces intrépides athlètes, quelque habitués qu'ils fussent à lutter avec la débauche. (10: 206)

The narrator even refers to the scene as a "tableau." "Le tableau fut complet" (10: 206). It displays the traditional leering face of death typical of the Dance of Death paintings and lithographs in Taillefer's amusement at his guests: "Vous eussiez dit la Mort souriant du milieux d'une famille pestiférée. . . " (10: 206). During the morning after, a notary appears to notify Raphaël of his inheritance. As the skin shrinks, Raphaël has a look of death on his face.

> Une horrible pâleur dessina tous les muscles de la figure flétrie de cet héritier, ses traits se contractèrent, les saillies de son visage blanchirent, les creux devinrent sombres, le masque livide, et les yeux fixèrent. Il voyait la MORT. (10: 209)

An interesting characteristic of these scenes is that there is no movement. They have the static quality of a painting.

The third tableaux is that of the antique dealer in the Savonnerie. Raphaël sees the dealer in the midst of a crowd.

> Les sourcils, les cheveux, la virgule à la Mazarin que montrait vaniteusement l'inconnu, étaient teints en noir; mais, appliqué sur une chevelure sans doute trop blanche, le cosmétique avait produit une couleur violâtre et fausse dont les teintes changeaient suivant les reflets plus ou moins vifs des lumières. (10: 221-22)

Again the description of Raphaël, squinting and contemplating, reinforces the image of the scene as a tableau. "Il s'avança en clignant les yeux fort insolemment vers cet être bizarre, afin de le contempler de plus près" (10: 221). If that does not categorize the scene, Raphaël's words do: "Quelle admirable peinture!" (10: 221) The antique dealer is described as having a grotesque face and a youthful body. Instead of resembling a picture of death, the character is a devil.

> En ce moment, un rire muet échappait à ce fantastique personnage, et se dessinait sur ses lèvres froides, tendues par un faux râtelier. A ce rire, la vive imagination de Raphaël lui montra dans cet homme, de frappantes ressemblances avec la tête idéale que les peintres ont données au Méphistophélès de Goethe. (10: 222)

Balzac frames the tableau with the following words.

> Cette espèce de poupée pleine de vie avait pour Raphaël tous les charmes d'une apparition, et il le contemplait comme un vieux Rembrandt enfumé, récemment restauré, verni, mis dans un cadre neuf. (10: 222)

Balzac adds the final brush strokes in the Dance of Death painting with specific references to death. One of the young men calls Euphrasie, the old man's mistress, a ghoul and the antique dealer a cadaver. "Dans quel cimetière cette jeune goule a-t-elle déterré ce cadavre?" (10: 223)

Raphaël throws the skin into a well and determines to begin a passionate love affair with Pauline, but the skin only returns to Raphaël, this time much smaller. Soon after he succumbs to his desire for Pauline, he develops a cough.

> Lorsque tu dors, ta respiration n'est pas franche, il y a dans ta poitrine quelque chose qui résonne, et qui m'a fait peur. Tu as

> pendant ton sommeil une petite toux sèche, absolument semblable à celle de mon père qui meurt d'une phtisie. (10: 255)

When awake, he becomes worse and develops a terrible coughing fit.

> . . . mais il eut alors un horrible accès de toux, de ces toux graves et sonores qui semblent sortir d'un cercueil, qui font pâlir le front des malades et les laissent tremblants, tout en sueur, après avoir remué leurs nerfs, ébranlé leurs côtes, fatigué leur moelle épinière, imprimé je ne sais quelle lourdeur à leurs veines. (10: 256)

When she looks at Raphaël's face, Pauline sees the hideous skeleton of death, in a Dance of Death image reminiscent of those of the Middle Ages.

> Elle se voila la figure de ses mains, car elle apercevait le hideux squelette de la Mort. La tête de Raphaël était devenue livide et creuse comme un crâne arraché aux profondeurs d'un cimetière pour servir aux études de quelque savant. Pauline se souvenait de l'exclamation échappée la veille à Valentin, et se dit à elle-même: "Oui, il y a des abîmes que l'amour ne peut pas traverser, mais il doit s'y ensevelir." (10: 256).

The last tableau contains a curious mix of anal and oral allusions, a Dance of Death superimposed on a caricature of the Madonna and child. When he returns, Raphaël finds Pauline's letters symbols of her smothering love, and attempts to destroy them. Just before his death, he explains to Pauline the importance of the skin and that he has little time left. In desperation, Pauline tries to commit suicide on Raphaël's bed. Raphaël, jumping on the bed in an effort to wrestle the shawl from her, dies from the desire he feels seeing her this last time. When he rushes to Pauline, he utters the double entendre that recalls a maternal state as well as a sexual one: "Je veux mourir à toi." (10: 292)[21] Consider the body language of the participants in the bedroom scene: as Pauline holds Raphaël in her arms, crouched above him, he attempts to bite her breasts:

> Le moribond chercha des paroles pour exprimer le désir qui dévorait toutes ses forces; mais il ne trouva que les sons étranglés du râle dans sa poitrine, dont chaque respiration creusée plus avant semblait partir des ses entrailles. Enfin, ne pouvant bientôt plus former de sons, il mordit Pauline au sein. Jonathas se présenta tout épouvanté des cris qu'il entendait, et tenta d'arracher à la jeune fille le cadavre sur lequel elle s'était accroupie dans un coin. (10: 292)

The last tableau is two in one, maternal images superimposed on a sexual scene: the first represents the death of Raphaël in his lover's arms, the triumph of anality; the second represents a caricature of the maternal image, madona and child, in which Raphaël nibbles at his mistress' breasts as a baby does in its mother's arms. This opposition of fantasies prevents either from dominating and generates little or no forward momentum in linear time. It creates an ending in which the static surface disintegrates and collapses on itself, leaving a void, a muddy nothingness, into which Raphaël falls. Raphaël does not just die; he disappears, as he becomes one with the holes in the narration. The only movement communicated in this last scene is dilation.

A study of the self-consuming narrative and the Dance of Death tableaux reveals that the rhythm we are seeking is not related to death, which is shown in images opposite to a dance, motionless and inert. It is before these tableaux that the reader pauses with the characters as they stop and contemplate death, the final void that lies below the narration. The self-consuming narrative disintegrates under the pressure of opposing forces of fantasy and reality, and of Raphaël's desire to preserve the skin opposed by the story's momentum to complete itself.

Stopping on the threshold of *La Peau de chagrin* and looking at the text with the paratext as a map reveals a pattern and system in Balzac's treatment of rhythm. The lithographs and Dance of Death tableaux represent the lack of motion and dilation in the novel, but our paratextual map reveals that this is merely half the story. The dilations created by these tableaux suggest a search for constriction along another paratextual path in order to complete the picture of rhythm and tempo in *La Peau de chagrin*.

Notes

[1]Most books entitled, *Dance of Death* postdate the appearance of the mural paintings which appeared in 1424. See, for example, Hans Holbein The Younger's *Dance of Death* lithographs published in 1538 in Lyons by Treschel. Werner L. Gundersheimer's introduction to *The Dance of Death: Hans Holbein The Younger: A complete Facsimile of the Original 1538 Edition, Lyons: Treshel. Les simulachres & historiees* (sic) *faces de la mort* (1538; New York: Dover Inc., 1971) ix-xiv.

[2]Jacques Derrida, "Living On: Border Lines," in Bloom et al., *Deconstruction and Criticism* (New York: Seabury, 1979) 93.

[3]Yvonne Bargues-Rollins, "Une 'danse-macabre': Du fantastique au grotesque dans *La Peau de chagrin*," *Romantisme : Revue du 19e siècle* 15.48 (1985): 33-46. Bargues-Rollins seems more interested in the connections between "real, symbol, caricature, supernatural, irony and the grotesque" than in how Balzac recreates the Dance of Death in *La Peau de chagrin* (34).

[4]Pierre Barbéris, *Balzac et le mal du siècle,* 2 vols. (Paris: Gallimard, 1970) 1: 130.

[5]Two other articles study movement in *La Peau de chagrin*. Stirling Haig, "Dualistic Patterns in *La Peau de chagrin*," *Nineteenth Century French Studies* 1 (1973): 211-18. He believes that Raphaël's path in the antique shop resembles Dante's construction of the *Divine Comedy*. Rivers, 138-42, connects a swirling motion with desire in the scenes involving beautiful women.

[6]There are a few references to a real dance in the *Dance of Death*: Leonard

P. Kurtz, *The Dance of Death and the Macabre Spirit in European Literature* (New York: Gordon P, 1975) 70, cites Jean Le Fèvre's statement, "Je fis de macabre la danse. . . " in his poem, "Le Respit de la mort," in 1376. He also studies the Danse macabre in drama, tracing its origins to a pantomime procession in which death leads its victims away by the hand (155). In spite of the research revealing that the Dance of Death appeared in different media, the traditional rendition of the Dance of Death was a mural painting depicting death taking people from all levels of society (Gundersheimer, xiv).

[7]Martin Kanes was correct in his "The Mythic Structure of *La Peau de chagrin* " when he connected the serpentine metaphors in the novel to the serpentine epigraph line of the Houssiaux edition and to Balzac's concept of *Pensée*. See "The Mythic Structure of *La Peau de chagrin,* " *Studi Francesi* 16(1972): 51 note 1.

[8]I. A. Richards, *Practical Criticism* (London: Routledge & Kegan Paul, 1929) 360.

[9]A. E. Sonnenschein, *What is Rhythm?* (Oxford: Blackwell, 1925) 16.

[10]Mieke Bal, *Narratology: Introduction to the Theory of Narrative*, trans. Christine van Boheemen (Toronto: U of Toronto P, 1985) 93.

[11]See François Bilodeau, "Espace et temps romanesques dans *La Peau de chagrin*," *L'Année balzacienne* (1969): 47-70; Lucienne Frappier-Mazur, "Espace et Regard dans *La Comédie humaine*," *L'Année balzacienne* (1967): 325-38; Georges Poulet, *La Distance intérieure* (Paris: Plon, 1952) 122-93, and " Espace et temps balzaciens," in *L'Oeuvre de Balzac publiée dans un ordre nouveau,* 16 vols. (1949-53; Paris: Club Français du Livre, 1967) 10: i-xxv.

[12]Martin Kanes, "The Mythic Structure of *La Peau de chagrin*" 47.

[13]Peter Brooks, "Balzac, Melodrama, and Metaphor," *The Hudson Review* 22 (1969) : 218-19.

[14]Erik Erikson, *Young Man Luther: A Study in Psychoanalysis and History* (New York: Norton, 1962) 118.

[15]Holland 10. See also Sigmund Freud, *Civilization and Its Discontents* in *The Standard Edition of the Complete Psychological Works of Sigmund Freud*, 24 vols. (1930 [1929]; London: Hogarth Press, 1953-74) 64-73.

[16]Pierre Danger, "La Castration dans *La Peau de chagrin*," *L'Année balzacienne* (1982): 234-37; 242-46. Danger sees Foedora as a kind of castrating amazon, and Pauline as a smothering mother figure, both of whom emasculate Raphaël.

[17]See Freud's "Character and Anal Erotism" Std. Edition 24 vols. (1908; London: Hogarth Press and the Institute for Psycho-analysis) 9: 167-77. See also Karl Abraham's "Contributions to the Theory of the Anal Character," in *Selected Papers of Karl Abraham, M. D.*, trans. Douglas Bryan and Alix Strachey (1927; New York: Basic Books, 1957) 370-92.

[18]"Logic and Language in *La Peau de chagrin*," 245. In *Introduction à la littérature fantastique* (Paris: Seuil, 1970), Tzvetan Todorov mentions *La Peau de chagrin* specifically when he speaks of treating "littérature fantastique" as a genre: "Examiner des oeuvres littéraires dans la perspective d'un genre est une entreprise tout à fait particulière. . . . Etudier *la Peau de chagrin* dans la perspective du genre fantastique est tout autre chose qu'étudier ce livre pour lui-même, ou dans l'ensemble de l'oeuvre balzacien, ou dans celui de la littérature contemporaine" (7). On the other hand, the following critics have emphasized the realistic side of the novel: Moïse Le Yaouanc, *Nosographie de l'humanité balzacienne* (Paris: Maloine, 1959) 203-04; Pierre-Georges Castex, *Le Conte fantastique en France de Nodier à Maupassant* (Paris: José Corti, 1951). Also Maurice Allem's editorial comments in his edition to *La Peau de chagrin*.

[19] Georges Jacques, *Paysages et Structures dans "La Comédie humaine"* (Louvain: Bibliothèque de l'Université, 1975) 159; 340-42, claims that what he refers to as the "l'entonnoir balzacien" is a maternal symbol. He believes that numerous passages in *La Comédie humaine* describe a long corridor ending in the center.

[20] Anne-Marie Garagnon, "Balzac et la 'métarhétorique' dans *La Peau de Chagrin*," *Mélanges de langue et de littérature française offerts à Pierre Larthomas,* ed. Jean-Pierre Séguin (Paris: Ecole Normale Supérieure de Jeunes Filles, 1985) 195-204. There is no reference to artistic metalanguage in this article, but Garagnon does study the tendency of Balzac to use metalanguage and its implications in the novel.

[21] The reprint of the 1831 edition of *La Peau de chagrin* reads: "Je veux mourir en toi." This is even more suggestive of sexual and foetal overtones.

Chapter Seven
The Serpent: Narrative Rhythm and Trajectory

In her work, *Narratology: Introduction to the Theory of Narrative*, Mieke Bal notes that there have been few studies devoted to narrative space.[1] Bal sees narrative space in two ways: as a frame or as a background for the action; when the space becomes thematized, an object of presentation itself, it becomes an "acting plane" rather than a "plane of action" (95). This is what happens in *La Peau de chagrin*. Space becomes an agent in the narration, an active player, which John O'Connor treats in his work, *Balzac's Soluble Fish*.[2]

The sinuous line of the epigraph of *La Peau de chagrin* and its undulations suggest a number of interpretations of narrative space. Although Balzac does not refer to the epigraph line in his preface, both Philarète Chasles and Félix Davin relate the serpentine line to a spatial interpretation of the text. Chasles refers to the "allure *serpentine*" of life's course (10: 1189), as does Davin in his "Introduction" to the *Etudes philosophiques* (10: 1213). As noted earlier, in his article "*Les Etudes philosophiques*" Lovenjoul criticizes the editor of the Houssiaux edition of 1855 for interpreting the epigraph line as a snake because such a reading is both a distortion of Sterne and of epigraphs approved by Balzac. The best reason for interpreting the epigraph line as a snake lies in the serpentine and sinuous narrative metaphor in the novel. Balzac's handling of rhythm and narrative space creates a serpentine trajectory that reinforces the "allure *serpentine* de la vie*" (10: 1213).

References to serpents are common in the *Comédie humaine* and in *La Peau de chagrin*.[3] Victor Brombert points out numerous serpent images in *Le Lys dans la vallée* which are described as having sexual connotations.[4] Another famous example of the serpent image is in *Sarrasine*, made famous by Roland Barthes's *S/Z*. La Zambinella sees a snake and Sarrasine kills it:

> Quand l'artiste tendit les bras à sa maîtresse pour l'aider à descendre, il la sentit toute frissonnante."Qu'avez-vous? Vous me feriez mourrir, s'écria-t-il en la voyant pâlir, si vous aviez la moindre douleur dont je fusse la cause même innocente.—Un serpent! dit-elle en montrant une couleuvre qui se glissait le long d'un fossé. J'ai peur de ces odieuses bêtes." Sarrasine écrasa la tête de la couleuvre d'un coup de pied.[5]

Sarrasine's squashing the serpent's head is an obvious castration symbol, image and theme that go hand in hand, as Pierre Danger has demonstrated in "La Castration dans *La Peau de chagrin*." Danger includes *La Peau de chagrin* with *Gobseck* and *Sarrasine* as works that contain castration as a predominant theme (227). Among the effeminate descriptions and castration symbols he proposes is the following image of Raphaël, a knife next to him and surrounded by the serpentine spirales of his pipe's smoke:

> Il avait laissé tomber à ses pieds le couteau de malachite enrichi d'or dont il s'était servi pour couper les feuillets d'un livre. Sur ses genoux était le bec d'ambre d'un magnifique houka de l'Inde dont les spirales émaillées gisaient comme un serpent dans sa chambre, et il oubliait d'en sucer les frais parfums. (Danger 227; Balzac 10: 216)

Danger calls the castration symbols that Balzac uses in despriptions of Raphaël "des images saisissantes du sexe abandonné" (227).

In *La Peau de chagrin* there are other serpent images. For example, in the antique store Balzac uses the serpent to describe the painting of Madame Dubarry.

> Madame Dubarry peinte au pastel par Latour, une étoile sur la tête, nue et dans un nuage, paraissait contempler avec concupiscence une chibouque indienne, en cherchant à deviner l'utilité des spirales qui serpentaient vers elle. (10: 69)

During the duel in Aix-les-Bains, toward the end of the novel, Raphaël's horrified opponent is described as "un oiseau devant un serpent" (10: 275). At the end of the novel, Balzac evokes a serpent image when he shows Raphaël in anger. The old men who had infuriated Raphaël seem frozen with fear, as if they were contemplating a snake. "A cet aspect, les deux vieillards furent saisis d'un trésaillement convulsif, comme deux enfants en présence d'un serpent " (10: 220).

Certain verbs and qualifiers such as "sinuosités" and "ondoyait," imply the serpent metaphor. *La Peau de chagrin* is teeming with such words. One is evoked after Raphaël loses his money in the gambling scene. His perception is shaky as if he were delirious. "Les tourmentes de cette agonie lui imprimaient un mouvement semblable à celui des vagues et lui faisaient voir les bâtiments, les hommes, à travers un brouillard où tout ondoyait" (10: 68). In the scene at the antique shop, the masses of objects appear sinuous, snake-like. "Enfin une poussière obstinée avait jeté son léger voile sur tous ces objects dont les angles multipliés et les sinuosités nombreuses produisaient les effets les plus pittoresques" (10: 70). The serpent image as phallic symbol has been included in long lists of other symbols of castration in Balzac's novels. Danger proposes that Raphaël is effeminate and that he is surrounded by symbols of castration, including the image of serpentine smoke spirals cited earlier (227). He sees the orgy scene and the scene at the antique shop as castrating, as are Foedora and Pauline: one in rejecting Raphaël, the other in mothering him. He even interprets the prostitute as a castrating agent (235). Among the phallic symbols Danger lists are Raphaël's hat, Raphaël's father's money bag and keys, and the long knife-like face of his father: "un grand homme sec et mince, le visage en lame de couteau" (10: 121). All of these are, as well, castration symbols for Danger.

In the extensive inventory of castration symbols that Danger lists, a number are of sexual desire and sterility rather than castration. Foedora is so powerful, she is a castrating agent. "Androgyne ou femme mécanique, à la fois amazone et castrat, Foedora est, comme l'antiquaire, un monstre froid; comme lui, elle est là pour proposer un contrat qui, pour celui qui signe, aboutit à la castration" (234). She is like a statue in the candlelight: "à la lueur des bougies, son corps blanc et rose étincela comme une statue d'argent qui brille sous son enveloppe de gaze" (10: 184).

While the visible signifiers of sexuality in the novel point to masturbation, sterility, castration, maternity, and incest, critics seem to focus on images that may be used to evoke the phallus, scrotum, or semen. Danger implies that phallic symbols are a necessary correlation to castration and images of separation. It is in this last type that one is most likely to see the snake. Critical attention to the snake seems to define it as a synecdochical device for castration when in fact it is one of many signifiers of sexuality in the novel. Its import goes beyond the male critic's preoccupation with damage or loss of masculine genitalia, because it is a metaphor that signifies both male and female sexual power. The serpent is a metaphor for Balzac's view of the flux of energy and power in his universe.

Lucienne Frappier-Mazur does an excellent job of sorting out contemporary criticism on metaphor as it applies to Balzac.[6] She excludes most of the "synecdoque d'individus" (25) which for her are more in the tradition of Jakobson who considers synecdoche as reciprocity of milieu and character typical of realistic novels.[7] Admitting that there is a fine line between metaphor and tropes that operate on the principle of contiguity or inclusion, as Genette would contend, Frappier-Mazur focuses on pure metaphor using six forms determined by the presence or absence of one or several of four elements: "*comparé, motif, modalisateur comparatif,* (comme, ressembler), *comparant*—qui constituent, dans cet ordre, la comparaison canonique. Mon amour / brûle / comme / une flamme."[8]

This discussion of metaphor, metonymy, and synecdoche does not mean that certain tropes may not be both at the same time. In *Introduction à la littérature fantastique* Todorov interprets the *peau de chagrin* as simultaneously a metaphor for life and a metonym for desire. "Remarquons la complexité formelle de l'image: la peau est la métaphore pour la vie, métonymie pour le désir et elle établit une relation de proportion inverse entre ce qu'elle figure ici et là" (72). The serpent image may be interpreted in a similar manner. Since numerous critics have focused on imagery based on contiguity (either metonymic or synecdochial), the serpent as metaphor for sexual power has been largely ignored.

Trajectory

A close look at Raphaël's way through Paris reveals a serpentine trajectory. We see him for the first time in a gambling house at the Palais Royal. Then he leaves, heads toward the Pont Royal on the Seine, and wanders along the river toward the Quai Voltaire (10: 64-68).

> Il continua donc son chemin, et se dirigea vers le quai Voltaire en prenant la démarche indolente d'un désoeuvré qui veut tuer le temps. Quand il descendit les marches qui terminent le trottoir du pont, à l'angle du quai, son attention fut excitée par les bouquins étalés sur le parapet; peu s'en fallut qu'il n'en marchandât quelques-uns. (10: 66)

Next, he is lured by a beautiful woman into a store, comes out, and continues to window-shop until there are no more boutiques.

> Il marcha d'un pas mélancolique le long des magasins, en examinant sans beaucoup d'intérêt les échantillons de marchandises. Quand les boutiques lui manquèrent, il étudia le Louvre, l'Institut, les tours de Notre-Dame, celles du Palais, le Pont des Arts. (10: 67)

He enters the antique shop and has a peculiar experience when he accepts the shagree's skin. He rises to the top level of the store and descends. When he leaves the store, his friends meet him and take him to a party at Taillefer's house. He crosses the Seine again, this time with his friends at the Pont des Arts, and goes to a party in a sumptuous apartment on the rue

Joubert (10: 89-93). The salient characteristic of this trajectory is a back and forth movement. This serpentine back and forth motion will repeat itself during the entire novel: his frequent trips from his garret on what seems to be a dead-end street, the rue de Cluny off the rue des Cordiers (10: 136), to Foedora's house in the Faubourg St. Honoré, and his desperate wanderings in the country. Raphaël makes the comment that Foedora's house and his quarters are far apart.

> Entre son hôtel et la rue des Cordiers il y a presque tout Paris; le chemin me parut court, et cependant il faisait froid. Entreprendre la conquête de Foedora dans l'hiver, un rude hiver, quand je n'avais pas trente francs en ma possession, quand la distance qui nous séparait était si grande! (10: 152)

This is a path that he takes many times while in favor with Foedora. He escorts her to the theater, to Paris night spots, to parks and museums, yet he returns to his mansard at the other side of Paris. During the romance with Foedora, Raphaël's back and forth motion beats the time of the narrative like a metronome.

After Foedora rejects him, Raphaël leaves the mansard and rents an opulent place on the rue Taitbout. "Le lendemain, j'achetai des meubles chez Lesage, je louai l'appartement où tu m'as connu, rue Taitbout, et chargeai le meilleur tapissier de le décorer" (10: 195). In the last part of the novel, *L'Agonie*, Raphaël moves to a house on the rue de Varennes.

> Dans les premiers jours du mois de décembre, un vieillard, septuagénaire allait, malgré la pluie, par la rue de Varennes en levant le nez à la porte de chaque hôtel, et cherchant l'addresse de M. le marquis Raphaël de Valentin, avec la naïveté d'un enfant et l'air absorbé des philosophes. (10: 211)

In another back and forth motion, he returns to the Théâtre des Italiens where he meets Pauline, his landlord's daughter, and returns with her to his old room on the rue des Cordiers. Later he visits the scientists at the Académie des Sciences.[9] After a hopeless session with them, he leaves Paris for Aix-les-Bains and the Mont d'Or in Auvergne, stops briefly in Burgundy, and finally moves back to Paris to his room where he dies. His path through the provinces is serpentine, going to the south, then veering from the West in Auvergne to the East in Burgundy before he returns to Paris.

From the initial gambling episode at the Palais Royal, across the Seine to the Quai Voltaire, across the Seine again on the Pont des Arts to Taillefer's house, from his mansard in the 5th *arrondissement* to Foedora's home in the Faubourg St. Honoré, Raphaël follows an undulating path through the Parisian jungle. If we were to plot the major points of Raphaël's journey, we would see more serpentine undulations back and forth across the Seine, from Foedora's apartment to Raphaël's mansard, from Paris to the provinces, from Aix-les-Bains to Auvergne, and then to Burgundy. If we were to connect these points we would recreate the serpentine epigraph line.

The Whirlpool

If one examined the movement of the snake in more detail, it would be clear that in addition to moving in an undulating fashion, it constricts, either in killing and eating its prey, or in recoiling for defense or preparation to strike. When the snake constricts, it creates an energy structure similar to a whirlpool which constricts and dilates as energy propels the whirlpool into motion. The opening created by the whirlpool is a vaginal image. If the serpent figure is a metaphor that permeates the space, trajectory, and rhythm of the narration, there must be constriction and dilation as well as undulation. This series of constrictions and dilations will create a throbbing, undulating, sexual rhythm, that advances the action. We will consider seven scenes in the narration that illustrate this constriction-dilation: the antique shop, the orgy, the description of Raphaël in his room, Raphaël in the casement of Foedora's bedroom window, the room in Auvergne, the hamlet in Burgundy, and finally Raphaël's bed.

In *La Pensée de Balzac*, Per Nykrog describes Balzac's view of the universe and society as having the form of spheres. One of the underlying principles governing these spheres is that of movement. Everything exists in a state of flux in Balzac's world. Quoting *Louis Lambert*, Nykrog reiterates Balzac's statement: "Tout ici-bas n'existe que par le Mouvement et par le Nombre. . . . Le Mouvement est en quelque sorte le Nombre agissant" (Nykrog 140-41; Balzac 11: 689-90). According to Nykrog, everything may be reduced to constant circulation and flux.

> Ainsi la formule du monde se résout pour Louis Lambert, (et, sans doute, pour Balzac aussi) en un flux permanent de combinaisons, en proportions toujours nouvelles, d'éléments qui, en eux-mêmes, ne sont que des manifestations (des "transmutations") d'une même substance à des dégrés différents de transformation (cf. la première série des Pensées). (141)

Movement is the passage from one state of distribution to another.

> Le Mouvement est donc, selon cette formule, un changement entre les proportions ou entre les dosages, la somme des passages incessants d'un état de distribution vers un autre. . . . En effet, les conflits qui font l'étoffe de ce roman sont invariablement présentés comme l'affrontement d'un certain nombre de personnages, disposant chacun d'un certain contingent de ressources: énergie, argent, position sociale, alliance, liaisons, avec d'autres personnages, etc. (141)

In his article on castration in *La Peau de chagrin*, Pierre Danger sees the description of the countryside that surrounds Raphaël as basically feminine (241). A number of these images in the novel are characterized by the curve. These would include water and descriptions that evoke water such as waves, rain, and fog.

> La matière dominante est l'eau, la forme dominante la courbe: il n'est question que de brouillard, de l'ondulation des toits, "océan de vagues immobiles," de mousses, de "couleurs ravivées par la pluie," et tout ce tableau s'incarne soudain dans la ravissante image, fugitivement entrevue, de "quelque

jeune fille faisant sa toilette," en laquelle se rejoignent le thème de l'eau et de la féminité. (241)

Both Danger's and Nykrog's work imply that Balzac saw the world in the form of curves because of the constant ebb and flow of energy. The snake, then, is not only a phallic symbol, but also a symbol of sexual energy behind the flux extant in the Balzacian universe. Since Balzac's universe is a dualistic one, for every male image there is a counterpart. Where there are virile, phallic and castration allusions, there will be its complement of female, sterile, and fertile images.

Three ingredients create the energy that propels the whirlpools in this narrative: sequestration, a spiral pattern, and motion. All three must coincide to create the whirlpool. Sometimes the whirlpool turns as a result of the motion generated from delirium and hallucination.[10] Sometimes however, the energy that turns the whirlpool is anger.

In *Balzac's Soluble Fish*, John R. O'Connor describes the symbolism of space in Balzac's novels. Often the locale, such as a closed room or a walled convent, suggests that the action is protected. Many of Balzac's novels take place in sequestered places.[11] The scene of *Ferragus* is a room in a convent. The action in *La Peau de chagrin* unfolds in several sequestered spaces: the antique shop, Raphaël's *mansard*, Foedora's salon, her bedroom, and Raphaël's bedroom. Sequestration is of paramount importance in creating the whirlpool because it must occur within a confined space. The sequestration can be anything from the walled effect of the crater in Auvergne to Raphaël's room at the rue de Varennes. Usually, however, it is patterned after the chambers in a nautilus, rooms within other structures. The nautilus pattern becomes a violent vortex when the energy of hallucination or anger is added to the scene. The vortex becomes a swirling maw that consumes Raphaël. A vaginal image, it provides a counterpoint to his serpentine trajectory though Paris.[12] After Raphaël is consumed into the vortex, his release usually occurs with his going outside into the Paris streets, causing a dilation.[13] This constriction and dilation effect creates a throbbing cadence that readers feel throughout the novel.

The opening scene in *La Peau de chagrin* shows Raphaël losing his money in the gambling house and wandering the streets thinking of throwing himself in the Seine. The first constriction occurs in the antique merchant's shop. This scene, perhaps the most studied of any in the novel, depicts a Raphaël in delirium.[14] Balzac uses a number of techniques to create the illusion of movement, among them the metaphor of the whirlpool to create the feeling of constriction. The antique shop becomes a vortex, and Raphaël becomes one and the same with all the avatars of civilizations past and present. Since the antique shop is a narrow shop with several floors, Raphaël climbs the stairs in order to see everything. He climbs three floors and enters three rooms on each level. His path creates a spiral pattern like a chambered nautilus as he enters the three rooms on each level, ascends to the last room where he meets the antique dealer, and accepts the wild ass' skin. At this point, the spiral is complete.

Raphaël's trajectory through the nautilus-like path creates the illusion of movement. Balzac accelerates this movement and constricts the whirlpool through a variety of techniques. The small room within the shop conveys a constriction effect, while Raphaël's movement creates a feeling of motion. The most effective method of communicating motion is simply through abundance. Balzac stocks the antique shops' rooms with objects from the great civilizations. There is complete disorder within the rooms; the objects are not organized, symbolic of Balzac's view of the eighteenth century concept of progress. Balzac saw no civilization as superior to the other (Nykrog 210). Nykrog considers this attitude not completely typical of Balzac.

> Une troisième famille d'opinions est plus rare; elle considère les Etats et les civilisations comme une poussière d'incidents sans valeur et sans conséquence. On la trouve surtout représentée chez les personnages du romancier, plus particulièrement chez ceux qui sont arrivés à un poste d'observation très élevé par rapport au quotidien .... (210)

Louis Lambert states in a letter to his uncle that all civilizations are equal, one not superior to the others.

> Les nations témoignent de leur grandeur par des monuments, ou de leur bonheur par le bien-être individuel. Les monuments modernes valent-ils les anciens? j'en doute. Les arts qui procèdent immédiatement de l'individu, les productions du génie ou de la main ont peu gagné. Les jouissances de Lucullus valaient bien celles de Samuel Bernard, de Beaujon ou du roi de Bavière. (11: 649-50)

The whirlpool may be interpreted as a symbol of Balzac's anti-progress philosophy. If the basis of Balzac's philosophy is that all is movement, one of the central themes of his thought must be movement and change.[15] Balzac explains that Raphaël's torpor causes him to see everything in the antique shop in movement.

> Il retomba bientôt dans ses vertiges, et continua d'apercevoir les choses sous d'étranges couleurs, et animées d'un léger mouvement dont le principe était sans doute dans une irrégulière circulation de son sang, tantôt bouillonnant comme une cascade, tantôt tranquille et fade comme l'eau tiède. (10: 68)

Chaos and disorganization create the illusion of movement.

> Les instruments de mort, poignards, pistolets curieux, armes à secret, étaient jetés pêle-mêle avec des instruments de vie: soupières en porcelaine, assiettes de Saxe, tasses diaphanes venues de Chine, salières antiques, drageoirs féodaux. (10: 69)

This process takes place in three stages. First there is the illusion of movement. An intermediate stage follows in which Raphaël becomes one with his surroundings, in this case the different periods of history. Balzac explains this process to the reader upon Raphaël's entry into the shop.

> Portant sa croix jusqu'au bout, il parut écouter son conducteur

> et lui répondit par gestes ou par monosyllables; mais insensiblement il sut conquérir le droit d'être silencieux, et put se livrer, sans crainte à ses dernières méditations, qui furent terribles. Il était poète, et son âme rencontra fortuitement une immense pâture: il devait voir par avance les ossements de vingt mondes. (10: 69)

Balzac describes what Raphaël sees as a multifaceted mirror, each facet representing a world (10: 69-70). The sight of all these civilizations together created a particular experience, similar to neoplatonic ecstasy: "il sortit de la vie réelle, monta par degrés vers un monde idéal, arriva dans les palais enchantés de l'Extase . . . " (10: 70). The action verbs that can be extracted from the following passage create the illusion of movement: "se heurtaient," "souriaient," "mordre," "courir," "grimper" (10: 69).

> Au premier coup d'oeil, les magasins lui offrirent un tableau confus, dans lequel toutes les oeuvres humaines et divines se heurtaient. Des crocodiles, des singes, des boas empaillés souriaient à des vitraux d'église, semblaient vouloir mordre des bustes, courir après des laques, ou grimper sur des lustres. (10: 69)

Balzac also creates the illusion of movement in the rapid changes from light to dark. "Ces monstrueux tableaux étaient encore assujettis à mille accidents de lumière par la bizarrerie d'une multitude de reflets dus à la confusion des nuances, à la brusque opposition des jours et des noirs " (10: 69-70). He accentuates the illusion of movement by hinting that the action has been interrupted. Efforts to restrain actions and extinguish light imply that a greater force stands behind what is visible in the text. Sensations struggle to be noticed and experienced. "L'oreille croyait entendre des cris interrompus, l'esprit saisir des drames inachevés, l'oeil apercevoir des lueurs mal étouffées" (10: 70). More movement is created with the serpentine description that Balzac adds to the picture. The teeming baroque images in the room reinforce the serpentine metaphor of Philarète Chasles and Félix

Davin. "Enfin une poussière obstinée avait jeté son léger voile sur tous ces objets, dont les angles multipliés et ces sinuosités nombreuses produisaient les effets les plus pittoresques" (10: 70). Furthermore, he describes the teeming room as an "océan de meubles, d'inventions, de modes, d'oeuvres, de ruines," but all incomplete, suggesting an unnamed immensity (10: 71). Again, Balzac reinforces this immensity by presenting an incomplete picture.

Balzac also conveys the illusion of movement by personifying the objets d'art in the antique shop. They seem to speak to Raphaël: "une statue de marbre assise sur une colonne torse et rayonnant de blancheur, lui parla des mythes voluptueux de la Grèce et de l'Ionie." (10: 70). He smiles contemplating the figure of a dancing girl on an Etruscan vase. "Ah! qui n'aurait souri comme lui de voir sur un fond rouge la fille brune dansant dans la fine argile d'un vase étrusque devant le Dieu Priape qu'elle saluait d'un air joyeux?" (10: 70) The remaining subjects are depicted as performing an action as if in reality, not as representation. This representation metamorphoses into a living scene:

> . . . le peuple courroucé défilaient lentement devant lui comme les vaporeuses figures d'un rêve. Enfin la Rome chrétienne dominait ces images. Une peinture ouvrait les cieux, il y voyait la Vierge Marie plongée dans un nuage d'or, au sein des anges, éclipsant la gloire du soleil, écoutant les plaintes des malheureux auxquels cette Eve régénérée souriait d'un air doux. (10: 71)

Later Raphaël becomes one with these creatures in the painting and statue. This is achieved by the use of the indirect and direct object pronouns receiving the action of the verbs. "Là dormait un enfant en cire, sauvé du cabinet de Ruysch, et cette ravissante créature *lui* rappelait les joies de son jeune âge" (10: 72; emphasis added). At the sight of a young native girl, his imagination "*lui* peignait la vie simple de la nature. . ." (10: 72; emphasis added).

Next, Raphaël is transported to the time and place which the characters depict. Cicero's head evokes ancient Rome for Raphaël. "Le jeune homme contempla Senatus Populusque romanus . . . " (10: 71). When he touches a mosaic he is transported to Italy during the Renaissance.

> . . . il assistait aux orgies des Borgia, courait dans les Abruzzes, aspirait aux amours italiennes, se passionnait pour les blancs visages aux longs yeux noirs. Il frémissait aux dénouements nocturnes interrompus par la froide épée d'un mari, en apercevant une dague du Moyen Age. . . . Une salière sortie des ateliers de Benvenuto Cellini le reportait au sein de la Renaissance, au temps où les arts et la licence fleurissaient. . . . Il vit les conquêtes d'Alexandre sur une camée, les massacres de Pizarre dans une arquebuse à mèche, les guerres de religion . . . au fond d'un casque. (10: 71)

That everything is described from Raphaël's point of view creates a circle with Raphaël at the center point of a swirl or whirlpool. After accepting the ass's skin, Raphaël descends the staircase and exits the antique shop. Upon stepping into the street, he meets friends who take him across the Seine a second time and then to a party.

Closure and sequestration are themes of this scene, as of all the others. Raphaël is again placed at the center of a sequestered space, two rooms in a sumptuous house in the midst of an orgy. Here again, the nautilus pattern reappears because Raphaël occupies a room within a room. The sense of closure and movement are created by the description of the number of people crowded into the space. Balzac's use of dialogue and description call the reader's attention to the energy created by many people talking.

> L'un venait de révéler un talent neuf. . . . L'autre avait hasardé la veille un livre plein de verdeur. . . . Plus loin, un statuaire dont la figure pleine de rudesse accusait quelque vigoureux génie, causait. . . . Ici, le plus spirituel de nos caricaturistes. . . guettait les épigrammes. . . . Là, ce jeune et audacieux écrivain. . . distillait la quintessence des pensées

politiques. . . . De jeunes auteurs sans style étaient auprès de jeunes auteurs sans idées. . . . (10: 94-95)

The feeling of movement created by the luxuries and richness of the apartment is analogous to that created by the abundant curiosities in the antique shop.

> La soie et l'or tapissaient les appartements. De riches candélabres supportant d'innombrables bougies faisaient briller les plus légers détails des frises dorées, les délicates ciselures du bronze et les somptueuses couleurs de l'ameublement. Les fleurs rares, de quelques jardinières artistement construites avec des bambous répandaient de doux parfums. Tout jusqu'aux draperies respirait une élégance sans prétention. . . . (10: 95-96)

A sumptuous meal is served to the group. Next, they move to another room within the hotel continuing the nautilus pattern. This room is even more seductive and voluptuous. Again, light accompanies the display. "Sous les étincelantes bougies d'un lustre d'or, autour d'une table chargée de vermeil, un groupe de femmes se présenta soudain aux convives hébétés dont les yeux s'allumèrent comme autant de diamants" (10: 109). The numerous place settings and the action of dishes served one after the other create the feeling of movement.

> Les cristaux répétaient les couleurs d'iris dans leurs reflets étoilés, les bougies traçaient des feux croisés à l'infini, les mets placés sous des dômes d'argent, aiguisaient l'appétit et la curiosité. Les paroles furent assez rares. Les voisins se regardèrent. Le vin de Madère circula. (10: 97)

Movement is also implied in the group's drunkenness: "quelques fronts pâles rougissaient, plusieurs nez commençaient à s'empourprer, les visages s'allumaient, les yeux pétillaient" (10: 97). Soon, everyone was talking at once (10: 97-98), as if in a battle.

> Mais cette mêlée de paroles où les paradoxes douteusement lumineux, les vérités grotesquement habillées se heurtèrent à travers les cris, les jugements interlocutoires, les arrêts souverains, et les niaiseries, comme au milieu d'un combat se croisent les boulets, les balles et la mitraille. . . . (10: 98)

Finally, the group's delirium sets the whirlpool in motion.

> Emportés par une espèce de tempête, ces esprits semblaient, comme la mer irritée contre ses falaises, vouloir ébranler toutes les lois entre lesquelles flottent les civilisations, satisfaisant ainsi sans le savoir, la volonté de Dieu. . . . Furieuse et burlesque, la discussion fut . . . un sabbat des intelligences. (10: 98)

To create the illusion of movement, Balzac uses a succession of short dialogues. The whirlpool accelerates and constricts with speed.

> —Monsieur. . . .
> —A quoi bon. . . .
> —Quelle horreur. . . .
> —Hé! Monsieur. . . . (10: 100)

They move to another room, more sumptuous than the other, to continue the orgy where there are beautiful women available to the men. Initially there is a pause in the action, and the men are described as if in ecstasy. "Elles restaient interdites, honteuses. . . . les convives, surpris dans un moment de faiblesse s'abandonnèrent aux délices d'une voluptueuse extase" (10: 110-11). Soon, the guests start talking, and the spoken word generates the feeling of movement.

> Des groupes se formèrent. Vous eussiez dit d'un salon de bonne

compagnie. . . . Mais bientôt quelques rires éclatèrent, le murmure augmenta, les voix s'élevèrent. L'orgie . . . menaça par intervalles de se réveiller. Ces alternatives de silence et de bruit eurent une vague ressemblance avec une harmonie de Beethoven. (10: 111)

Sound and socializing continue the illusion of movement and activity.

At the end of the orgy, we hear in a flashback the story of Raphaël's life in his garret and of his courtship of Foedora. Within a small room, Raphaël relates events that occur in three sequestered places: the garret, Foedora's salon, and finally her bedroom. The interplated story mirrors the nautilus structure because Raphaël describes this appartment's closed quarters from within a room. The quick, drunken exchanges convey the illusion of movement.

Raphaël's garret was, as in other rooms in Balzac's novels, a sequestered place. The adjectives Raphaël uses to describe his quarters are: "emprisonné" and "captivé " (10: 138). During Raphaël's flashback, he relates his life of poverty in this little room. The street appeared to be a dead end, the rue de Cluny, off the rue des Cordiers: "la rue n'aboutissait à rien, et ne devait pas être très passante" (10: 136). His apartment was in the Hôtel St. Quentin, a mansard, small and poorly decorated. Again light comes in through a small window which surprises him with "des effets nouveaux" (10: 138). In this room the illusion of movement is achieved through delirium. Raphaël's ideas and mental activity overwhelmed him: "quand j'écoutais les voix terribles et confuses de l'inspiration, quand d'une source inconnue les images ruisselaient dans mon cerveau palpitant" (10: 137). Sometimes in his delirium, words would come alive for him. "A force de contempler les objets qui m'entouraient, je trouvais à chacun sa physionomie, son caractère; souvent ils me parlaient . . . les toits . . . se coloraient, pâlissaient, brillaient, s'attristaient, ou s'égayaient. . . " (10: 138). Because of hunger, Raphaël had hallucinative day dreams.

> Par une sorte de mirage ou de calenture, moi, veuf de toutes les femmes que je désirais, dénué de tout et dans une mansarde d'artiste, je me voyais alors entouré de maîtresses

> ravissantes. . . . J'étais rongé de vices, plongé dans la débauche, voulant tout, ayant tout; enfin ivre à jeun, comme Saint Antoine dans sa tentation. Heureusement le sommeil finissait par éteindre ces visions dévorantes; le lendemain la science m'appelait en souriant, et je lui étais fidèle. (10: 139)

Hallucination is the motor that turns the whirlpool. The same delirium occurs again after Raphaël has been rejected by Foedora, and Pauline visits his little room. He is so delirious that he cannot comprehend Pauline's words when she tries to speak to him: "j'avais entendu sa voix, sans comprendre le sens de ses paroles" (10: 191). Later, when he returns to the Hôtel St. Quintin and they declare their love, he learns that Pauline is rich. The same delirium returns in the sequestered room. He describes himself as "en proie à une sorte de délire." (10: 229).

Another scene that combines sequestration and delirium occurs in Raphaël's voyeur scene in Foedora's bedroom. It is there, after he hears Foedora described as an enigma, that he experiences delirium. "Ces paroles excitèrent en moi une sorte d'ivresse . . ." (10: 149). This delirium is more developed in a bizarre scene in which Raphaël sneaks into Foedora's bedroom and hides in her window casement. Foedora's presence lights the small deserted room. Undressed, she exudes bright light: "à travers sa chemise et à la lueur des bougies, son corps blanc et rose étincela comme une statue d'argent qui brille sous son enveloppe de gaze" (10: 184). As in the orgy scene, the whirlpool's movement is communicated first with light, then with sound. In the orgy, the room's light reflects on crystal and luxurious accoutrements; sound comes from the guests' excited chatter. In this scene, Foedora provides light with her presence and sound with her singing: "elle était agitée, elle soupirait; ses lèvres laissaient échapper un léger bruit perceptible à l'ouïe et qui indiquait des mouvements d'impatience. . ." (10: 184). It is interesting to note that when Raphaël is sequestered in the smallest enclosure, he is capable of hearing everything. When he hears Foedora sing he succumbs to the illusion that she is capable of kindness. He remarks that this sound has changed his image of her: "ce lambeau d'une pensée inconnue, que je devais remporter pour toute lumière, avait tout à coup changé mes idées sur Foedora" (10: 184). Raphaël describes her music as language. "Les fantaisies du souffle qui passait entre ses dents, tantôt faible, tantôt accentué, grave ou leger, formaient une sorte de langage auquel j'attachais des pensées et des sentiments" (10: 185).

This protected enclosed space affords Raphaël the opportunity to see without being seen. He passes through three areas: the salon, the bedroom, and finally its window casement where he hides in order to spy on Foedora. The structure contains again the nautilus-like chambers. This time, however, the image of Raphaël in the window casement creates a pause in the whirlpool's momentum because of the paradoxical qualities of the nautilus structure, which resembles a whirlpool but also negates it by being static. This whirlpool is propelled by Raphaël's delirium, recreated by his illusion of the room's spinning and whirling. Paradoxically, he describes himself in the window as a spider in its web. "Pour ne pas me fatiguer inutilement, je me tins debout en attendant le moment critique pendant lequel je devais rester suspendu comme une araignée dans sa toile" (10: 180).[16] In this room Raphaël is in the smallest and most protected place that he has experienced. Balzac's description makes his hiding place seem sealed and impervious. "La moire blanche et la mousseline des rideaux formaient devant moi de gros plis semblables à des tuyaux d'orgue, où je pratiquai des trous avec mon canif à fin de tout voir par ces espèces de meurtrières." (10: 180) The room is full of sounds, sounds from the salon and of Foedora singing as she enters her bedroom. She becomes a siren, a goddess.

> De note en note, la voix s'éleva, Foedora sembla s'animer, les richesses de son gosier se déployèrent, et cette mélodie prit alors quelque chose de divin. La comtesse avait dans l'organe, une clarté vive, une justesse de ton, je ne sais quoi d'harmonique et de vibrant qui pénétrait, remuait, et chatouillait le coeur. . . . elle paraissait s'écouter elle-même. . . . mais quand elle se tut, sa physionomie changea. . . . (10: 182)

The delirium that Raphaël feels is similar to the delirium of Ulysses upon hearing the Sirens that lured sailors to shipwreck. Raphaël is seduced into thinking that perhaps Foedora is really kind. The siren Foedora changes as a result of the song. She tempts Raphaël, making him believe that she is kind and would listen to his feelings if he were to try again.

> Je rêvais avec elle, j'espérais m'initier à ses secrets en pénétrant son sommeil, je flottais entre mille partis contraires, entre mille jugements. A voir ce beau visage, calme et pur, il me fut impossible de refuser un coeur à cette femme. Je résolus de faire encore une tentative. (10: 185)

Raphaël turns within a mental whirlpool. The contradiction at the end of the paragraph illustrates his confusion. "En lui racontant ma vie, mon amour, mes sacrifices, peut-être pourrais-je réveiller en elle la pitié, de lui arracher une larme, à celle qui ne pleurait jamais" (10: 185). Raphaël was tortured by desire for Foedora, being so close and enticing, yet so inaccessible. Again delusion changes the motion of the whirlpool from the static image of Raphaël suspended in the window to him spinning at the center of a whirlpool.[17] After Foedora goes to bed, Raphaël goes down the servants' stairs and out into the street. Two days later he returns to the countess, declares his love, and she rejects him. Later he refers to his love for Foedora as "la folie." "Il fallait oublier Foedora, me guérir de ma folie, reprendre ma studieuse solitude, ou mourir" (10: 190).

In the last part of the novel, entitled *L'Agonie*, there is a different kind of sequestration. In order to avoid desire and the shrinking of the shagreen's skin, Raphaël has returned to his sumptuous apartments and uses his valet, Jonathas, as a shield against the outside world and situations that would tempt him to express desire.

Jonathas calls himself Raphaël's "père nourricier" (10: 213). The narrateur presents Jonathas as a sixth sense who screens life's emotions before they reach Raphaël. Jonathas describes his master's sequestration in the following manner:

> Monsieur n'a voulu voir personne. Il mène une drôle de vie, M. Porriquet, entendez-vous? une vie inconciliable. Monsieur

se lève tous les jours à la même heure. Il n'y a que moi, moi seul, voyez-vous? qui puisse entrer dans sa chambre. (10: 213)

Their conversations are one-sided, with Jonathas anticipating Raphaël's every desire and asking him only yes or no questions. His menus are planned. He wears the same clothes that Jonathas replaces when they wear out. Elimination of all desire changes the description of the enclosure in which Raphaël finds himself. He has never escaped sequestration, but now the swirl of desire is driven by something other than desire, i.e., anger. The energy of anger replaces the energy of desire which sets the whirlpool in motion. When Raphaël finds himself trapped into wishing for his teacher's success, he becomes furious, then falls into reverie.

> La colère avait blanchi le visage de Raphaël; une légère écume sillonnait ses lèvres tremblantes, et l'expression de ses yeux était sanguinaire. A cet aspect, les deux vieillards furent saisis d'un tressaillement convulsif, comme deux enfants en présence d'un serpent. (10: 220)

After Raphaël fails in an attempt to control the shrinking skin through science, he leaves Paris in a desperate search for a way to stop desire and the subsequent shrinking of the skin. The sequestration theme resonates in each locale, even in the provinces. Consider the description of the Auvergne landscape after Raphaël's disasterous visit to Aix-les-Bains:

> Figurez-vous un cône renversé, mais un cône de granit largement évasé, espèce de cuvette dont les bords étaient morcelés par des anfractuosités bizarres: ici des tables droites sans végétation, unies, bleuâtres, et sur lesquelles les rayons solaires glissaient comme sur un miroir.... (10: 277)

At the bottom of the crater was a lake, and next to it was a little house. Even the outside scene is sequestered, and the crater gives the image its verticality. In his sequestered place, it is the people and their pronouncement of death that inspire Raphaël's anger. Although the whirlpool is not described in this scene, its ingredients are here: sequestration and energy that create the illusion of movement, this time propelled by anger.

Raphaël flees to Burgundy and finds another sequestered spot. This time it is a hamlet at the bottom of a gorge: "des hameaux modestement cachés au fond d'une gorge de roches jaunâtres montraient la pointe de leurs clochers..." (10: 286). The sounds of people and music awake Raphaël and the sight of an old blind man playing a violin with no dancers seems fantastic to him (10: 287). He becomes angry and returns to Paris. Again, anger propels the motion of the whirlpool.

After these giant hops from one sequestered spot to another in the provinces, Raphaël's pendulate trajectory comes to an end, as he returns to his apartment in Paris. His sequestration continues in the shrinking size of his quarters. He retreats to his bed and remains in a dream-like state. Even then, he can't prevent himself from thinking of desirable things. In his bed, the last and smallest place of Raphaël's sequestration, it is dreams that provide the engine for the whirlpool. The narrator speculates on Raphaël's dreams because of his contented look:

> ... il souriait transporté sans doute par un rêve dans une belle vie. Peut-être était-il centenaire, peut-être ses petits enfants lui souhaitaient-ils de longs jours; peut-être de son banc rustique, sous le soleil, assis sous le feuillage, apercevait-il, comme le prophète, en haut de la montagne, la terre promise, dans un bienfaisant lointain. (10: 290)

To see the serpent as a castration symbol is excessively narrow and phallocentric, and it prevents us from fully understanding the complexity of sexual imagery in Balzac's work. It is the critics' insistence on pondering the phallic synecdochial images that prevents them from perceiving the larger metaphor of sexual power which I believe is linked to Balzac's concept of immensity. If we take an androgenic approach to the interpretation of the serpent, it becomes a metaphor that permeates several levels of the narrative.[18] Consistent interpretation of the synecdoche as metaphor explains why several fine critics maintain that the concept of immensity goes beyond the metaphorical.[19] The serpent metaphor not only dictates the form and character of Raphaël's trajectory through the novel but governs the use of space and narrative rhythm through the novel. This rhythm does not refer exclusively to the male aspects of sexuality, as some male critics (victims of "castration fixation") would infer, but contains an important female counterpart in the sinuous curves of Raphaël's serpentine trajectory and in the constriction and dilation of the whirlpools in the seven sequestered scenes discussed here. This feminine complement to the serpentine metaphor gives it its infinite and mythological character. It is the constriction and dilation of its whirlpools that beats the throbbing cadence of the ebb and flow of sexual energy, propels the novel's action forward, and keeps time to the tune of Raphaël's Dance of Death.

Notes

[1] Bal 93.

[2] John R. O'Connor, *Balzac's Soluble Fish* (Madrid: José Porrúa Turanzas, 1977). O'Connor does not focus on *La Peau de chagrin* in his study, but some of his findings are applicable here.

[3] Michel Thérien makes no mention of serpents in his article, "Métaphores animales et écriture balzaciennes: Le portrait et la description." *L'Année balzacienne* (1979): 193-208.

[4] Victor Brombert, "Natalie ou le lecteur caché de Balzac," *Etudes critiques offertes à Georges Poulet* (Paris: Librairie José Corti, 1972) 183. Numerous works have explored the symbolism of the phallus. Jean-Joseph Goux, in *Freud, Marx. Economie et symbolique* (Paris: Seuil, 1973) 66, explores the parallel between Freudian and economic analysis. He believes that the phallus and gold are related in that they both transcend partial meaning to stand for the whole. The phallus substitutes for sexual energy and gold for merchandise.

[5] Balzac, 6: 1070. In *S/Z* Barthes says that this image signifies castration "L'épisode du serpent est à la fois un exemplum (arme inductive de l'ancienne rhétorique) et un signifiant (renvoyant à un sème de caractère fixé en l'occurrence sur le castrat)." (176-77)

[6] Lucienne Frappier-Mazur, *L'Expression Métaphorique dans "la Comédie humaine"* (Paris: Klincksieck, 1976).

[7] Roman Jakobson, *Essais de linguistique générale* (Paris: Seuil, 1963) 63-65.

[8] Frappier-Mazur 19. See also Gérard Genette, "La rhétorique restreinte," *Figures III* (Paris: Seuil, 1972) 38; in the same volume, "La rhétorique restreinte," 41-63. Other sources for my definition of metaphor are Monroe C. Beardsley, "The Metaphorical Twist," *Philosophy and Phenomenological Research* 22 (1962): 293-307. He sees the definition of metaphor as one based on opposition of meaning rather than comparison (298). For the définitive work on metaphor see Paul Ricoeur, *La Métaphore vive* (Paris: Seuil, 1975).

[9] Raphaël situates the Académie des Sciences between "La Halle aux Vins, immense recueil de tonneaux, et la Salpétrière, immense séminaire d'ivrognerie" (10: 237).

[10] In *La Poétique de l'espace* (Paris: PUF, 1958), Gaston Bachelard treats the whirlpool structure as a "shell." He sees all three ingrédients, confined space, the spiral structure, and the resulting energy as a consequence of verticality (35: 105-29).

[11] In *Balzac's Soluble Fish*, John R. O'Connor concentrates on *Ferragus*.

[12] Bachelard makes the connection between the spiral, the shell, and female sexual images (112-13).

[13] See Charles D. Minahen's "Tourbillons de lumière: The symbolism of Rimbaud's illuminating vortices," *Stanford French Review* 9 (1985): 358-64. He treats the history of this image in literature from the Greeks to Rimbaud. The whirlpool is a metaphor that has existed since the Greeks. According to Minahen, in the *Ancilla* the pre-Socratic philosophers compared logos to a "fiery water spout." Lucretius refers to a recurrent sea image in *De Rerum Nature*. One of the major characteristics of the vortex is

the whirlwind, whose entry into a vision of transcendent unity forces a synthesis of disorder at the vortical core. This image, not a new or infrequent one in literature, has a simple meaning. All things correspond and are one. According to Minahen, the observer and his surroundings combine as well. Minahen's word is "interchangeable" (364). The past, future, and present all become one in the same.

14Among the many studies of the antique shop scene, Stirling Haig's "Dualistic Patterns in *La Peau de chagrin*," is the best. He sees Raphaël's entering the antique shop as a descent into the underworld. This Dantesque view is not inconsistent with the interpretation of the whirlpool structure. For some other studies that treat the antique shop scene see: Anne-Marie Garagnon, 195-204; also Nicole Cazauran, "Le Tableau du magasin d'antiquités dans *La Peau de chagrin*," in *Mélanges de langue et de littérature française offerts à Pierre Larthomas,* ed. Jean-Pierre Séguin (Paris: Ecole Normale Supérieure de Jeunes Filles, 1985) 87-98.

15The first rule of his laws of the universe as described in *Louis Lambert* and quoted by Per Nykrog: "Tout ici-bas n'existe que par le Mouvement et par le Nombre" (140; also Balzac 11: 689). "In this instance, mouvement means more than action. Perhaps a better term is flux. "Ainsi la formule du monde se résout pour Louis Lambert (et, sans aucun doute, pour Balzac aussi) en un flux permanent de combinaisons, en proportions toujours nouvelles. . ." (141).

16Samuel W. Weber discusses this metaphor as a Freudian image in *Unwrapping Balzac: A Reading of "La Peau de chagrin"* (Toronto: U of Toronto P, 1979) 97.

17The whirlpool is a mythological image, and it is fitting that a mythological reference like that of the Sirens would propel the whirlpool. Although Martin Kanes does not mention these images in his article, he does treat the mythological nature of *La Peau de chagrin* in "The Mythic Structure of *La Peau de chagrin*," 46-59.

18See any of the French feminists' works in Elaine Marks and Isabelle de Courtivron, eds., *New French Feminisms: An Anthology* (Amherst: U of Mass. P, 1980). See especially Hélène Cixous who argues for a kind of bisexual writing in which each person writes and does not exclude the other (254). For a feminist critique of Freudian sexual analysis read, Luce Irigaray. *Ce Sexe qui n'en est pas un* (Paris: Minuit, 1974) and *Speculum de l'autre femme* (Paris: Minuit, 1974). Shoshana Felman, "Women and Madness: The Critical Phallacy" *Diacritics* 5.4 (1975): 2-10 provides a feminist's interpretation of Balzac.

19See Lucienne Frappier-Mazur, "Espace et Regard and *La Comédie humaine*" 327; Georges Poulet, *La Distance intérieure* 122-93 and "Espace et temps balzaciens" 10: i-xxv.

Lithograph, 1851-53 Marescq edition
Oeuvres illustrées

Chapter Eight
Strewn Goblets and Fallen Crowns: Balzac's Carnival

In the Marescq edition of *La Peau de chagrin* there is an interesting lithograph at the end of the novel. It contains a small engraving of a table strewn with cornucopias, goblets, and crowns. This small lithograph captured and summarized the carnivalesque elements in *La Peau de chagrin* long before critics ever broached the subject. The goblet and fruit refer to carnival oral imagery, and the cast off crown recalls the burlesque reversal of order and hierarchy typical of the carnival.

The term "carnivalization" coined by Bakhtin in his *Rabelais and His World*, was written in 1940, but not published until 1965.[1] Pomorska describes this work as "semiotic" because it is the first to underscore the importance of "verbal, pictorial, and gestural . . . sign systems" (Pomorska x). The subject of *Rabelais and His World* is laughter and the way it appears in different forms of folk rituals and festivals. The path from Bakhtin to Balzac might appear circuitous, but the former devotes a portion of his work to a romantic interpretation of the carnival theme, listing Balzac as an author who used carnival imagery. [2]

The carnival's source can be traced to the banquets of antiquity. Feasts were donated during times of crisis, usually by the socially and politically powerful establishment.[3] One critic traces the carnival tradition to the *deipnon* of the Greeks and the Latin *cena*, whose traditions continued into the Middle Ages.[4] Although there are references to the festivals of antiquity (Petronius) in the banquet scene attended by Raphaël and his friends in

La Peau de chagrin, the episode's source is clearly Rabelais. Rabelais is expressly mentioned or implied several times, as when the guests say they are going to spend the evening "à la Panurge" (10: 91).

That Balzac was inspired by Rabelais is a known and documented fact.[5] Jean Claude Fizaine states that Rabelais was a model for *La Peau de chagrin*, a model he describes as simultaneously devouring, producing, and creating.[6] He sees Balzac's use of laughter and contemporary irony as a recreation of Rabelais' style. Another critic, Elisheva Rosen, relating Balzac and Rabelais, mentions Bakhtin's analysis of carnival themes and images in the banquet scene at the beginning of *La Peau de chagrin*, thereby establishing a link with Rabelais' rendition of the carnival.[7]

Bakhtin defines carnival in both sociological and philosophical terms. He sees festivals of the carnival type (comic rites and cults, clowns, fools, giants, dwarfs, and jugglers), all that is grotesque, and the vast and manifold literature of parody, as having one element in common; they belong to the "culture of folk carnival humor."[8]

> In spite of their variety, folk festivities of the carnival type, the comic rites and cults, the clowns and fools, giants, dwarfs, and jugglers, the vast and manifold literature of parody—all these forms have one style in common: they belong to one culture of folk carnival humor.
>
> The manifestations of this folk culture can be divided into three distinct forms.
> 1. Ritual spectacles: carnival pageants, comic shows of the market-place.
> 2. Comic verbal compositions: parodies both oral and written, in Latin and in the vernacular.
> 3. Various genres of billingsgate: curses, oaths, popular blazons. (Bakhtin, *Rabelais and His World* 4-5)

The best examples of carnivalization include ritual spectacles: carnival pageants and market place shows, comic verbal compositions (parodies), and verbal denigration (billingsgate and curses) (Bakhtin, *Rabelais and His*

World 5). Because of the ritual aspect of folk carnival festivities, there are certain recurring images that appear within carnival literature implying certain philosophical views.

Bakhtin sees laughter as the major image recurring through carnival literature. Reflecting philosophically ambivalent attitudes, carnival laughter reverses hierarchical order, bringing the sovereign down to the level of serf and elevating the serf to that of the king. Sometimes there is a mock crowning of a lowly character during carnival festivities, and the laughter added to the social ritual produces a combination of exaltation and derision.

> Let us say a few initial words about the complex nature of carnival laughter. It is, first of all, a festive laughter. Therefore it is not an individual reaction to some isolated "comic" event. Carnival laughter is the laughter of all the people. Second, it is universal in scope; it is directed at all and everyone, including the carnival's participants. The entire world is seen in its droll aspect, in its gay relativity. Third, this laughter is ambivalent: it is gay, triumphant, and at the same time mocking, deriding. It asserts and denies, it buries and revives. Such is the laughter of carnival. (Bakhtin, *Rabelais and His World* 11-12)

Laughter is healthy, eliminating fear and disgust through references to the grotesque and the "lower bodily strata" (Bakhtin, *Rabelais and His World* 21). Stock images include anything that refers downward as earthly and carnivalesque. References to digestion (food, drink, buttocks, intestines) anything that digests food is typical of the carnival, as well as anything that suggests procreation (genitals, breasts, the phallus, a potbelly or the nose). These images allude to the higher philosophical ambiguity of birth and death. Birth and death recur because they are natural life processes. They are potentially ambivalent, because there is rebirth in death, and birth starts the disintegration and dismemberment of old age.

One of the fundamental tendencies of the grotesque image of

> the body is to show two bodies in one: the one giving birth and dying, the other conceived, generated, and born. This is the pregnant and begetting body, or at least a body ready for conception and fertilization, the stress being laid on the phallus or the genital organs. From one body a new body always emerges in some form or other. (Bakhtin, *Rabelais and His World* 26)

Carnival laughter is typical of contemporary satire in Rabelais' time. Rabelais' laughter attacks Medieval institutions, destroying the medieval in the creation of a new Renaissance philosophy. A similar pattern of destruction takes place in *La Peau de chagrin*, in which contemporary satire mocks the July Revolution as a symbol of the fall of the *ancien régime* and leads to the triumph of the bourgeoisie, the press, and financiers (Rosen 121-22).

The critical attention given to carnival in *La Peau de chagrin* has erred in assuming that the carnivalesque is only to be found in the banquet scene, when in fact, it goes far beyond it.[9] According to Bakhtin, carnivalesque elements penetrate "the very construction of the major strong characters and the development of the passions" rather than manifest themselves in "plot, in external carnivalistic antitheses and contrasts, in abrupt changes of fate . . . mystifications, and so on."[10] The banquet scene is but the crescendo of a carnival motif which starts at the beginning of the novel, appears and disappears with serpentine movement, and dissipates with Raphaël's collapse into a drunken sleep at the end of the orgy. Comparing *La Peau de chagrin* to a concerto, we could say that carnivalesque images appear as a theme in the opening movement, gradually achieve a crescendo and diminuendo during the orgy at Taillefer's house, and reappear in the final movement like a leitmotif.

Balzac's signature on the carnivalesque is characterized by three elements: metamorphosis, substitution, and ludicity. An overview of how the carnival appears and disappears in the course of the novel will show how Balzac uses metamorphosis to weave the carnival into the fabric of the text to create an ebbing and flowing effect.

In the first part of the novel, Raphaël's peripatetic activities serve to metamorphose a scene in and out of the carnival mode. Raphaël encounters carnival activities and images as he walks along the river. During his walk, light and sound announce the reemergence of the carnival, while silence announces its disappearance. "Ma vie a été un trop long silence" (10: 203). The entire first part of the novel is a long silence covered by a carnivalesque orchestration which struggles with a philosophical theme. The reader begins with the silence and darkness of the gambling scene and ends with the silence and darkness of Raphaël's drunken sleep at the end of the orgy. All that suggests the carnival is accompanied by light and heralded by noise and laughter. Carnivalesque enjoyment of the present and philosophical contemplation of the past compete and alternate to shape a metamorphosing picture that forms and then dissipates as it throbs through the novel. Philosophical contemplation for Raphaël is a preoccupation with the past, whereas the carnival concerns the present. Both represent a further attempt to hold the future in abeyance, the result of which is a polyphony, a combination of differing voices with different messages.[11] These voices represent the past (in Raphaël's reminiscing), the carnivalesque present (in the laughter of Emile, the two party girls, and the other party-goers), and Raphaël's future, his inevitable death, in the powerful silence that dominates all.

In *Problems of Dostoevsky's Poetics,* Bakhtin stated that carnivalization was "combined organically with all other characteristics of the polyphonic novel" (159). Although Bakhtin saw Balzac as a precursor of the polyphony in Dostoevsky's works, he believed that the former fell short of "Dostoevsky's multivoicedness." He states that one can only speak of polyphonic elements in Balzac's work.[12] Nevertheless, the dialogues and the varieties of discourse in *La Peau de chagrin* put Balzac closer than anyone had been at the time to Dostoevsky's polyphony.[13]

The opening scenes of the novel take place in a gambling house. The gambling house is a carnival institution going back in time to the folk celebrations or games played at the early market places (Bakhtin, *Rabelais and His World* 231).

Le soir, les maisons de jeu n'ont qu'une poésie vulgaire, mais

> dont l'effet est assuré comme celui d'un drame sanguinolent. Les salles sont garnies de spectateurs et de joueurs, de vieillards indigents qui s'y traînent pour s'y réchauffer, de faces agitées, d'orgies commencées dans le vin et décidées à finir dans la Seine. . . . Si l'Espagne a ses combats de taureaux, si Rome a eu ses gladiateurs, Paris s'enorgueillit de son Palais-Royal dont les agaçantes roulettes donnent le plaisir de voir couler le sang à flots, sans que les pieds du parterre risquent d'y glisser. Essayez de jeter un regard furtif sur cette arène, entrez.. . . Quelle nudité! (10: 59)

The passage above is replete with the vocabulary of carnival literature: "drame," "spectateur," "joueurs," "orgies," "vin," "la Seine," "gladiateurs." Elisheva Rosen notes that during the banquet episode Balzac departs from his usual meticulous precision in favor of hyperbolae and cliché, suggesting that Balzac deliberately remains vague when describing these activities (Rosen 118). The gambling scene also lacks the author's usual precision. Balzac evokes other carnival folk celebrations with references to bull fights, Roman gladiators, and his description of the Palais Royal as an "arena" (10: 59). It is significant that at the end of this scene Raphaël leaves without asking for his hat, thereby reinforcing the image that he has been uncrowned, like a carnival king.

Outside the gambling house Raphaël mulls over the possibility of drowning himself in the Seine. As he stands in the middle of a bridge contemplating death, an old lady passing by laughs and jokes about suicide. "Mauvais temps pour se noyer, lui dit en riant une vieille femme vêtue de haillons. Est-elle sale et froide, la Seine!" (10: 65) This scene abounds in carnivalesque images: poverty, old age, death, and the good-natured, unafraid laughter of all classes and ages presupposing a kind of equality. After Raphaël leaves the old woman, the image disappears into silence, and with the silence, the carnival ebbs.

The sounds of activity at the market place attract Raphaël, and the carnivalesque again gathers momentum. The scene takes place outside, in an area where several people have congregated. Different social levels are represented in the group: two beggars, a stamp merchant, and a beautiful rich woman who leads Raphaël to the area filled with shops. The mixture of classes and the outdoor quality are typical of the carnival. The beautiful young woman provides the link between the outside scene and of the antique shop's interior which provides more carnival images. Many scholars have studied the antique shop, and it is tempting (but erroneous) to treat it as a separate entity, apart from the novel. In this scene Balzac again abandons his traditionally precise descriptive technique in favor of a vague, unrealistic style, thus signaling a departure from reality upon Raphaël's entry into the story: "il sortit de la vie réelle, monta par dégrés vers un monde idéal, arriva dans les palais enchantés de l'Extase où l'univers lui parut par bribes et en traits de feu . . . " (10: 70).

In *Rabelais and His World*, Bakhtin discusses the utopian quality in *Gargantua* and in carnival literature in general. All social classes are treated as equals and the future has no importance during the carnival celebration (Bakhtin 324-29). The abundance of objects depicting the divine and the grotesque in Balzac's store is clearly in the carnival tradition, implying equality among civilizations.

> Une peinture ouvrait les cieux, il y voyait la Vierge Marie plongée dans un nuage d'or, au sein des anges, éclipsant la gloire du soleil, écoutant les plaintes des malheureux auxquels cette Eve régénérée souriait d'un air doux. . . . Un monstre de la Chine dont les yeux restaient tordus, la bouche contournée, les membres torturés, réveillait l'âme par les inventions d'un peuple qui, fatigué du beau toujours unitaire, trouve d'ineffables plaisirs dans la fécondité des laideurs. . . .
> Il vit les conquêtes d'Alexandre sur un camée, les massacres de Pizarre dans une arquebuse à mèche, les guerres de religion échevelées, bouillantes, cruelles, au fond d'un casque. Puis, les riantes images de la chevalerie sourdirent d'une armure de Milan supérieurement damasquinée, bien fourbie, et sous la visière de laquelle brillaient encore les yeux d'un paladin. (10: 71)

Several words from the passage above reenforce the carnival theme: "régenéré," "la bouche contournée," "massacres," "riantes images." Rising from one level of the store to the next, Raphaël sees more and more objects, with Balzac using the carnivalesque term "bazar" to describe the display. As Raphaël slowly ascends, the reader is confronted with a disorganized and overwhelming catalogue of objects without Balzac's usual precise descriptions.

When the images disappear, silence marks the ebbing of the carnival theme, as it occurred earlier in the novel, separating the gambling episode from the exchange with an old woman, and the old woman from the outdoor scene.[14] Raphaël says little in the long ascent to the top floor of the antique shop. At one point the narrator describes the silence. "Le silence régnait si profondément autour de lui, que bientôt il s'aventura dans une douce rêverie . . . " (10: 76). The appearance of a bright light which is described in auditory terms maintains the silence and fantasy motifs. "Il ne l'avait entendu ni venir, ni parler, ni se mouvoir" (10: 77). The light awakens him like a "voix terrible" (10: 77) might awaken him from a nightmare. There are numerous references to Raphaël's pitiful state and his near-death. In the carnival, the lowliest person rises to success, and death is replaced by renewal and regeneration. At the point in the novel when Raphaël's morale is at its lowest, the old man promises riches and offers the shagreen skin. Again the tension shifts as philosophizing and contemplation replace the carnivalesque. The old man tries to explain to Raphaël that if he accepts the talisman he must learn to temper his desires in order to survive. The shagreen's skin implies the carnivalesque because the wild ass is a lowly creature evoking the "lower bodily strata," and in folklore there is a carnival mass called the Feast of the Ass (Bakhtin, *Rabelais and His World* 78). Raphaël's walk is accompanied by what may be characterized as a struggle between contemplative silence and the carnival in which silence is disrupted and subverted by a crescendo of carnival elements starting with the old woman in rags and climaxing in the swirl of carnival images at the top of the antique shop.

Extolling the hedonistic philosophy of living only for the moment, the very essence of carnival philosophy, Raphaël abruptly ends the old man's philosophizing by rejecting the contemplation of philosophical subjects, grabing the talisman, and making his first wish, to live in excess.

After accepting the skin and stepping out onto the street, Raphaël meets friends who want to take him to a party. The same ingredients appear in this scene as in the first part of the novel. As Raphaël walks, he encounters people who bring the carnival to him. In this case they take him to Taillefer's house to celebrate the July revolution. The party has the carnival elements of a banquet: laughter, political satire, and bawdiness. It is full of billingsgate which begins immediately upon Raphaël's exit from the shop. "Animal!—Imbécile!" (10: 89). With the July revolution as an excuse, the participants plan to have a celebration with Raphaël as king. "Nous te destinions les rênes de cet empire macaronique et burlesque. . . . nous t'y saluerons roi de ces esprits frondeurs que rien n'épouvante . . . " (10: 91). The egalitarian quality of the carnivalesque is made evident through the use of the "tu" form to refer to the man they are making king. The candid humor is apparent as well as the obvious good will of the participants. There is neither cynicism, nor fear, nor preoccupation with the future.

> Nous, véritables sectateurs du dieux Méphistophélès, avons entrepris de badigeonner l'esprit public, de rhabiller les acteurs, de clouer de nouvelles planches à la baraque gouvernementale, de médicamenter les doctrinaires, de recuire les vieux républicains, de réchampir les bonapartistes et de ravitailler le centre. . . . Oui, nous t'instituerons le souverain de ces puissances intelligentes qui fournissent au monde les Mirabeau, les Talleyrand, les Pitt, les Metternich, enfin tous ces hardis Crispins qui jouent entre eux les destinées d'un empire comme les hommes vulgaires jouent leur kirschenwasser aux dominos . . . . Taillefer, notre amphitryon, nous a promis de surpasser les étroites saturnales de nos petits Lucullus modernes. (10: 91-92)

These passages are filled with terms suggesting the carnivalesque: "les actes," "recuir" (cooking vocabulary is carnivalesque), "kirchenwasser," "saturnales," "Lucullus." Raphaël answers his friends with more carnival vocabulary such as "ivres," "vins," "digérant." "Jusqu'à présent nous avons fait de l'impiété entre deux vins, nous avons pesé la vie étant ivres, nous avons prisé les hommes et les choses en digérant" (10: 92).

An important carnival image is regeneration. During the celebration Raphaël expresses the feeling that through the orgy he has been reborn (10: 92). The party continues in luxurious surroundings, where laughter and luxury abound. During the celebration wine flows freely, reminiscent of Rabelais'*Gargantua*.The celebration continues with Emile, Raphaël's friend, drawing a crown in the air over Raphaël's head.[15] The feast represents a crescendo in the narrative, a temporary triumph of the carnival over the philosophical, present over past or future, desire over denial, death over life, and the regeneration inherent in death. Before the carnival dialogue accelerates, light imagery reappears as in the previous scenes; rich candelabra with numerous candles illuminate the room (10: 95-96). The exchanges become shorter, closely resembling the exchanges in *Gargantua*, compete with insults and bragging, punctuated with references to food. "Passez-moi du canard !" (10: 106)

The appearance of two girls at the party affords the opportunity to discuss the carnival view of time.[16] Euphrasie, looking neither forward nor backward, describes the future as nonexistent (10: 114). This is consistent with carnivalesque philosophy which emphasizes enjoyment with no regard for the future. When the valet tells Taillefer that the neighbors are complaining about the noise of the revelers, Raphaël laughs in a manner described by Balzac as exhibiting a "joie brutale" (10: 118). It again marks a shift, this time to a philosophical exchange. The carnival subverts the philosophical discussion, changing it to play as the interlocutors make allusions to various philosophers. Emile persists in the philosophical vein, remarking to Raphaël: "Tu me fais douter de la puissance de Dieu, car tu es plus bête qu'il n'est puissant. . . " (10: 119).

Next, Raphaël seeks to depart from the carnival to undertake a serious account of his sad experiences with Foedora. The interpolated story is consistent with carnival literature in that the account is framed by the carnival orgy and punctuated by Emile's carnivalesque dialogue. Raphaël becomes depressed during the account, completely engrossed with contemplating the past. Emile retains the gay carnival posture by laughing and making light of Raphaël's account. "Oh! de grâce, épargne-moi ta préface," says Emile, "d'un air moitié riant moitié pieux, en prenant la main de Raphaël" (10: 120). This scene contains a struggle, a tension between Raphaël's philosophizing and Emile's carnivalesque counterpoint, with the latter gradually prevailing. After an account of the loss of his family's fortune, Emile says gaily, "Joliment tragique ce soir!" (10: 130) An account of Raphaël's friendship with Pauline, and his obsession with Foedora lasts for pages, contemplation thereby subduing any carnivalesque counterpoint offered by Emile or the others. Finally contemplation of the past yields to the carnival when Raphaël, exhausted and overwhelmed by his own words, exclaims that he wants to live in the present (10: 202), thus giving up the struggle and flowing with the torrent. Raphaël insults the guests, hits Emile, and declares himself regenerated, stating that his life to that point had been but a long silence. Raphaël revels and then falls into a drunken sleep (10: 203), with all sound reduced to that of the two sleeping friends. The carnival motif ebbs as silence takes over, and the light of the last candles goes out. A new mode begins with the light of the next day, and Raphaël awakens to live the philosophical dilemma of pleasure and death versus denial and life.

Another strategy of Balzac's is the use of conflicting styles of discourse which account for the metamorphosis as the carnival dominates, then loses momentum.[17] Carnivalesque discourse struggles with philosophical contemplation and confession. Raphaël's confession demonstrates this subversion of the carnivalesque. In the confession it is he who competes with the carnival in his effort to relate the story of his lost love for Foedora. Emile's interjections evoke the carnival throughout Raphaël's narration, preventing it from becoming a classic confession, and turning his words into a parody. As the metamorphosis continues, the carnival dissolves into the récit as the men fall asleep. The lights dim, the novel falls into complete silence and darkness. In the last part, *L'Agonie,* carnival elements cease to appear except near the very end of the novel when Jonathas plans a luxurious party for Raphaël. It is as if Balzac were briefly replaying the carnival theme.

Balzac puts his signature to the carnival through substitution which appears on several levels. The party is a celebration in which the burlesque reigns, and all carnival burlesque is based on an exchange of roles. While the serf substitutes as king, the king is uncrowned. In *La Peau de chagrin*, the antique merchant is referred to as a prince while he owns the shagreen's skin. He is looking for someone, anyone, to take the skin and replace him as the owner, a role which Raphaël assumes when he accepts the skin. During the party, the revelers need a person to play the role of king; anyone would do. The king's role waits for a player, implying a certain lack of discrimination. Raphaël substitutes again, taking on yet another role. The burlesque in the carnival treatment of the first section of *La Peau de chagrin* reverses the established political order through substitution. The party is a celebration of the substitution of one monarch for another:

> Il s'agit donc de nous inculquer une opinion royalement nationale en nous prouvant qu'il est bien plus heureux de payer douze cents millions trente-trois centimes à la patrie représentée par messieurs tels et tels, que onze cents millions neuf centimes à un *Roi* qui disait *moi* au lieux de dire *nous*. (10: 90-91)

The revelers make Raphaël the mock king of their wild party, in classic carnival practice, taking him at the moment when he is at his lowest. "Nous te destinions les rênes de cet empire macaronique et burlesque, ainsi nous t'emmenons de ce pas au dîner donné pour le fondateur dudit journal. . . . nous t'y saluerons roi . . ." (cited earlier, 10: 91). His distinguished ancestry is recited, and he is crowned with a fork.

> Nous ne sommes pas un enfant trouvé, mais le descendant de l'empereur *Valens*, souche des *Valentinois*, fondateur des villes de Valence, en Espagne et en France, héritier légitime de l'empire d'Orient. Si nous laissons trôner Mahmoud à Constantinople, c'est par pure bonne volonté, et faute d'argent ou de soldats.

Emile décrivit en l'air, avec sa fourchette, une couronne au-dessus de la tête de Raphaël. (10: 99)

Substitution is merely a ritual which enhances the most important element of Balzac's carnival. Although the basis of the carnival is laughter, Balzac's special signature is more complicated. It is a ludicity that takes the form of intertextual references. It functions by a playful and consistent pattern of distortion which evokes an author by citation, by style (or by both), and reproduces it with a less than perfect facsimile. An example is his treatment of Jean Jacques Rousseau. Balzac evokes him on two levels: Raphaël lives at the same address in Paris where Rousseau lived; and Raphaël's interpolated love story is a confession which unfolds during the carnival banquet orgy. Emile, who serves as a reluctant listener, ridiculing and interrupting Raphaël's "confession" with interjections and a slap-stick fight, burlesques Raphaël's confession and makes light of his suffering. His counterpoint not only interferes with Raphaël's account, but lampoons the confession as an ancient and respected genre (dating back to St. Augustine).

He also parodies folk and fairy tales by presenting fractured versions. The title itself evokes the folk tale *La Peau d'âne*, while structures of the powerful talisman evoke *Alladin's Lamp* and many other tales in which a talisman brings about the demise of the recipient.[18] Balzac also burlesques Rabelais by using oral imagery and other references to Rabelais which he then distorts. Rabelais is evoked throughout the novel through references to eating and drinking in grand style. The old man's laughter and the laughter of the people at the party are also reminiscent of Rabelais, but in a different way. Rabelais' laughter is healthy, but that of Balzac is an ironic and Mephistophelean cackle, one layered with decadence.[19] It is so frightening that Raphaël stops talking. "Un éclat de rire, parti de la bouche du petit vieillard, retentit dans les oreilles du jeune fou comme un bruissement de l'enfer, et l'interdit si despotiquement qu'il se tut" (10: 88).

This unhealthy laughter highlights Balzac's distortion of his references to *Gargantua*, and in this distortion lies the answer to how Balzac's carnival differs from that of Rabelais. In *Gargantua*, the carnival dominates from the first word "buveurs" to the last word "trinc," as Rabelais uses the metaphor of drinking to refer to accumulating knowledge. His carnival provides the metaphor that underpins the entire work. The joyous feasting on food and drink is the joyous feasting and drinking of knowledge. Rabelais' carnival images are a vehicle for the political satire and criticism at the heart of his work. Bakhtin does not elaborate on Balzac's use of the carnival because it is incidental. Using the carnival like a musical theme that appears and disappears in a concerto, Balzac refers to the carnival elements of food, drink, and celebration to evoke Raphaël's desire. Since objects of desire are contiguous to desire, their relation to the narrative must be metonymic, not metaphoric. Because Balzac's carnival slithers in and out of the narrative, emanating from characters and particular situations rather than from the narrator, as in Rabelais, it is not seriously carnivalesque.[20] The carnival ebbs before one third of the novel is complete, being reduced to one theme among numerous others. In *La Peau de chagrin* the carnival becomes a leitmotif for debauchery, subordinate to the real subject of the work. Balzac's use of the carnival as an accessory betrays his lack of comprehension of its philosophical implications. In *La Peau de chagrin*, the carnival supports, but is subordinate to, only one of the conflicting philosophical views: living wildly will rapidly exhaust one's vital energies.

Both authors express their ludicity through intertextuality, a playful combination of lampoons of great works, the burlesque of conventional literary genres and of famous works being typical of the carnival. However, Rabelais' intertextuality refers most often to works of antiquity, whereas Balzac lampoons the carnival itself, bringing sophistication and self-consciousness to it. This self-conscious use of the carnival soon makes it a parody of itself, and as a burlesque of the burlesque, it becomes sophisticated beyond the carnivalesque. The ludic manner in which the carnival elements are evoked crosses the line from carnival to satire of the carnival, the key difference which separates Balzac from Rabelais. Balzac's carnival enables him to imitate Rabelais' style, but the imitation becomes a pastiche of Rabelais, a self-conscious parody.

Carnival elements appear and disappear in the novel as accessory and decor rather than as metaphor. The carnival evokes Raphaël's desire, rather than communicates a vision of society. It is a metanymic device in which carnivalesque elements and style refer to debauchery and desire. The philosophy of excess that they evoke competes with an ascetic philosophy for dominance in the novel. This struggle is recreated in the conflict between silence and sound. Silence signifies economy, and the carnival signifies expenditure, in a never-ending struggle where the ultimate result of expenditure is death, and the philosophical implication of energy is flux. Balzac uses the carnival in *La Peau de chagrin* as a device which conflicts with other discourse in the novel to create a stylistic dialectic mirroring the philosophical dialogue. The carnival serves as counterpoint and camouflage for the true subject of the work, which is its philosophical premise: riches flow through society pumped by force of human desire.

Notes

¹For a short history of Bakhtin's publishing career and analysis of the evolution of his criticism see Krystyna Pomorska's foreword to Mikhail Bakhtin's *Rabelais and His World*, trans. Helene Iswolsky (Cambridge: MIT P, 1968). The best description of Bakhtin's place in the history of literary criticism is by David Lodge, *After Bakhtin: Essays on Fiction and Criticism* (London: Routledge, 1990) 5 : "Such a poetics of fiction exists. Pioneered by the Russian formalists, such as Victor Shklovsky and Boris Tomashevsky, developed and elaborated by the French critics of the 1960s and 1970s, such as Tzvetan Todorov, A. H. Greimas, Gérard Genette and Roland Barthes, incorporating some of the ideas of linguistic and anthropological structuralism as practiced by Roman Jakobson and Claude Lévi-Strauss, it has since been assimilated and synthesized with Anglo-American criticism in such books as Seymour Chatman's *Story and Discourse* (1978)." See Tzvetan Todorov, *Mikhail Bakhtin: The Dialogic Principle* (Manchester: Manchester UP, 1984); Seymour Chatman, *Story and Discourse: Narrative Structure in Fiction and Film* (Ithaca: Cornell UP, 1978).

²See Mikhail Bakhtin, *Rabelais and His World*, trans. Helene Iswolsky (Cambridge: MIT P, 1968) 36-51, for a history of the carnival theme through the ages. Bakhtin's *Problems of Dostoevsky's Poetics*, trans. Caryl Emerson (Minneapolis: U of Minnesota P, 1984) 158-59, shows Balzac's importance in the history of carnivalization. Bakhtin states that Dostoevsky found a more "profound assimilation of the carnival tradition" in Balzac, George Sand, and Victor Hugo. He further says that these authors have a "deeper carnival sense of the world."

³Mikhail Bakhtin, *Rabelais and His World* 9.

4Elisheva Rosen, "Le Festin de Taillefer ou les 'Saturnales' de la Monarchie de Juillet," *Balzac et "La Peau de chagrin,"* ed. Claude Duchet (Paris: SEDES-DCU, 1979) 116.

5See, for example, Maurice A. F. Lecuyer, *Balzac et Rabelais,* Etudes françaises fondées sur l'initiative de la Société des professeurs français en Amérique 47 (Paris: Société d'Editions "Les Belles Lettres," 1956).

6See Jean Claude Fizaine's, "Ironie et Fiction dans l'oeuvre de Balzac" in *Balzac: L'Invention du roman,* eds. Claude Duchet and Jacques Neefs (Paris: Belfond, 1982) 159-80. He mentions what has been quoted here. Throughout the article he draws a parallel with Rabelais and mentions carnivalization and Bakhtin (166).

7For a discussion of the banquet scene in *La Peau de chagrin* of the varied types of banquet conventions that exist in literature from the symposium to the carnival see Elisheva Rosen's article, "Le Festin de Taillefer ou les 'Saturnales' de la Monarchie de Juillet," in *Balzac et "La Peau de chagrin"* (Paris: SEDES-DCU, 1979) 115-26.

8Bakhtin, *Rabelais and His World* 4.

9In *Rabelais and His World*, Bakhtin mentions Balzac only briefly in the following reference: "Renaissance grotesque imagery, directly related to folk carnival culture, as we find it in Rabelais, Cervantes, and Shakespeare, influenced the entire realistic literature of the following centuries. Realism of grand style, in Stendhal, Balzac, Hugo, and Dickens, for instance, was always linked directly or indirectly with the Renaissance tradition" (52). There are, however, copious references to Hugo in this volume. See also Bakhtin's *Problems of Dostoevsky's Poetics* 33-34, in which Bakhtin compares Balzac and Dostoevsky, indicating that Balzac is one of the first novelists to demonstrate polyphony in his novels.

10*Problems of Dostoevsky's Poetics*, 158-59. Bakhtin thought that Balzac,

George Sand, and Victor Hugo demonstrated a deeper assimilation of the carnival tradition than Soulié, Sue, Dumas fils, or de Kock.

11In Bakhtin, *Problems of Dostoevsky's Poetics* 29.

12In *Problems of Dostoevsky's Poetics* he writes: "One may also speak of elements of polyphony in Balzac's work—but only of elements. Balzac belongs to the same line of development in the European novel as Dostoevsky, and is one of his direct and most immediate predecessors. Points in common between Balzac and Dostoevsky have been frequently noted (especially well and thoroughly by Leonid Grossman), and there is no need to return to them here. But Balzac did not transcend the object-ness of his characters, nor the monologic finalization of his world" (34). See also Leonid Grossman, *Balzac and Dostoevsky*, trans. Lena Karpov (USA: Ardis, 1973).

13See Marie Pierrette Malcuzynski, "Polyphony, Polydetermination and Narratologic Alienation Since 1960," in the *Proceedings of the Xth Congress of the International Comparative Literature Association*, eds. Anna Balakian and James Wilhelm, 2 vols. (New York: Garland,1982) 1: 21-26.

14Samuel Weber, discusses the element of silence at the beginning of the gambling scene in the first chapter of *Unwrapping Balzac: A Reading of "La Peau de chagrin"* 25-29.

15Balzac 10: 99. Rosen cites this incident as an example of carnivalization.

16See Emile Talbot's article, "Pleasure/Time or Egoisme/Love: Rereading *La Peau de Chagrin*" in *Nineteenth Century French Studies* 11 (1982-83): 72-82, for a discussion of time in *La Peau de chagrin*.

17Ruth Amossy, in "La Confession of Raphaël: Contradiction et Interferences," in *Balzac et "La Peau de chagrin,"* ed. Claude Duchet

(Paris: CDU and SEDES, 1979) 59, sees the confession as "carnivalized" and "subverted" by the presentation of a realistic confession with a first person point of view framed by a different form of fantastic discourse. In the same volume, André Vanoncini, in "La Dissemination de l'objet fantastique," sees these varying discourses as held together by "semantic networks" (61).

[18]Susan Bershtel, "Fairy Tales and Success in Balzac's *Comédie humaine*," *Comparative Literature* 31 (1977): 50. See also Vladimir Propp, *Morphology of the Folktale*.

[19]Jean Claude Fizaine notes this distorted intertextual reference to Rabelais. See especially 163-66.

[20]Genette has already established in *Figures III*, that it is easy to take almost any trope for a metaphor. Gérard Genette, *Figures III* 38; 41-63. See also Roman Jakobson's *Essais de linguistique générale* (Paris: Seuil, 1963) 63-65. Lucienne Frappier-Mazur, *L'Expression Métaphorique dans "la Comédie humaine"* (Paris: Klincksieck, 1976) 29, writes: "Sans nul doute aussi, les exigences du portrait et de la description font naître chez lui une abondance de détails synecdochiques semblables à ceux que Jakobson considère comme caractéristiques du roman réaliste: la première vision qu'a Félix de Madame de Mortsauf . . . 'toutes ces épaules' qu'il baise, ce 'blason' du corps de l'héroïne qu'il évoque ensuite, relèvent à coup sûr de la relation synecdochique."

Conclusion

In *Allegories of Reading*, Paul de Man expresses concern that he had planned to write a "historical study" but finished with an examination of reading, a synchronic work.[1] He considers reading as part of a two-part struggle, something done in a sheltered place defended against the outside world (de Man 59). We see the concepts of binary opposition and monologism when he speaks of reading Proust.

> Thus reading is staged, from the beginning of the text, as a defensive motion in a dramatic contest of threats and defenses: it is an inner, sheltered place (bower, closet, room, cradle) that has to protect itself against the invasion of an outside world, but that nevertheless has to borrow from this world some of its properties. (59)

Even a modern critic such as de Man sees theories of reading in terms of a binary system, inside/outside. In the preface to *Allegories of Reading* de Man seems to see the structuralism/deconstruction dialectic as thrust upon him because he defends deconstruction while tiptoeing around the question of whether he is or is not a deconstructivist critic (x).

> I consciously came across "deconstruction" for the first time in the writings of Jacques Derrida, which means that it is associated with a power of inventive rigor to which I lay no

claim but which I certainly do not wish to erase. Deconstruction, as was easily predictable, has been much misrepresented, dismissed as a harmless academic game or denounced as a terrorist weapon, and I have all the fewer illusions about the possibility of countering these aberrations since such an expectation would go against the drift of my own readings. (x)

In an aside, Pierre Barbéris, the great Balzac scholar, comments that Balzac is no longer read by those who know only traditional criticism. "Balzac n'est plus lu aujourd'hui par ceux qui ne connaissaient que l'ancienne critique prémarxiste, préfreudienne, prélinguisitique et présémiologue. . . ."[2] Barbéris sees critics as aligned in either the historical or ahistorical camp. He complains that critics eschew history to consider the text alone. "J'insiste. Univers du signifiant, univers du symbolique: c'est toujours une manière de ne pas être l'univers de l'Histoire, un moyen de ne pas en parler et donc de ne gêner personne" (183). You are a respectable person if you speak of signs, language, or symbols (183). He complains that those who bring up politics or history are considered old fashioned bores. "Vous êtes un emmerdeur, un cuistre, un archaïque, si vous parlez institutions, finances publiques . . . dérives politiques, origines et entreprises des pouvoirs" (183). He implies that if a critic mentions history or politics he will be viewed as an old fashioned marxist.

> . . . bref, si vous entendez parler du capitalisme, de ses crises, de ses effets, des solutions et des ruses qu'il engendre ou finance, des diverses social-démocraties (sic) sans lesquelles il ne saurait survivre ni simplement passer certains caps dangereux, alors vous êtes vraiment un homme sans goût et pour tout dire un empêcheur de rocardiser la critique littéraire. . . . (184)

Barbéris seems to imply another binary system in his reference to what is perhaps now considered an obsolete concern, marxist versus nonmarxist criticism. It is not surprising that a critic who has seen numerous theories come and go would group them monologically. It is perhaps surprising to catch Paul de Man writing of critics who focus on either inside or outside the text. When he speaks of outside/inside, he is defining critics according to a monologic principle. He reenforces a monologic view of contemporary theory when he complains that the terms have changed, but not the polarities. "The polarities of the inside and outside have been reversed, but they are still the same polarities that are at play. . . " (4).

Barbéris' comments must not be misconstrued as the complaints of a last voice of the positivistic nineteenth century-style critics. His comments have more credibility in the face of the New Historicism. Consider the attention that Stephen Greenblatt has received for proposing that we "shift the ground of literary study away from the notion of a text as an autonomous artifact."[3] This is not merely another variation on de Man's inside/outside dialectic. Although some might fear that the New Historicism returns to the critical methods of yore, Greenblatt and his followers would state that the method is one that focuses on the "margins" of the text, rather than its presumed center."[4] Anton Kaes writes:

> The new historicists's attention has moved to the "borders" of the text where it connects with the material world, where traces of the negotiations and transactions between the social and the aesthetic realm are still visible, where classical concepts such as representations, authorship, and autonomy of art are called into question. (Kaes 213)

It can be said that the New Historicism is a method that succeeds in reconciling synchronic and diachronic study. It combines several theories and their languages to create a composite method based on Foucault, Derrida, Geertz, Bakhtin, and Kristeva (Kaes 210-11). The latter underlines the simultaneous play of synchrony and diachrony that has always existed in linguistic study.

Enfin, ce que nous appelons langage a une histoire qui se

> déroule dans le temps. Du point de vue de cette diachronie, le langage se transforme durant les différentes époques, prend diverses formes chez les différents peuples. Pris comme un système, c'est-à-dire synchroniquement, il y a des règles précises de fonctionnement, une structure donnée et des transformations structurales obéissant à des lois strictes.[5]

It is important that Derrida and Barbéris seem to move in the same direction, away from a monologic view of literary theory, if not toward a polyphonic or dialogic one. These terms evoke Bakhtin with good reason. In his works on Rabelais and Dostoevsky, Bakhtin wrote dialogically as he described dialogics because his work was both synchronic and diachronic.[6]

The advent of the New Historicism validates paratextual studies of *La Peau de chagrin*. Because paratext occupies the grey area between text and reality, it forces the reader to look around the text before reading. Although this work can not be classified as a perfect example of New Historicism because it remains too close to the object of study, it is connected to it in one respect. It treats an idea essential to Greenblatt's view of art and culture, that one can expand the boundaries of the work of art by relating it to other texts and events. Seeming to leap over the line of demarcation between the work of art and the world, Stephen Greenblatt says the following about his perceptions: "I seem to have moved to the place where I now see the art object as being so completely dispersed in the world that you don't see it as an object anymore, It's everywhere."[7] While Greenblatt travels far for "textual traces" that reveal much about the culture he examines, in this study I remain closer to the text, preoccupied with paratextual traces that diffuse and erase the line of demarcation between the work of art and the culture it mirrors.

David Lodge defines Derrida's inside/outside dialectic through Seymour Chatman's schematic representation of the relationship between the real author and the real reader and their various reflections within textual boundaries. Chatman places the implied author, narrator, narratee, and implied reader, respectively, in a straight line within a box, their counterparts in reality outside on either side (143). Paratext is the mysterious territory that may be mimetic, like a fictional preface, or diagetic, as is the case with Balzac's prefaces. It is like the mysterious territory between the unknown foam on the horizon and the sky in Mallarmé's "Brise marine," neither sea, nor sky, but in-between. They establish the zone where history and culture meet text and where fictional time and space bump up against each other in reality. Because of the infinite permutations and combinations that paratext provides, the possibilities are inlimited. Paratext constitutes the area where real author meets implied author, where the real reader metamorphoses into the implied reader, and where the reality of text, culture, and history converge.

Notes

¹Paul de Man, preface, *Allegories of Reading: Figural Language in Rousseau, Neitzsche, Rilke, and Proust* (New Haven: Yale UP, 1979) ix.

²Pierre Barbéris, "Dialectique du Prince et du Marchand," *Balzac, L'Invention du roman*. eds. Claude Duchet and Jacques Neefs (Paris: CDU-SEDES, 1980) 182.

³Russell Schoch, "A Conversation with Stephen Greenblatt," *California Monthly* (April, 1988) 9. Quoted by Anton Kaes, "The New Historicism and the Study of German Literature," *The German Quarterly* 62.2 (1989): 211.

⁴Stephen Greenblatt, *Shakespearean Negotiations: The Circulation of Social Energy in Renaissance England* (Berkley; Los Angeles: U of California P, 1988) 4.

⁵Julia Kristeva, *Le Language, cet inconnu: Une Initiation à la linguistique* (Paris: Seuil, 1981) 14.

⁶In his conclusion to *Problems of Dostoevsky's Poetics*, Mikhail Bakhtin writes that "While continuing the 'dialogic line' in the development of European artistic prose, Dostoevsky created a new generic variety of the novel—the polyphonic novel—whose innovative features we have tried to illuminate in this book" (270). He was quite aware of using both strategies at the same time.

⁷This is a direct quote from Greenblatt in an interview by Schoch, "A Conversation with Stephen Greenblatt," 9. I see my project and Genette's work on paratextuality as closer to Greenblatt and the New Historicists than

to Genette's latest work, *Fiction et Diction*. Although it treats the latest issues in literary theory, it lacks the simultaneous diachrony and synchrony implied in the New Historicism and in his earlier work, *Seuils*.

Appendix A

Foedora, Poème de jeunesse

A 83: Fragment de la main de Balzac. Manuscrit autographe, lettres. Lovenjoul Collection.

This fragment is illegible in places. The file is almost exclusively devoted to the notes and text of one poem, "Foedora." It also contains one letter from Grogniart, a tailor from Tours dated August 4, 1823; a second letter is to Mme Doutremont, dated August 1, 1823. Some of the text is scrawled on the backs of envelopes. Parts of this manuscript were transcribed by Claude Serval in "Une énigme balzacienne, La Foedora de *la Peau de chagrin*," and reproduced by Maurice Allem in his preface to the Classiques Garnier edition of *La Peau de chagrin* (xiii-xv). A more recent transcription of parts of this file is by Thierry Bodin in "Balzac poète."

Elle glissait si légèrement qu'elle avait l'air d'une ombre
dansant, le soir, au clair de lune, sur l'herbe fraîche des prairies, et la jeune fille, le matin, cherchera vainement quelles fleurs le fantôme a fauchées.[1]

Elle enviera pendant une seconde le sort et les plis gracieux de la robe flottante de l'ombre. Pour le moment, elle valse, non pas dans une prairie, non; le salon de l'ambassadeur de Russie est le théâtre sur lequel elle déploie la grâce de ses mouvements. L'abandon de sa tête est si grand, qu'à chaque effort on croit qu'elle va se détacher d'un col blanc comme le lait. . . .

Pourquoi son partenaire ne séparerait-il pas cette blonde tête de ce corps charmant? Pourquoi? Il n'en a pas le droit, mais il peut l'acquérir. Elle l'aime, voilà. Sans doute ce qui augmente la légèreté de Foedora, voilà pourquoi elle est aussi peu pesante que lorsque dans un rêve on croit marcher sur les airs et qu'on y marche.

Pouvait-elle concevoir qu'il y eût une barrière entre elle et lui? Elle est veuve, comtesse, riche, jeune, belle, bienfaisante, douce, et son mari étant mort avant de franchir le seuil nuptial, l'avait laissée vierge. . . . Tout Moscou l'avait comparée à l'arche du Seigneur, dont l'approche donnait la mort. . . . Son partenaire est une arche sacrée—il donne aussi la mort—il est ce que les hommes rappellent le plus.

Leurs têtes charmantes sont confondues; les mains de Georges tiennent cette taille que des femmes seules ont pressée jusqu'ici. Foedora est pure comme le premier matin de la création—toutes les femmes lui envient ce Georges, l'objet de leurs regards.

Mille bougies, mille cristaux, mille parures, des glaces fidèles, des tableaux ornent le salon. Mais, parmi les femmes, Foedora brille comme le lustre[2] étincelant qui descend de la voûte qui tient le lustre, car, sans lui, Foedora n'est rien.

Il est là dans un coin, le visage pâle, les yeux inquiets, sa chevelure noire est en désordre; il cache toujours ses mains, il semble le Dieu du mystère. Chacun se demande: Quel est ce jeune homme? On répond: "C'est l'ami de Foedora; dans peu ils seront époux, et il veut qu'elle retourne au sein des forêts de la Russie."

Foedora interrogée dit. "J'ignore qui il est, mais ce que je sais c'est qu'il a tout mon coeur, nos âmes rendent le même son, quoi qu'il soit triste et que j'aime la gaîté vive de la France, et le son des grelots de la folie."

"Je l'ai vu à l'assemblée brillante qui dans les longues allées de notre promenade favorite, se réunit aux jours où la terre célébra la féconde naissance du Sauveur. J'étais dans un char élégant, il montait à cheval . . . je le vois encore . . . son regard candide est tombé sur mon coeur comme la flamme céleste sur une hécatombe. Je lui ai fait signe, il l'a compris, et. . . . Depuis ce jour-là nous nous aimons."

Une rivale de Foedora fut à l'ambassadeur lui demander quel était la famille de

Georges. L'Ambassadeur l'ignorait. Elle fut à Georges, prit une chaise, le regarda, voulut lui parler mais un regard de Georges la glaça de terreur. Elle attendit, que son frisson fût passé pour l'interroger.

Une pâleur livide était répandue sur son visage; il ne voyait que Foedora mais son sein était gros d'une infortune qu'il voulait se dissimuler à lui-même. L'Anglaise lui fit plusieurs questions. Il dédaigna de répondre et lorsqu'elle lui dit, "Qui êtes-vous?" Un sourire sardonique plus amer que l'onde de l'océan, plus terrible que le regard d'un frère courroucé, fit trembler les cheveux de la rivale de Foedora quand il vint errer sur la lèvre du jeune homme....

Elle revint à côté de Foedora, lui prit la main, la regarda. L'Anglaise était superstitieuse, elle montra à Foedora, comme L'M qui signifiait Mort était exactement formée dans la main charmante—Foedora soutint en riant qu'elle voulait dire qu'elle serait mariée--et de loin elle sourit à son bien aimé.

Il lui répondit dans le même langage, il sourit, aussi. Elle en était joyeuse.... elle n'était inquiète que d'une seule chose c'est qu'il lui cachait la demeure. Elle aurait voulu y aller, pour un matin le voir dormir, lui sourire à son réveil et le servir comme un maître.

Georges avait un amour immense; Foedora l'aurait envoyé mourir, si elle avait pu le vouloir; par toutes ses actions, il témoignait d'une âme grande et généreuse. On apercevait dans ses paroles les traces d'une gaîté qui s'éteignait de jour en jour. Sa mélancolie commença avec son amour.

Souvent il doutait de la tendresse de Foedora.—Si j'étais criminel," disait-il,--m'aimerais-tu?"—Toujours."—mais nous serions un jour séparés."—ou dans la vie future."—Je t'obtiendrais ton pardon." ... A ces mots, Georges fondait en larmes.

—Si j'étais un lâche," —tu ne le dirais pas"—mais enfin.—Cela n'est pas car tu méprises la mort."—Non Foedora, mais bien la vie." Souvent Foedora voulait lui prendre la main, mais il s'en défendait, et ce n'était jamais que par surprise et en jouant qu'elle pouvait s'ensaisir.

Quand elle y déposait furtivement un baiser, Georges plissait son front, lui jetait un regard qui l'épouvantait et lui disait—tu en auras peut-être regret un jour."—Jamais," disait-elle. Alors la sueur froide sur le front, Georges répondait--partons pour ton pays . . . Paris m'étouffe."

La veille de son départ, Foedora, accompagnée de sa tante, était en calèche et revenait à son hôtel; "Avancez doucement," disait la comtesse à son cocher. La voiture n'avançait pas, la foule était trop immense. L'image d'une prairie émaillée de fleurs est incomplète pour donner l'idée de ce rassemblement d'un peuple entier. . . . Foedora, étonnée, lève les yeux. Elle voit la main chérie qu'elle couvrait de baisers. . . . Cette main tenait une tête sanglante et la montrait au peuple.[3]

Foedora ne poussa qu'un soupir: "Foedora! Foedora!" disait sa tante en la tenant par la manche. Il ne restait plus d'elle que le nom, et les formes qu'un ange prit pour apparaître aux mortels. La tante, voyant le doigt de sa nièce, qui, tout mort qu'il était, montrait l'échafaud, y jeta les yeux. . . . Ce jour-là la mort eut quatre victimes![4]

Mais, la plaintive Isis, les couvrant de ses voiles, vint emporter leur âme au séjour des étoiles en un songe éternel, et le marin, le soir, assis sur le rivage, de leurs pieds lumineux reconnaît le passage en consultant le ciel.[5]

The following are verse scattered throughout the document that seem to have no place in the poem's final plan.

Foedora étonnée leva les yeux.
Elle voit la main chérie qu'elle couvrit de baisers—
Cette main tenait une tête sanglante, objet d'horreur et la montrait au peuple. (f° 5)

Lui préférant d'un squelette agitant une tête
Dans le bruit fantastique est
D'un spectre que la mort. (f°13)

Pourquoi de Foedora, l'épouvantable guide,
Soulevant un couteau justement homicide
Ne fait-il pas rouler cette tête où pour moi
Son regard fait éclore un sourire plus doux que le (the rest is illegible.) . . . . f°19

Cette main tendait une tête sanglante, objet d'horreur et la montrait au peuple.

Notes to Appendix A

[1]Thierry Bodin transcribes it as "foulées" in "Balzac poète," 157. I have chosen not to transcribe incomplete strophes here. In his article. Bodin reconstructs several from "Foedora," 156-58.
An alternate introductory strophe is to be found among the papers:
Par ses deux bras de neige, enveloppant son guide,
Gracieuse elle glisse, or,
　　De son pied rapide
Voltige dans les airs;
Comme on voit le soir, une ombre Diaphane . . . .

(The following strophe was crossed out)
Par deux bras de neige enveloppant son guide
Gracieuse elle glisse, et de son pied rapide
Voltige dans les airs;
　　. . . une vierge champêtre

[2]I read this as "astre."

[3]Elle voit la main chérie qu'elle couvrit de baisers.

[4]Sometimes the last line is indented as a new paragraph. In the manuscript that is not the case.

[5]Among small pages and envelopes of letters addressed to Balzac in Vouvray is the following variation:
Lui préférant d'un squelette agitant une tête
Dont le bruit fantastique est d'un (text stops)
D'un spectre que la mort . . . .

Appendix B
"Foedora," copié par Lovenjoul

A 168: f°150-59 "Foedora," poème. Lovenjoul Collection. Oeuvres diverses. Faites sur les manuscrits autographes, notamment par Lovenjoul.[1]

Dédicace

Les poètes anciens avaient autour d'eux de nobles divinités; des vierges au doux sourire, des âmes grandes, et lorsque leur imagination, fatiguée par son propre vol vers le ciel, s'inclinait vers la terre, ils reprenaient un essor plus sublime, encouragés par les amis, des maîtresses. Beaux jours où ces hommes divins étaient vantés, honorés avec enthousiasme, vous n'êtes plus, et lorsqu'un poète rencontre une de ses belles âmes, ne doit-il pas lui consacrer ses chants? C'est à elle que sera dédié cet essai d'une jeune muse.

Foedora

Par ses deux bras de neige enveloppant son guide,[2]
Gracieuse, elle glisse, et, de son pied rapide,
Voltige dans les airs;
Comme on voit, dans les prés, une ombre diaphane
Célébrer en dansant, sous les yeux de Diane.
Ses suaves concerts;

Et si la pure aurore a tardé de paraître,
Devançant le soleil, une vierge champêtre

Ira chercher en vain
Quelles brillantes fleurs le fantôme a fanées.
De quelles perles d'or toutes son(t) couronnées
Par les feux du matin;

Car nulle n'est en deuil de sa tige brisée,
Et toutes mollement balancent la rosée
De même Foedora valsant sur la prairie
Laisserait la verdure immobile et fleurie
Sous son rapide essor.

Mais les champs ne sont point le curieux théâtre
Où cette ombre légère et réjouie et folâtre[3]
Comme un ange aux pieds d'or
D'un messager des Czars la demeure sacrée
Admire en ses lambris cette belle adorée
Eblouir tous les yeux.

Par ces brillants contours de sa robe flottante
Le poli de ses flancs, leur souplesse élégante.
Et l'or de ses cheveux
Où le plaisir éteint dans son regard humide,
Et sa bouche entr'ouverte où le sourire réside
Et des baisers, le lieu.

Où le nid abondant d'une tête divine.
Comme un lys virginal, que le soleil courtise
Se penche vers les eaux, espérant qu'une brise
Rafraîchira son coeur !
Et de loin, Foedora, vers lui tourne la tête
Sollicite un sourire et se fait une fête
D'un seul mot de douceur!

Alors, tu n'avais pas ce sourire si tendre,

Ce regard fier et pur, si facile à comprendre.
Et ce front virginal
Où brille avec l'amour l'audace du génie.

Mais la plaintive Isis, les couvrant de ses voiles,
Vint emporter leur âme au séjour des étoiles,
En un songe éternel.

Et le marin, le soir, assis sur le rivage,
De leur pieds lumineux reconnaît le passage,
En consultant le ciel.

Fin

Plan

Elle glissait si légèrement, qu'elle avait l'air d'une ombre dansant, le soir, au clair de lune, sur l'herbe fraîche des prairies, et la jeune fille, le matin, cherchera vainement quelles fleurs le fantôme a fauchées, car toutes se balancent malheureusement sur leurs tiges et chaque calice semble une couronne de diamant parce que les rayons du soleil levant font briller les gouttes de rosée.[4]

Elle enviera pendant une seconde le sort [et le plus gracieux de la robe flottante] (All brackets are in the original document.) de l'ombre. Pour le moment elle valse, non pas dans une prairie, non; le salon de l'ambassadeur de Russie est le théâtre sur lequel elle déploie la grâce de ses mouvements. L'abandon de sa tête est si grand, qu'à chaque effort, on croit qu'elle va se détacher d'un [col blanc] comme le lait:

[Elle glissait] Comme une ombre brillante au contours diaphanes célébrant à la nuit sous les yeux de Diane.[5] Pourquoi son (partenaire) ne séparerait-il pas cette blonde tête de ce corps charmant? Pourquoi? Il n'en a pas le droit; mais il peut l'acquérir. Elle l'aime. Voilà sans doute à qui augmente la légèreté de Foedora; voilà pourquoi elle est aussi peu pesante que, lorsque [vapeur éphémère] dans un rêve on croit marcher sur les airs et qu'on y marche.

Pouvait-elle concevoir qu'il y eût une barrière entre elle et lui? . . . Elle était veuve, comtesse, riche, belle, bienfaisante, douce, et son mari était mort avant de franchir le seuil nuptial, l'avait laissée vierge. Tout Moscou l'avait comparée à l'arche du seigneur, dont l'approche donnait la mort. . . . Son partenaire est une arche à un autre sacrée—il donne aussi la mort—il est ce que les hommes respectent le plus. Leurs têtes charmantes sont confondues, les mains de Georges tiennent cette taille que des femmes seules ont pressée jusqu'ici! Foedora est pure comme le premier matin de la création. Toutes les femmes lui envièrent à Georges, l'objet de leurs regards.

Il est là, dans un coin, le visage pâle, les yeux inquiets; sa chevelure noire est en désordre; il cache toujours ses mains; il semble le Dieu du Mystère. Chacun se demande quel est ce jeune homme? On répond: c'est l'ami de Foedora; dans peu ils seront époux, et il veut qu'elle retourne au sein des forêts de la Russie. Foedora, interrogée, dit "J'ignore qui il est, mais ce que je sais c'est qu'il a tout mon coeur, nos âmes rendent le même son, quoi qu'il soit triste, et que j'aime la gaîté vive de la France, et le son des grelots de la folie."

"Je l'ai vu à l'assemblée brillante qui dans les longues allées de votre promenade favorite, se réunit aux jours où la terre célèbre la seconde naissance du sauveur. J'étais dans un char élégant: il montait un cheval . . . . Son regard candide est tombé sur mon coeur comme la flamme céleste sur une hécatome. Je lui ai fait un signe, il l'a compris, et depuis ce temps nous nous aimons."

Une rivale de Foedora fut à l'ambassadeur, lui demande quelle était la famille de Georges. L'ambassadeur l'ignorait. Elle fut à Georges, prit une chaise, le regarda, voulut lui parler. Mais un regard de Georges la glaça de terreur. Elle attendit que son frisson fût passé pour l'interroger.

Elle revint à côté de Foedora, lui prit la main, la regarda. L'Anglaise était superstitieuse. Elle montra à Foedora comme l'M qui signifiait Mort était exactement formée dans sa main charmante. Foedora soutient en riant qu'elle voulait dire qu'elle serait Mariée . . . et de loin, elle sourit à son bien aimé. Il lui répondit dans le même langage. A elle seule dans la nature il souriait ainsi. Elle en était joyeuse. . . . Elle n'était inquiète que d'une seule chose: c'est qu'il lui cachait sa demeure. Elle aurait voulu y aller, pour au matin, le voir dormir, lui sourire à son réveil, et le servir comme un maître.

Georges avait un amour immense. Foedora l'aurait envoyé mourir, si elle avait pu le vouloir. Par toutes ses actions, il témoignait une âme grande et généreuse. On apercevait dans ses paroles les traces d'une gaieté qui s'éteignait de jour en jour. Sa mélancolie commença avec son amour.

Une pâleur livide était répandue sur son visage . . . il ne voyait que Foedora. Mais son sein était gros d'une infortune qu'il voulait se dissimuler à lui-même. L'Anglaise lui fit plusieurs questions.

Il dédaigna répondre, et lorsqu'elle lui dit, "Qui êtes-vous?" Un sourire sardonique, plus amer que l'onde de l'Océan, plus terrible que le regard d'un Dieu courroucé, fit trembler les cheveux de la rivale de Foedora, quand il vint errer sur la lèvre du jeune homme.—Si j'étais un lâche, tu ne le dirais pas."—Mais enfin. Cela n'est pas car tu méprises la mort."—Non Foedora, mais bien la vie." Souvent Foedora voulait lui prendre la main, mais il s'en défendait, et ce n'était jamais que par surprise et en jouant qu'elle pouvait s'en saisir.

Quand elle y déposait furtivement un baiser, Georges plissait son front, lui jetait un regard qui l'épouvantait, il lui disait: "Tu en auras peut-être regret un jour."—Jamais disait-elle.—Alors, la sueur froide sur le front, Georges répondait, "Partons pour ton pays, Paris m'étouffe."

Ils devaient partir bientôt, les apprêts d'un long voyage étaient faits. La joie brillait dans les yeux de Foedora. Georges se trouvait dans la chambre à coucher de son amie. La voix envolée d'un crieur public arriva jusqu'à lui. Il pâlit, et tomba dans les bras de son amie.

La veille de son départ Foedora, accompagnée de sa tante, était en calèche et revenait à son hôtel.—Avancez donc," disait doucement la comtesse à son cocher. La voiture n'avançait pas. La foule était trop immense.

L'image d'une prairie émaillée de fleurs est incomplète pour donner l'idée de ce rassemblement d'un peuple entier . . . Foedora, étonnée, lève les yeux. Elle voit la main chérie qu'elle couvre de baisers. . . . Cette main tenait une tête sanglante, et la montrait au peuple!

Foedora ne poussa qu'un soupir. --Foedora! Foedora! " disait sa tante, en tenant par la manche de sa robe,—Foedora." Il ne restait plus d'elle que le nom, et les formes qu'un ange prit pour apparaître aux mortels. La tante voyait le doigt de la nièce, qui, tout morte qu'elle était, montrait l'échafaud, y jeta les yeux. Ce jour-là la mort eut quatre victimes.

Notes to Appendix B

[1] In the manuscript, the poem and the plan were copied side by side, the plan to the right of the poem.

[2] Because of the similarities in Arrigon's references to the "Plan," it is apparent that he transcribed the Lovenjoul copy instead of Balzac's manuscript in *Les Débuts littéraires de Honoré de Balzac* (156-57).

[3] Arrigon transcribes it as "se joue et folâtre."

[4] Lovenjoul made a note that these lines were written in pencil next to the title.

[5] These notes occurred at the bottom of the page with the brackets as shown.

Appendix C
Lovenjoul A84 f°6-8
Le Livre de Job, poème [1]

En la terre de Hus vivait un très-saint homme,
De la diphtongue Job l'Ecriture le nomme.
Il s'écartait du mal par crainte du Seigneur,
Et n'allait point au vice, étant simple de coeur.
Pourtant il eut bientôt une grande famille;
Trois fois madame Job accoucha d'une fille,
Mais Job, y prenant garde, eut après sept garçons.
Trois fois mille chameaux et sept mille moutons
Paissaient avec des boeufs, dont le millier indique
Que Job avait encore un nombreux domestique,
Dont par deux mots la Bible évite le détail,
Donnant, comme toujours, préséance au bétail.
Veuves de leurs époux, plus de cinq cents ânesses,
Par leur lait pectoral augmentaient ses richesses,
Ou le rendaient dispos pour peu qu'il en eût bu . . . .
Tel est des biens de Job le fidèle inventaire,
Que l'Esprit-Saint a fait aussi bien qu'un notaire.
Si, par un grand malheur, l'Ecriture a perdu
La carte du village où ce monde a vécu.
Toujours est-il que Job fut grand propriétaire
Admis dans les congrès chez les Orientaux,
Et de son double vote ôtant les libéraux.

Aussi, tous ses enfants, plongés dans la liesse,
L'un chez l'autre invités et couronnés de fleurs,
Là, fêtés, fortunés, consommaient leur jeunesse[2]
Et, pour plus grand plaisir, à leurs trois jeunes soeurs
Envoyaient les landaus qui roulaient en Judée;
De leurs petits soupers l'ivresse était guidée
Par ces tendres beautés qui buvaient des liqueurs,
Et d'entremets friands savouraient les douceurs.
Quand le cercle trop court de ces belles journées,
Séparait par sa fin leurs troupes étonnées,
Soudain de ces repas Job narguant [3] les effets,
Pour les purifier détachait ses valets;
Et du lit conjugal se levant dès l'aurore,
Au nom de ses enfants qui sommeillaient encore,
D'un pieux holocauste il présentait l'encens;
Car du sieur Azaïs Job ayant tout le sens,
Des compensations connaissait le système.
Et voici comme au texte il se parle à lui-même:[4]

Notes to Appendix C

[1] In *Histoire des Oeuvres de Balzac*, Lovenjoul reads the line as follows: " En fêtes, en festins, consumaient leur jeunesse. . . ."

[2] copied by Lovenjoul, published in his *Histoire des oeuvres de Balzac*.

[3] I read "craignant."

[4] The text stops with a curious reference. "Ici Balzac s'interrompt. Tout à coup le bonhomme Job l'emmène [pour la] santé et il était tenté par les merveilleuses aventures de Mobu-le-Diable."

Appendix D

Balzac Editions: 1850-1900[1]

Date	Edition	Group	Epigraph Line	Dedication	Original Prefaces
1851-3	Marescq	II &III	0	X	None
1853-5	Houssiaux	II	X	X	1845
1856-67	Librairie Nouvelle (Lévy)	I	X	X	1845
1869-76	Lévy	II	X	X	1845
1891-99	Lévy	II & III	X	X	XXXX
1899	Rouff	II	X	X	1845
1900	Ollendorf	II	X	X	1831

Balzac Editions: 1901-1939

Date	Edition	Group	Epigraph Line	Dedication	Orig Prefaces
1901	Flammarion	I*	0	0	0
1903	Librairie Populaire	II,III*	0	0	0
1909; 10; 12; 21; 25	Larousse	I*	0	0	0
1910;31;34; 36;39;69	Nelson	I*	0	X	0
1923	Grès et Cie	I*	X	X	0
1927	Conard	I	0	X	XXXX
1928	Tallandier	I	0	0	XXXX
1933	Garnier	II*	X	X	0
1933	Hilsum	I*	0	0	0
1936	Béziat	I*	0	0	0

228

Balzac Editions 1940-1950

Date	Edition	Group	Epigraph Line	Dedication	Orig Prefaces
1942	Corbeil	I*	0	0	0
1942	Nouvelle France	II*	0	0	0
1945	Gasmier	II*	0	0	0
1945	Panthéon	I*	0	0	0
1946	Gibert	I*	X	X	0
1946	Martel	III	0	0	XXXX
1946	Ratier	I*	0	0	0
1047	Vautrain	I*	X	0	0
1947	Rasmussen	I*	0	0	0
1948	Gründ	II*	X	X	0
1950	Dauphin	I*	X	X	0

Balzac Editions: 1951-1970

Date	Edition	Group	Epigraph Line	Dedication	Orig Prefaces
1952	Guillot	II*	0	0	1831
1953	Hazan	II	0	0	0
1956	Club des libraires de France	I*(1838)	X	0	1831
1956-63	Club de l'honnête homme	I	X	X	XXXX
1949-53	Formes et Reflets	III	X	X	0
1949-65	Gallimard	I	X	X	XXXX
1958-62	Rencontre	I	X	X	XXXX
1962	Le Monde en 10/18	I*	0	0	0
1966	Livre de Poche	I	0	0	0
1967-74	Bibliophile de l'original	I	X	X	1845
1969	B.P.	II*	0	0	0
1969	Seuil	I	X	X	XXXX
1970	Société Encyclop. française	I* (1838)	X	0	0

Balzac Editions: 1971-1984

Date	Edition	Group	Epigraph Line	Dedication	Orig Prefaces
1971	Garnier-Flammarion	I*	0	0	0
1972;84	Livre de Poche	I,II (1831)	0	0	1831
1973	Michel de l'Ormeraie	I*(1838)	X	0	0
1978-79	Rencontre	I	X	X	
1976-81	Gallimard	I	X	X	XXXX
1982	Imprimerie National	I*	X	X	0

---

[1]The following abreviations may prove helpful:
0 the element is missing from this edition.
X the element is present.
XXXX *La Peau de chagrin* is part of a critical edition with much of the paratext in notes.
I, II, III categories are given in Roman numerals.
*the work is not part of a complete works edition.

Selected Bibliography

I. Primary

a. Manuscripts and Correspondance

Balzac, Honoré de. *Correspondance*, Ed. Roger Pierrot. 5 vols. Paris: Garnier Frères, 1960-69.

---. "Foedora," poème. Lovenjoul ms. A 83. Bibliothèque de L'Institut de France, Paris. All Lovenjoul manuscripts are from the "Collection du Vicomte de Spoelberch de Lovenjoul" which has been moved from Chantilly to Paris.

---. "Foedora," poème. Lovenjoul ms. A 168 f° 150-59. Bibliothèque de l'Institut de France, Paris. Copied by Spoelberch de Lovenjoul.

---. *Furne corrigé*, Lovenjoul ms. A 30. Bibliothèque de l'Institut de France, Paris.

---. *Lettres à Mme Hanska*. Ed. Roger Pierrot. 4 vols. Paris: Bibliophiles de l'Originale, 1967-68.

---. "Lettres sur la littérature." Vol. 40. *Oeuvres complètes de Honoré de Balzac*. Paris: Louis Conard, 1940. 40 vols. 271-329.

---. "Le Livre de Job," poème. Lovenjoul ms. A 84 f° 6-8. Bibliothèque de L'Institut de France, Paris.

---. *La Peau de chagrin*. Lovenjoul ms. A 177. Bibliothèque de l'Institut de France, Paris. Hand-corrected copy of first edition.

b. Chronological list of *La Peau de chagrin* editions

Balzac, Honoré de. *La Peau de chagrin*. 2 vols. Paris: Gosselin and Canel, 1831.

---. *La Peau de chagrin*. 2 vols. Bruxelles: Hauman, 1831.

---. *Romans et contes philosophiques*. 3 vols. Paris: Gosselin, 1831.

---. *La Peau de chagrin*. 2 vols. Bruxelles: Méline, 1833.
---. *Romans et contes philosophiques*. 4 vols. Paris: Gosselin, 1833.
---. *Etudes philosophiques*. 5 vols. Paris: Werdet, 1835.
---. *Balzac illustré. La Peau de chagrin. Etudes sociales*. Paris: Delloye et Lecou, 1838.
---. *La Peau de chagrin*. Paris: Charpentier, 1839.
---. *La Peau de chagrin*. 2 vols. 1901. Paris: Flammarion, 1932. Listed in Talvart and Place as one volume of an *Oeuvres complètes* edition in 36 volumes (1902-25).
---. *La Peau de chagrin*. Paris: Librairie populaire, 1903.
---. *La Peau de chagrin, Le Curé de Tours, et Le Colonel Chabert*. 1910. Paris: Nelson, 1961.
---. *La Peau de chagrin*. Paris: Crès et Cie., 1923.
---. *La Peau de chagrin*. 1909. Paris: Larousse, 1925.
---. *La Peau de chagrin et Le Medecin de campagne*. 1925. Paris: Larousse, 1930.
---. *La Peau de chagrin*. Paris: Barrie, 1925.
---. *La Peau de chagrin*. Paris: Tallandier, 1928.
---. *La Peau de chagrin*. Paris: Trianon, 1930.
---. *La Peau de chagrin et Massimilia Doni*. 2 vols. Paris: Gallimard, 1932.
---. *La Peau de chagrin*. 2 vols. 1933. Paris: Hilsum, 1953.
---. *La Peau de chagrin*. Ed. Maurice Allem. 1933. Paris: Garnier, 1978.
---. *La Peau de chagrin*. Paris: Henri Béziat, 1936.
---. *La Peau de chagrin*. Paris: Gründ, 1939.
---. *La Peau de chagrin*. Paris: Corbeil, 1942.
---. *La Peau de chagrin*. Paris: La Nouvelle France, 1943.
---. *La Peau de chagrin*. Paris: Marcel Gasmier, 1945.
---. *La Peau de chagrin*. Paris: Panthéon, 1945.
---. *La Peau de chagrin*. Paris: Gibert, 1946.
---. *La Peau de chagrin*. Paris: Vie réelle, 1946.
---. *La Peau de chagrin*. Paris: Ratier, 1946.
---. *La Peau de chagrin*. Paris: Rasmussen, 1947.
---. *La Peau de chagrin*. Paris: Vautrain, 1947.
---. *La Peau de chagrin*. Paris: Editions du Dauphin, 1950.

---. *La Peau de chagrin. Les Etudes philosophiques.* 4 vols. Paris: Albin Michel, 1951.
---. *La Peau de chagrin. Les Etudes philosophiques.* Paris: Albert Guillot, 1952.
---. *La Peau de chagrin.* Paris: Hazan, 1953.
---. *La Peau de chagrin.* Paris: 1838. Club des libraires de France, 1956.
---. *La Peau de chagrin.* Paris: Le Monde en 10/18, 1962.
---. *La Peau de chagrin.* Paris: Un gen d'éditeurs, 1962.
---. *La Peau de chagrin.* Paris: Baudelaire, 1964.
---. *La Peau de chagrin.* Paris: Livre de poche, 1966. Preface by André Pieyre de Mandiargues. Edited and annotated by Jean A. Ducourneau.
---. *La Peau de chagrin.* 1966. Paris: Gallimard, 1974. Preface by André Pieyre de Mandiargues. Edited and annotated by S. de Sacy.
---. *La Peau de chagrin.* Paris: Editions G. P., 1969.
---. *Balzac illustrée. La Peau de chagrin. Etudes sociales.* 1838. Paris: Société encyclopédique française, 1970.
---. *La Peau de chagrin.* Ed. Pierre Citron. Paris: Garnier-Flammarion, 1971.
---. *La Peau de chagrin.* 1831. Paris: Livre de poche, 1984. First published in 1972. Preface by Pierre Barbéris.
---. *La Peau de chagrin.* 1838. Paris: Michel de l'Ormeraie, 1973.
---. *La Peau de chagrin.* Paris: Garnier-Flammarion, 1974. Preface by Pierre Citron.
---. *La Peau de chagrin.* Paris: Hachette, 1980.
---. *La Peau de chagrin.* Ed. Madeleine Ambrière. Paris: Imprimerie Nationale, 1982.

c. Chronological list of *Oeuvres complètes* editions
Because titles of *Oeuvres complètes* editions of Balzac's works vary, I have listed them chronologically.

Balzac, Honoré de. *La Comédie humaine.* 17 vols. Paris: Furne, 1842-48. vols. 18-20 by Houssiaux.

---. *Oeuvres illustrées de Balzac*. 10 vols. Paris: Marescq et Cie, 1851-53.
---. *Oeuvres complètes illustrées*. 20 vols. Paris: Houssiaux, 1853-55. This edition contains Georges Sand's "Notice."
---. *Oeuvres complètes*. 55 vols. Paris: Librarie nouvelle, 1856-67. Publishing house purchased by Michel Lévy Frères. Later printed by Calmann Lévy.
---. *Oeuvres complètes de H. de Balzac*. Ed. Charles Spoelberch de Lovenjoul. 24 vols. Paris: Michel Lévy Frères, 1869-76. Later printed by Calmann Lévy, 1875-92.
---. *La Comédie humaine*. 52 vols. Paris: Calmann Lévy, 1891-99. Also published from 1899-1902.
---. *Oeuvres de Honoré de Balzac*. 27 vols. Paris: Rouff, 1899. Originally issued in fascicles. Volume numbering by library.
---. *Oeuvres complètes illustrées*. 50 vols. Paris: Ollendorf, 1900-02. Later published by Ollendorf as the Société d'éditeurs littéraires et artistiques.
---. *Oeuvres complètes de H. de Balzac. Comédie humaine. Théâtre. Contes drôlatiques*. 3 vols. Paris: La Renaissance du Livre, 1911.
---. *Oeuvres complètes*. 40 vols. Eds. Marcel Bouteron and Henri Longnon. Paris: Conard, 1912-40.
---. *La Comédie humaine*. Ed. Marcel Bouteron. 10 vols. Paris: Gallimard, 1935-37. Bibliothèque de la Pléiade.
---. *Oeuvres complètes illustrées de Balzac*. 31 vols. (Givors: Martel, 1946-51).
---. *L'Oeuvre de Balzac publieé dans un ordre nouveau*. Eds. A. Béguin et J. A. Ducourneau. 16 vols. Paris: Formes et Reflets, 1949-53.
---. *La Comédie humaine*. Ed. Roger Pierrot. 11 vols. Paris: Gallimard, 1949-65. Bibliothèque de la Pléiade.
---. *Oeuvres complètes*. 28 vols. Paris: Société d'Etudes balzaciennes, 1956-63. In association with the Club de l'Honnête homme under the direction of Maurice Bardèche.
---. *Oeuvres de Balzac*. Ed. R. Chollet. 37 vols. 1958-62. Genève: Rencontres, 1967-74. Later published as *Oeuvres complètes*, Lausanne, 1978-79.

---. *La Comédie humaine.* "Préface" by Pierre-Georges Castex. 7 vols. Paris: Seuil, 1965. "Présentation" and "Notes" by Pierre Citron.
---. *Oeuvres complètes.* 37 vols. Paris: Cercle du Bibliophile, 1965-68.
---. *Oeuvres complètes illustrées.* Ed. Jean Ducourneau. 25 vols. Paris: Bibliophiles de l'Originale, 1967-74. First published as a facsimili of the *Furne corrigé* manuscript of *La Comédie humaine* in 17 volumes.
---. *Oeuvres compètes.* 24 vols. Paris: Club de l'Honnête homme, 1968-71.
---. *La Comédie humaine.* Ed. Pierre-Georges Castex. 12 vols. Bibliothèque de la Pléiade. Paris: Gallimard, 1976-81.

II. Secondary

Abraham, Karl. *Selected Papers of Karl Abraham, M.D.* Trans. Douglas Bryan and Alix Strachey. 1927 New York: Basic Books, 1957.

Arrigon, Louis J. *Les Débuts littéraires de Honoré de Balzac.* Paris: Perrin et Cie. , 1924.

Bachelard, Gaston, *La Poétique de l'espace.* (Paris: PUF,1958).

Bakhtin, Mikhail. *Problems of Dostoevsky's Poetics.* Trans. Caryl Emerson. Manchester: Manchester UP, 1984.

---. *Rabelais and His World.* Cambridge: MIT P, 1968.

Bal, Mieke. *Narratology: Introduction to the Theory of Narrative.* Trans. Christine von Boheeman. Toronto: U of Toronto P, 1985.

Baldensberger, Fernand. *Orientations étrangères chez Honoré de Balzac.* Paris: Champion, 1927.

Balakian, Anna, and James Wilhelm, eds., *Proceedings of the Xth Congress of the International Comparative Literature Association.* 2 vols. New York: Garland, 1982.

Banfield, Ann. *Unspeakable sentences: Narration and Representation in the Language of Fiction.* Boston: Routledge & Kegan Paul, 1982.

Barbéris, Pierre. "L'Accueil de la critique aux premières grandes oeuvres de Balzac (1831-1832)," *L'Année balzacienne* (1968): 165-95.

---. *Aux Sources de Balzac: les romans de jeunesse.* Paris: Bibliophiles de l'Originale, 1965.

---. *Balzac et le mal du siècle.* 2 vols. Paris: Gallimard, 1970.

Bargues-Rollins, Yvonne. "Une 'dance-macabre:' Du fantastique au grotesque dans *la Peau de chagrin*," *Romantisme: Revue du Dix-neuvième siècle* 15.48 (1985): 33-46.

Barrière, Pierre. *Honoré de Balzac, les romans de jeunesse*. Paris: Hachette, 1928.

Barthes, Roland. *S/Z*. Paris: Seuil, 1970.

---. "Barthes puissance trois," *Quinzaine Littéraire*. 1-15 March 1975: 3-5.

Barton, Francis Brown. *Etude sur l'influence de Laurence Sterne en France au dix-huitième siècle*. Paris: Hachette, 1911.

Baudelaire, Charles. *Petits poèmes en prose*. Paris: Bordas, 1986.

Beardsley, Monroe C. "The Metaphorical Twist." *Philosophy and Phenomenological Research* 22 (1962): 293-307.

Bellos, David. *Balzac Criticism in France, 1850-1900: The Making of a Reputation*. Oxford: Clarendon P, 1976.

Bénabou, Marcel. *Pourquoi je n'ai écrit aucun de mes livres*. Paris: Hachette, 1986.

Benveniste, Emile. *Problèmes de linguistique générale*. Paris: Gallimard, 1966.

Berne, Mauricette and Jean-Yves Mollier. *Une Aventure d'éditeurs au XIXe Siècle*. Paris: Bibliothèque Nationale, 1986.

Bershtel, Susan. "Fairy Tales and Success in Balzac's *Comédie humaine*," *Comparative Literature* 31 (1979): 47-62.

Bilodeau, François. "Espace et temps romanesques dans *La Peau de chagrin*," *L'Année balzacienne* (1969): 47-70.

---. *Balzac et le Jeu des Mots*. Montréal: Presses de l'Université de Montréal, 1971.

Bodin, Thierry. "Balzac poète," *L'Année balzacienne* (1982): 151-66.

Booth, Wayne C. *The Rhetoric of Fiction*. Chicago: U of Chicago P, 1961.

Brombert, Victor. "Natalie ou le lecteur caché de Balzac," *Etudes critiques offertes à Georges Poulet*. Paris: José Corti, 1972. 177-90.

Brooks, Peter. "Narrative Desire," *Style* 18.3 (1984): 312-27.

---. "Balzac, Melodrama, and Metaphor." *The Hudson Review* 22 (1969): 213-28.

Castex, Pierre-George, *Le Conte fantastique en France de Nodier à*

Maupassant. Paris: José Cortí, 1951.

Chatman, Seymour Benjamin. *Story and Discourse: Narrative Structure in Fiction and Film.* Ithaca: Cornell UP, 1978.

Chollet, Roland H. "Une Heure de ma vie, ou Lord R'Hoone à la découverte de Balzac," *L'Année balzcienne* (1968): 121-34.

Cross, Wilbur. *The Life and Times of Laurence Sterne.* New Haven: Yale UP, 1929.

Culler, Jonathan. *On Deconstruction: Theory and Criticism after Structuralism.* Ithaca: Cornell UP 1982.

Danger, Pierre. "La Castration dans *La Peau de chagrin.*" *L'Année balzacienne* (1982): 227-46.

De Man, Paul. *Allegories of Reading: Figural Language in Rousseau, Neitzsche, Rilke, and Proust.* New Haven: Yale UP, 1979.

Derrida, Jacques. *La Dissémination.* Paris: Seuil, 1972.

---. *Glas.* Paris: Galilée, 1974.

---. "Living On: Border Lines," Bloom et al. *Deconstruction and Criticism* (New York: Seabury, 1979) 75-175. French "Survivre." Unpublished.

Di Fazio Alberti, Margherita. *Il titolo e la funzione paraletteraria.* Torino: ERI, 1984.

Donnelly, Sandra Suares. *Balzac and Sterne.* Diss. Florida State U, 1973. Ann Arbor: UMI, 1989. 34:7227A (Fla.).

Duchet, Claude., ed. *Balzac et "La Peau de chagrin."* Paris: CDU and SEDES, 1979).

--- and Jacques Neefs., eds. *Balzac et l'Invention du roman.* Paris: Belfond, 1982.

---. "La Fille abandonnée et la Bête humaine, éléments de la titrologie romanesque." *Littérature* 12 (1973): 49-73.

Erikson, Erik. *Young Man Luther: A Study in Psychoanalysis and History.* New York: Norton, 1962.

Eco, Umberto. *A Theory of Semiotics.* Bloomington: Indiana UP, 1976.

Falconer, Graham. "Le travail de style dans les révisions de *la Peau de chagrin.*" *L'Année balzacienne* (1969): 71-106.

Felman, Shoshana. *La Folie et la chose littéraire.* Paris: Seuil, 1978. UP, 1985. Translated as *Writing and Madness* by Martha Noel Evans.

Ithaca: Cornell UP, 1985.
---. "Rereading Feminitiy," *Yale French Studies* 62 (1981): 19-44.
---. "Women and Madness: The Critical Phallacy," *Diacritics* 5.4 (1975): 2-10.
Flaubert, Gustave. *Madame Bovary*. Paris: Flammarion, 1986.
Fluchère, Henri. *Laurence Sterne, de l'homme à l'oeuvre; biographie critique et essai d'interpretation de "Tristram Shandy."* Paris: Gallimard, 1961.
Fortassier, Rose. *Les Mondains de "la Comédie humaine."* Paris: Klincksieck, 1974.
Frappier-Mazur, Lucienne, "Espace et regard dans *La Comédie humaine.*" *L'Année balzacienne* (1967): 325-38.
---. *L'Expression métaphorique dans "La Comédie humaine."* Paris: Klincksieck, 1976.
Freeman, Kathleen, trans. *The Ancilla to the Pre-Socratic philosophers*. Cambridge: Harvard UP, 1948.
Freud, Sigmund. *The Standard Edition of the Complete Psychological Works of Sigmund Freud*. Trans. and Ed. James Strachey. 24 vols. London: Hogarth Press and the Institute for Psycho-analysis, 1953-74.
Genette, Gérard. *Fiction et Diction*. Paris: Seuil, 1991.
---. *Figures I*. Paris: Seuil, 1966.
---. *Figures II*. Paris: Seuil, 1969.
---. *Figures III*. Paris: Seuil, 1972.
---. *Introduction à l'architexte*. Paris: Seuil, 1979.
---. *Narrative Discourse: An Essay in Method*. Trans. Jane E. Levin. Ithaca: Cornell UP, 1980.
---. *Palimpsestes*. Paris: Seuil, 1982.
---. *Seuils*. Paris: Seuil, 1987.
George, Albert J. *Books by Balzac*. Syracuse: Syracuse UP, 1960.
Goux, Jean-Joseph. *Freud, Marx. Economie et symbolique*. Paris: Seuil, 1973.
Greenblatt, Stephen. *Shakespearean Negotiations: The Circulation of Social Energy in Renaissance England*. Berkley and Los Angleles:

U of California P, 1988.
Grossman, Leonid Petrovich. *Balzac et Dostoevsky*. Trans. Lena Karpov. Ann Arbor: Ardis, 1973.
Guise, René. "Balzac et l'étranger." *L'Année balzacienne* (1970): 3-19.
Gurney, A.R. *The Rape of Bunny Stunz*. New York: Samuel French, 1964.
Greimas, A. J. *Sémantique structurale*. Paris: Larousse, 1966.
---. "Sur l'histoire événementielle et l'histoire fondamentale," *Geschichte-- Ereignis und Erzählung*. Eds. von R. Koselleck und W.D. Stempel, *Poetik und Hermeneutik*. 5 Munich: Fink, 1973. 139-53.
Haig, Stirling. "Dualistic Patterns in *La Peau de chagrin*," *Nineteenth Century French Studies* 1 (1973): 211-18.
Hamburger, Käte, *The Logic of Literature*. Trans. Marilynn J. Rose. Bloomington: Indiana UP, 1973.
Holbein, Hans. *The Dance of Death: Hans Holbein the Younger: A Complete Facsimili of the Original 1538 Edition. Les simulachres et histoiries faces de la mort*. (sic) Lyons: Treschel, 1538. New York: Dover, 1971.
Holland, Norman. *The Dynamics of Literary Response*. New York: Oxford UP, 1968.
Hédouin, A. *Sterne inédit. Le Koran. Oeuvres posthumes complètes nouvelles*. Paris: Librairie nouvelle, 1853.
Iser, Wolfgang. *The Implied Reader: Patterns of Communication in Prose Fiction from Bunyon to Beckett*. Baltimore: Johns Hopkins UP, 1974.
Irigaray, Luce. *Ce sexe qui n'en est pas un*. Paris: Minuit, 1977.
---. *Speculum de l'autre femme*. Paris: Minuit, 1974.
Jakobson, Roman. *Essais de linguistique générale*. Paris: Seuil, 1963.
Jacques, Georges. *Paysages et Structures dans "La Comédie humaine."* Louvain, Belgium: Bibliothèque de l'Université, 1975.
Kaes, Anton. "The New Historicism and the Study of German Literature," *The German Quarterly* 62.2 (1989): 210-19.
Kanes, Martin. *Balzac's Comedy of Words*. Princeton: Princeton UP, 1975.
---. "Logic and Language in *La Peau de chagrin*," *Studi Francesi* 14 (1970): 244-56.
---. "The Mythic Structure of *La Peau de chagrin*," *Studi Francesi* 16

(1972): 46-59.
Keesey, Donald. *Contexts for Criticism.* Palo Alto: Mayfield, 1987.
Kristeva, Julia. *Semiotike.* Paris: Seuil, 1969.
---. *Le Language, cet inconnu: Une Initiation à la linguistique.* Paris: Seuil, 1981.
Kurtz, Leonard P. *The Dance of Death and the Macabre Spirit in European Literature.* New York: Gordon P, 1975.
Lacan, Jacques. *Ecrits.* Paris: Editions du Seuil, 1966.
Lastinger, Michaël. "Narration et 'Point de vue' dans deux romans de Balzac: *La Peau de chagrin* et *Le Lys dans la vallée*," *L'Année balzacienne* (1988): 271-90.
Lecuyer, Maurice A. *Balzac et Rabelais.* Paris: Société d'Edition Les Belles Lettres, 1956. Etudes françaises fondées sur l'initiation de la Société des Professeurs français en Amérique, 47.
Le Huenen, Roland and Paul Perron, eds. *Le Roman de Balzac: recherches critiques, méthodes, lectures.* Montreal: Didier, 1980.
Le Yaouanc, Moïse. *Nosographie de l'humanité balzacienne.* Paris: Maloine, 1959.
Lodge, David. *After Bakhtin: Essays on Fiction and Criticism.* London: Routledge, 1990.
Lotte, Fernand. "Indexe des Personnnes réelles et des allusions littéraires." *La Comédie humaine.* Ed. Roger Pierrot. Vol. 11. Paris: Gallimard, 1965. 11 vols. 1951-65.
Lucretius, Carus, Titus. *De Rerum Natura.* Ed. J. D. Duff. London: Cambridge UP, 1958.
Mallarmé, Stéphane. *Oeuvres complètes.* Paris: Flammarion, 1983.
Marivaux, *La Vie de Marianne ou, Les aventures de Madame la contesse de xxxx.* Paris: Garnier frères, 1982.
Marks, Elaine and Isabelle de Courtivron, eds. *New French Feminisms: An Anthology.* Amherst: U of Mass P, 1980.
Martin, A., V. G. Mylne, and R. Frautschi. *Bibliographie du genre romanesque français.* 1751-1800. London: Mansell, 1977.
McCarthy, Mary Susan. *Balzac and his Reader: A study of the Creation of Meaning in "La Comédie humaine."* Columbia: U of Missouri P, 1982.

Minahen, Charles D. "Tourbillons de lumière: The Symbolism of
    Rimbaud's illuminating Vortices," *The Stanford French Review*. 9
    (1985): 358-64.
Mitterand, Henri. *Le Discours du roman*. Paris: PUF, 1980.
Molière, *Oeuvres complètes*. Paris: Seuil, 1962.
Nykrog, Per. *La Pensée de Balzac dans "La Comédie humaine."*
    Copenhague: Munksgaard, 1965.
O'Connor, John R. *Balzac's Soluble Fish*. Madrid: José Porrúa Turanzas,
    1977.
Poulet, Georges. *Etudes sur le temps humain* 1950; *II La Distance inté-
    rieure*. Paris: Plon, 1952.
---. "Espace et temps balzaciens," *L'Oeuvre de balzac publiée dans un
    ordre nouveau*. Eds. A. Béguin and J. A. Ducourneau. 16 vols. Paris:
    Formes et Reflets, 1967. 10: i-xxv.
Prince, Gerald. "Introduction à l'étude du narrataire." *Poétique* 14 (1973):
    178-96.
---. "Notes Towards a Categorization of Fictional 'Narratees'." *Genre* 4
    (1971): 100-05.
---. "On Presuppostion and Narrative Strategy." *Centrum* 1 (1973): 23-31.
Prioult, A. *Balzac avant "la Comédie humaine."* Paris: Courville, 1936.
Prendergast, Christopher, *Balzac: Fiction and Melodrama*. New York:
    Holmes and Meier Publishers, 1978.
Propp, Vladimir. *Morphology of the Folktale*. Trans. Laurence Scott.
    Bloomington: U of Indiana Research Center, 1958.
Pugh, Anthony. *Balzac's Recurring Characters*. Toronto: U of Toronto P,
    1974.
Quérard, Josephe Marie. *La France littéraire, ou Dictionnaire
    bibliographique*. 12 vols. Paris: Firmin Didot, 1824-64.
Raimond, Michael. "Balzac vu par les romanciers français de Zola à
    Proust." Thesis: La Sorbonne, 1966.
Reboussin, Marcel. *Balzac et le mythe de Foedora*. Paris: Nizet, 1966.
Reeder, Claudia. "Paradoxe du (para) text," *Esprit Créateur* 24.2 (1984):
    36-38
Reznik, Raïssa. "Sur l'épigraphe de *La Peau de chagrin*," *L'Année*

balzacienne (1972): 373-75.
Ricoeur, Paul. *La Métaphore vive.* Paris: Seuil, 1975.
Rivers, Kenneth. "The Swirl: Eroticism in Balzac and Flaubert," *Eroticism in French Literature.* Columbia: U of South Carolina French Literature Series 10 (1983): 140.
Richards, I. A. *Practical Criticism.* London: Routledge & Kegan Paul, 1929.
Roche, Denis. *Dépots de savoir et de technique.* Paris: Seuil, 1980.
---. *Notre Antéfixe.* Paris: Flammarion, 1978.
Romains, Jules. *Les Hommes de bonne volonté.* 4 vols. Paris: Laffont, 1988.
Rothe, Arnold, *Der Literarische Title: Funktionen, Formen, Geschichte.* Frankfurt: Klostermann, 1986.
Royce, William Hobert. *A Balzac Bibliography: Writings relative to the Life and Works of Honoré de Balzac.* 2 vols. Chicago: U of Chicago P, 1929.
Schoch, Russell. "A Conversation with Stephen Greenblatt," *California monthly* (April, 1988): 8-9.
Séguin, Jean-Pierre, ed. *Mélanges de langue et de littérature française offerts à Pierre Larthomas.* Paris: Ecole Normale Supérieur de Jeunes Filles, 1985.
Serval, Claude. "Une énigme balzacienne, La Foedora de *La Peau de chagrin*," *Bulletin de la Société Historique et Archéologique des VIIIe et XVIIIe Arrondissements de Paris.* ns 5 (1925-6): 387-441.
Sherman, Carol. "The Deferral of Textual Authority in *La Religieuse.*" *Postscript: Publication of the Philological Society of the Carolinas.* 2 (1985): 57-65.
Sonnenschein, Adolf Edward.*What is rhythm?* Oxford: Blackwell, 1925.
Spoelberch de Lovenjoul, Charles Victor. "*Etudes philosophiques* de Honoré de Balzac." *Revue d'Histoire littéraire de la France.* Juillet-septembre. (1907): 393-441.
---. *Histoire des oeuvres de Honoré de Balzac.* 1888. Geneva: Slatkine, 1968.
Sterne, Laurence. *La Vie et les opinions de Tristram Shandy.* Trans. Joseph-

Pierre Frenais and Charles-François de Bonnay. 4 vols. York and Paris: Ruault, Volland, 1776-85.

---. *La Vie et les opinion de Tristram Shandy.* Trans. Joseph-Pierre Frenais and Griffet de la Baume. 4 vols. Paris: Bibliothèque de la Rue Richelieu, 1776-85.

---. *Oeuvres complètes de Laurent Sterne.* Trans. Joseph-Pierre Frenais et al. 6 vols. Paris: Bastien, 1803.

---. *Oeuvres complètes de Laurent Sterne.* Trans. Joseph-Pierre Frenais and Griffet de la Baume. 4 vols. Paris: Ledoux et Tenré, 1818.

---. *Oeuvres complètes.* Trans. Joseph-Pierre Frenais and Charles-François de Bonnay. 6 vols. Paris: Ledoux and Tenré, 1818.

---. *Oeuvres de Sterne.* Trans. Une société de gens de lettres. 4 vols. Paris: Salmon, 1825.

---. *Tristram Shandy.* Ed. James A. Work. New York: Odessy, 1940.

---. *The Works of Laurence Sterne.* 6 vols. New York: The Clonmel Society, 1899.

Talbot, Emile. "Pleasure/Time or Egoisme/Love: Rereading *La Peau de chagrin.*" *Nineteenth Century French Studies* 11.1-2 (1982-83): 72-82.

Talvart, Hector and Joseph Place. *Bibliographie des auteurs modernes de langue française.* Vol. 1. Paris: Editions de la Chronique des lettres françaises, 1928. 22 vols. 1928-76. Continued by Georges Place.

Thérien, Michel. "Métaphores animales et écriture balzaciennes: Le portrait et la description." *L'Année balzacienne* (1979): 193-208.

Tilby, Michael. "A partir d'une allusion à Sterne dans *La Peau de chagrin.*" *Année balzacienne* (1985): 247-62.

Todorov, Tzvetan. *Mikhail Bakhtin: The Dialogic Principle.* Manchester: Manchester UP, 1984.

---. *Introduction à la littérature fantastique.* Paris: Seuil, 1970.

Undank, Jack, and Herbert Josephs, eds. *Diderot, Digression, and Dispersion: a Bicentennial Tribute.* Lexington: French Forum, 1984.

Weber, Samuel W. *Unwrapping Balzac: A Reading of "La Peau de chagrin."* Toronto: U of Toronto P, 1979.

Weinberg, Bernard. *French Realism: The Critical Reaction, 1830-70*. Chicago: U of Chicago Libraries, 1937.

West, Catherine Jones. "La Mise en Jeu de l'autorité dans la préface de roman." Diss. U of North Carolina, 1989.

Wurmser, André. *La Comédie inhumaine*. Paris: Gallimard, 1965.

Page Index

A

Abraham, 151
Abruzzes, 166
Academy of Sciences, 14
Académie, 158
Académie des Sciences, 159, 177
Académie française, 122
actoriale, 3, 4, 14
L'Agonie, 12, 134, 139, 158, 172, 191
Aix, 140
Aix-les-Bains, 138, 139, 155, 159, 173
Aladin, 16
Alcofribas, 13, 129
Alexandre, 166, 187
Alladin's Lamp, 193
Allem, M., 45, 46, 51, 62, 151, 209
L'Allier (river), 139
allographe, 3, 4, 13
allographic, 13, 15, 16, 17, 18, 23
Ambassadeur, 211
Amossy, R., 198
Ancilla, 177
Andrieux (illustrator-lithographer), 37
Androgyne, 156
Anglaise/ L'Anglaise, 115, 211, 218, 219
antipréface, 4
l'Antiquité, 94
apocryphe, 4
Arabic, 90
Arrigon, 111, 122, 124, 126, 221
L'Auberge rouge, 54
auctoriale, 3
auctoricale, 20
authentic, 23
authorial, 14, 17, 18, 22, 23
Auvergnat, 134
Auvergnate, 139
Auvergne, 141, 159, 161, 173
Avant-propos, 6, 18, 19, 26, 47, 51, 84, 88, 99, 102, 103
Avis du Libraire-Editeur, 27
Azaïs, 224

B

B., Alexandre de, 20, 74
Bachelard, G., 177
Bakhtin, M., 181, 182, 183, 184, 185, 187, 188, 194, 196, 197, 198, 203, 204, 206
Bal, M., 131, 150, 153, 176
Balakian, A., 59, 198
Baldensberger, F., 79
Balzac illustré, 29, 35, 36, 37, 41, 48, 49, 55, 56, 60
bande, 6
Banfield, A., 83, 100, 104
Barbéris, P., 32, 33, 53, 59, 79, 86, 87, 104, 105, 122, 130, 131, 136, 149, 202, 203, 204, 206
Bargues-Rollins, Y., 130, 149
Baron, H., 35
Barrière, P., 79
Barthes, R., 1, 3, 6, 20, 110, 123, 154, 176, 196
Barton, F., 65, 74, 79
Baschet, A. 122
Baudelaire, C., 12
Baume, G. de la, 73, 74, 75, 76, 77, 78, 80, 81, 82

Bavière, 163
Beardsley, M., 177
Béatrix, 37
Beaucé (illustrator-lithographer), 37
Beaujon, B. de., 163
Beethoveen., L., 169
Bellos, D., 26, 94, 104
Bengale, 140
Benveniste, E., 83, 99, 100, 104
Bernard, C. de, 74, 105, 106
Berne, M., 61
Bershtel, S., 199
Bertall (illustrator-lithographer), 37, 51
Beuville (illustrator) 46
Béatrice, 116
Béguin, A., 25, 50, 59
Bénabou, M., 3
Bible, 119, 120, 125, 223
Biblical, 116, 118, 120
Bibliothèque de l'Arsenal, 94
Bibliothèque de l'Institut de France, ii, iii, 45, 52, 60, 124
Bibliothèque nationale, ii, iii, 37
Bilodeau, F., 50, 62, 131, 132, 150
Bodin, T., 112, 122, 124, 209, 214
Boheemen, C. van, 150
Bonnay, C. de, 74, 75, 82
Booth, W., 26, 28
Borgia, 166
Bossuet, J., 100
Le Bourgeois gentilhomme, 7
Le Bourget (lake) 138
Bouteron, M. 45, 46, 62
Brillat-Savarin, A. 85
Brombert, V., 154, 176
Brooks, P., 126, 132, 151
Brunellière (engraver), 35
Bryan, D., 151
Burgundy, 138, 139, 159, 174

C

Calmann-Lévy, 42, 48
Canel, U., 13, 32, 42, 80
Cappatti, P., 46
"Le caractère de Semei," 125
La Caricature, 19, 80
carnival, 181, 182, 183, 184, 185, 186, 187, 188, 189, 190, 191, 192, 193, 194, 195, 196, 197, 198
carnivalesque, 181, 183, 184, 185, 186, 188, 189, 190, 191, 194, 195
carnivalization, 181, 182, 185, 196, 197
Carrouges, M., 51
Castex, P. G., 23, 25, 26, 55, 79, 81, 151
catalogue, 21, 27
Cazauran, N., 178
Cellini, B., 166
cena, 181
Cervantes, M. de, 197
Chantilly, 45, 52, 122
Charpentier, 35, 50, 55, 60, 70, 72, 80
Chasles, P., 16, 17, 26, 35, 69, 84, 89, 90, 91, 92, 93, 94, 95, 96, 97, 98, 99, 102, 104, 153, 164
Chatman, S., 196, 204
Chaucer, G., 134
Le Chef d'oeuvre inconnu (*Gillette*), 54, 60
Chine (Chlna), 163, 187
Chollet, R., 25, 53, 59, 63, 69
Christ, 120
Cicero, 166
Citron, P., 26, 53
Cixous, H., 179
Le Collège de Vendôme, 122
La Comédie du diable, 60
Constantinople, 192
Le Constitutionnel, 106
Contes philosophiques, 20, 27
Le Contrat de mariage, 113
Cornélius, 54
Le Correspondant, 21
Courtivron, I. de., 179
Crispins, 179
Cross, W., 80
crypto-auctorial, 18
Culler, J., 6
Le Curé de Village, 51
Czars, 216

D

dada, 111
Dance of Death, 35, 41, 47, 53, 129, 130, 131, 132, 141, 143, 144, 145, 146, 147, 149, 150, 175
Danger, P., 151, 154, 155, 156, 160, 161

danse-macabre, 46, 130, 149, 150
Dante Alighieri, 178
Darwin, C., 102
Daumier, H., 37, 51
Davin, F., 17, 18, 19, 26, 35, 60, 72, 84, 92, 93, 94, 95, 96, 97, 98, 99, 103, 105, 153, 165
Les Débats, 106
"La Débauche," 19
deconstruction/*déconstruction*, 1, 6, 87, 149, 201, 202
deconstructive, 1, 5
deconstructivist, 201
Dédicace, 36, 125, 215
dedication, 4, 14, 41, 42, 43, 44, 46, 47, 48, 49, 50, 51, 52, 55
deipnon, 181
De Man, P., 201, 203, 206
"Le Dernier Napoléon," 19
Derrida, J., 22, 27, 87, 88, 127, 130, 149, 201, 203, 204
Deslignères (illustrator), 48
Les Deux Rêves (Le Petit Souper), 60
Di Fazio Alberti, M., 3
diachronic, 4, 5, 88, 103, 203, 204
diachronie, 204
diachrony, 5, 203, 207
dialectic, 204
dialogic, 204
dialogics, 204
Diane, 217
Diaphane, 214
Dickens, 197
Diderot, 63, 64, 65
diegesis/diagetic, 22, 130, 205
Dieu, 66, 70, 117, 165, 168 190, 210, 218, 219
The Divine Comedy, 149
Don Quichotte, 66
Donnelly, S., 65, 73, 76, 77, 79
Doré, G., 51
Dostoevsky, F., 185, 196, 197, 198, 204, 206
Une Double Famille, 37
Doutremont (Madame, from Tours), 209
Dow, G., 66
Dubarry, J. (Countess), 154, 155
Duchet, C., 3, 7, 105, 197, 198, 206
Ducourneau, J., 25, 50, 59
Lady Dudly, 115

Dumas fils, A., 198

E

Eco, U., 110, 123, 127
Ecole Polytechnique, 14
El verdugo, 37, 60
L'Elixir de longue vie, 37, 60
Emerson, C., 196
Emile, 89, 131, 185, 190, 191, 193
L'Enfant Maudit, 37, 60
England, 206
English, 72
L'Envers de l'histoire contemporaine, 116
epigraph/*épigraphe*, 2, 4, 6, 11, 14, 18, 26, 30, 35, 36, 37, 41, 42, 43, 44, 45, 46, 47, 48, 49, 50, 51, 52, 53, 54, 65, 69, 70, 71, 72, 73, 74, 75, 76, 79, 81, 83, 94, 109, 130, 150, 153, 159
Epilogue, 126
epitext/*épitexte*, 3, 4, 14, 15, 18, 19, 20, 21, 23
Erikson, E., 133, 151
L'Espagne (Spain), 186, 192
Esprit-Saint, 223
Etruscan, 165
L'Etude de femme, 60
Etudes, 58
Etudes analytiques, 18
Etudes de moeurs, 17, 18, 19, 101, 102
Etudes de moeurs au XIXe siècle, 31
Etudes philosophiques, 12, 13, 17, 18, 19, 26, 29, 31, 35, 37, 42, 43, 44, 45, 48, 50, 55, 58, 60, 61, 68, 70, 71, 72, 73, 81, 84, 92, 93, 95, 99, 102, 103, 153
Etudes sociales, 35, 41, 60
Eudes, G., 62, 145
Euphrasie, 145, 190
European, 150, 206
Evans, M., 124
Eve, 187

F

Falconer, G., 29, 58, 59
Fargeaud, M. Ambrière, 54, 55, 63, 79
Faubourg St. Honoré, 158, 159

Feast of the Ass, 188
Felman, S., 111, 123, 179
La Femme de trente ans, 37
La Femme sans coeur, 12
Ferragus, 161
Félix (de Vandenesse), 199
fête des morts, 130
Fiction et Diction, 105, 207
Figures, 3
Figures III, 3, 177, 199
La Fille aux yeux d'or, 103, 111, 123
Madame Firmiani, 54
Fizaine, J., 182, 197, 199
Flaubert, G., 112, 125
Fluchère, H., 82
Foedora, 109, 110, 111, 112, 113, 114, 115, 116, 118, 120, 122, 124, 125, 126, 134, 138, 151, 155, 156, 158, 159, 161, 169, 170, 171, 172, 190, 191, 209, 210, 211, 212, 213, 214, 215, 216, 217, 218, 219, 220
formalist, 1, 2, 7, 196
Fortassier, R., 114, 125
Foucault, M., 203
France, 79, 192, 210, 218
Frappier-Mazur, L., 79, 131, 150, 156, 176, 177, 179, 199
Frautschi, R., 73, 74, 76, 79
Frenais, P., 68, 74, 75, 77, 78, 80, 81, 82
French, 43, 65, 66, 72, 74, 75, 76, 77, 78, 102, 111
Freud, S., 123, 133, 151, 176, 178, 179
frontispiece, 45, 50, 54, 55, 68
Furne, 22, 28, 30, 31, 33, 35, 36, 37, 41, 42, 44, 47, 48, 49, 50, 51, 52, 55, 56, 60
Furne corrigé, 33, 44, 50, 52

G

Gambara, 37, 51
Garagnon, A., 152, 178
Gargantua, 13; 17, 18, 187, 190, 193
Gautier, T., 65
Gavarin (illustrator), 51
La Gazette de La Franche-Comté, 74
Geertz, C., 203
Genette, G., ii, 2, 3, 4, 5, 6, 7, 11, 12, 13, 15, 18, 20, 21, 22, 23, 25, 27, 28, 31, 47, 52, 56, 58, 59, 63, 105, 129, 156, 177,
196, 199, 206, 207
Genettean, 78
George, A., ii, 29, 36
Georges, 113, 114, 115, 210, 211, 212, 218, 219
German, 206
Gobseck, 80, 154
God, 116, 117, 135
Goethe, 69, 80, 145
Gosselin, 13, 19, 42, 59, 60, 80,
Gothic, 118
Goux, J., 176
La Grande Bretèche, 37
Greeks, 177, 181
Greenblatt, S.,203, 204, 206
Greimas, A., 59, 110, 123, 196
La Grèce, 165
La Grenadière, 37
Griffith, R. 26, 69, 73, 76, 79, 80
Grogniart (taylor from Tours), 209
Grossman, L., 198
Guillot., A. 48
Guise, R., 69, 73, 75, 81, 125
Gundersheimer, W., 149, 150
Gurney, A. 63

H

Haig, S., 149, 178
La Halle aux Vins, 177
Hamburger, K., 104
Hanska, Madame (Madame Balzac), 37
Hédouin, A., 69
Hémard, J. 47
Hilarion The Hermit, 67
Hobbes, T., 100
hobby-horse, 111
Holbein The Younger, H., 149
Holland, N., 63, 133, 134, 135, 139, 141, 151
Holy Innocents (Church of the), 129
Homer, 4
Les Hommes de bonne volonté, 12, 25, 31
Honorine II, 116
Hôtel St. Quentin, 89, 169, 170
Huard, C., 45
Hugo, V., 65, 196, 197
Hus, 223

I

Illusions Perdues, 116
illustrated, 22, 30, 35, 36, 41, 42, 48, 52, 53, 56
illustration, 22, 46, 47, 48, 49
illustrations, 2, 6, 22, 23, 36, 37, 41, 42, 43, 46, 47, 48, 50, 51, 52, 54, 130
illustrators, 51
illustré (e), 36, 46, 54
Inca, 109
Inde, 154
Institut (de France), 157
intertextuality, 3
intertitle(s)/*intertitre*, 6, 12, 13, 23, 28
introduction, 2, 4, 17, 20, 26, 43, 46, 54, 72, 84, 92, 103, 153
Introduction à l'architexte, 3, 6
Ionie, 165
Irigaray, L., 179
Isis, 126, 212, 217
Iswolsky, H., 196
Italy, 166

J

jackets, 3
Jacques, G., 152
Jakobson, R., 156, 177, 196, 199
Janet, A., 35
Janin, J., 69
jaquette, 6
Jesus, 119, 120
Jésus Christ en Flandre, 54, 60
Job, 109, 116, 117, 118, 119, 120, 125, 126, 223, 224, 225
Johannot, T., 37, 51
Jonathas, 139, 140, 141, 142, 147, 172, 173, 191
Josephs, H., 64
La Judée, 224
July revolution, 86, 184, 189

K

Kaes, A., 203, 206
Kaërnavan, 68
Kanes, M., 45, 61, 98, 106, 132, 136, 139, 140, 150, 178
Kant, I., 100
Kantian, 57
Karpov, L., 198
Keesey, D., 7
Kock, P. de, 198
Kristeva, J., 3, 6, 203, 206
Kurtz, L., 150

L

Lacan, J., 123, 124
Lamartinian, 138
Lampsonius, E., 37, 51
Lanternois, 13
Larthomas, P., 152, 178
Lastinger, M., 6
Latin, 181
Latour, M., 155
"Lazare et l'homme riche," 120
Lazarus, 109, 111, 119, 120
"Lazarus and the rich man," 120
Lecuyer, M., 197
Leibnitz, G., 100
Lejay, 37, 61
Lettres à Madame Hanska, 21, 27
Lettres à Mme Hanska, 105
Lettres de l'auteur, 75
Lettres sur la littérature, 27
Lévi-Strauss, C., 196
Lévy, 37, 42, 44, 51, 60, 61
Le Yaouanc, 151
lithograph(s), 35, 41, 44, 45, 46, 49, 50, 52, 53, 56, 129, 130, 143, 144, 147, 149, 181
"Le Livre de Job," 109, 110, 118, 223
Lodge, D., 196, 204
logocentrism, 5
La Loire (river), 139
Longnon, H., 45
Lord R'Hoone, 69
Lotte, F., 66, 67, 68, 69, 79, 116, 120, 125
Louis Lambert, 37, 98, 100, 160, 162, 178
Louvre (Palais du), 157
Lovenjoul, Charles Spoelberch de 29, 32, 36, 42, 44, 45, 55, 58, 60, 70, 73, 74, 80, 81, 109, 111, 112, 113, 115,

118, 124, 125, 126, 153, 209, 221, 225
Lucretius, 177
Lucullus, 163, 189
Luke, 120
Luther, M., 151
Le Lys dans la vallée, 6, 101, 115 116, 154

M

macabre, 150
Macbeth, 130
Machiavelli, N., 100
Madame Bovary, moeurs de province, 25
Madame Firmiani, 54
Madère, 167
Madonna, 146
Mahmoud, 192
Maison de Balzac, iii
Maître, X., 65
Malcuzynski, M., 198
Mallarmé, S., 205
Mareschal-Duplessis(school administrator), 109, 122
Marivaux, P., 4
Marks, E., 179
Marquis, 103
Martin, A., 73, 74, 76, 79
Les Martyrs Ignorés, 120
Marx, K., 176
marxist, 202
Massimilla Doni
Mazarin, J., 144
McCarthy, M., 111, 122
Medieval, 184
Meissonier, J., 51, 37
Mémoires de Sterne, 69, 73, 75, 76, 79, 82
Méphistophélès, 145, 189
Mephistophelean, 193
Mephistophelian, 141
*Le Messag*e, 54
Le Messager, 93
metonymic, 12
Metternich, C., 189
Middle Ages, 64, 129, 143, 146, 181
Milan, 187
Minahen, C., 177, 178

Mirabeau, H., 189
Mitterand, H., 83, 104
Mobu-le-Diable, 126, 225
Molière, 7, 102
Mollier, J., 61
La Monarchie de Juillet, 51, 197
Monnier, H., 37, 51
monologic, 203, 204
monologism, 5
Mont d'Or, 138, 139, 159
Montalembert, C. de, 21, 27
Montesquieu, C., 100
"Moralité," 13, 25, 33, 42, 44, 46, 47, 48, 51, 53, 60, 90, 129, 130
Moreau, A., 42
Mortsauf, Madame de, 101, 199
Moscou, 210, 218
Moscow, 210, 218
Moses, 120
Moyen Age, 90, 166
Mozet, N., 86, 87, 105, 106
muse, 215
La Muse du département, 120
Mylne, V., 73, 74, 76, 79

N

Nanteuil, C., 37
narrataire, 2, 6
narratees, 6
Naumann, M., 59
Neefs, J., 197, 206
Nietzsche, F., 206
new historicism, 1, 203, 204, 206, 207
New Historicists, 206
Nodier, C., 65, 69
"Note de l'éditeur pour la Quatrième édition," 25
Notre-Dame, 157
Nykrog, P., 105, 106, 159, 160, 161, 162, 178

O

O'Connor, J., 153, 161, 176, 177
O'Flaharty, 140
OCLC, ii, iii, 32, 37
Oeuvres complètes illustrées, 25, 36, 42, 54, 59, 62

Oeuvres de Balzac illustrées, 61
Oeuvres de jeunesse, 31, 32
Oeuvres illustrées, 32, 35, 36, 37, 41, 42, 49, 51, 55, 61
"On the character of Shimei," 116
Opéra, 132
Orient, 192
Orientaux, 223

P

Palais Royal, 157, 159, 186
Palimpsestes, 3, 4, 6
Pança (Sancho), 66
Pantagruel, 18
Panurge, 182
Paquita, 103
"Parable of the Rich Man and Lazarus Considered," 126
paratext/*paratexte*, ii, iii, 2, 3, 4, 5, 6, 11, 22, 23, 29, 30, 32, 33, 35, 43, 44, 45, 47, 48, 50, 51, 52, 53, 54, 55, 56, 57, 63, 77, 105, 204, 205
paratextual, ii, iii, 4, 5, 11, 14, 23, 27, 29, 30, 31, 32, 33, 35, 36, 37, 41, 42, 43, 45, 46, 47, 48, 49, 50, 51, 52, 53, 55, 57, 58, 69, 83, 87, 88, 89, 103, 204
paratextuality, 2, 3, 4, 5, 7, 11, 55, 58, 64, 81
Paris, 52, 70, 114, 122, 129, 137, 157, 158, 159, 161, 173, 174, 186, 193, 212, 219
Parisian, 102, 159
Parisienne, 114
Pauline, 68, 115, 134, 140, 145, 146, 147, 151, 155, 158, 170, 191
La Peau d'âne, 193
peritext/*péritexte*, 3, 4, 5, 11, 13, 15, 18, 22, 27
Perrault, C., 102
Petronius, 181
Père Goriot, 113
Physiologie, 86
La Physiologie du mariage, 14, 15, 17, 18, 20, 73, 75, 85, 86, 88, 89, 91, 94
Piel, A., 52
Pierrot, R., 26, 27, 79, 104, 105
Pitt, W., 189
Pizarre, F., 187

Place, J., ii, 53, 60, 63
"Plaintes de Job," 118
"Plaintes de Job sur les malheurs de la brièveté de la vie," 117
Planchette, 66
Pléiade, 23, 28, 54, 69
Poe, E., 69, 134
polyphonic, 204
Pomorska, K., 181, 196
Le Pont des Arts, 137, 157, 159
Le Pont Royal, 157
Porriquet, 141, 172
post-structuralist, 1
postface(s), 6, 13
Poulet, G., 131, 150, 176, 179
preface(s)/*préface*, 2, 3, 4, 6, 7, 11, 13, 14, 15, 16, 17, 18, 19, 20, 23, 25, 30, 32, 33, 35, 42, 43, 44, 46, 47, 48, 49, 50, 51, 53, 54, 55, 59, 60, 64, 72, 83, 84, 85, 86, 87, 88, 89, 90, 91, 92, 93, 94, 95, 96, 97, 98, 99, 100, 102, 103, 104, 105, 122, 191, 201, 205, 209*
préfacier, 83, 84
Prendergast, C., 26
Priape, 165
prière d'insérer, 6, 20, 21, 27
Prince, G., 6
Prioult, A., 69, 73, 75, 81, 82
proleptic, 12
Propp, V., 110, 123, 199
Les Proscrits, 37, 54, 60
prospectus, 20, 21
Proteus, 29, 56
Proust, M., 3, 105, 131, 201, 206
pseudo-allographic, 23
pseudo-auctorial, 18
pseudo-authorial, 18
Pugh, A., 125

Q

Quai de Conti, 122
Quai Voltaire, 157, 159
Quérard, 75, 82
La Quotidienne, 106

R

Rabelais, F., 13, 14, 15, 16, 18, 85, 89,

90, 102, 181, 182, 183, 184, 185, 187, 188, 190, 193, 194, 196, 197, 199, 204
Rabelaisian, 29
La Rabouilleuse, 120
Raimond, M., 105
Raphaël, 16, 17, 66, 67, 88, 89, 94, 111, 113, 115, 116, 118, 119, 120, 126, 129, 131, 132, 134, 136, 137, 138, 139, 140, 141, 142, 143, 144, 145, 146, 147, 149, 151, 154, 155, 157, 158, 159, 160, 161, 162, 163, 164, 165, 166, 169, 170, 171, 172, 173, 174, 175, 177, 178, 181, 184, 185, 186, 187, 188, 189, 190, 191, 192, 193, 194, 198
Rastignac, E. de, 114, 132
Reboussin, M., 112, 124
Recherche, 25, 31
Reeder, C., 3, 7
La Religieuse, 58, 63
Rembrandt, H., 145
Renaissance, 143, 166, 184, 197, 206
La Réquisitionnaire, 54, 60, 98
Retailleau, J., 52, 53
La Revue des deux mondes, 19
Reznik, R., 79
rhematic/*rhématique*, 12
Richards, I. A., 131, 150
Ricoeur, P., 177
Rilke, R., 206
Rimbaud, A., 177
Rivers, K., 112, 113, 125, 149
Roche, D., 3
Roman philosophique, 48
Romans et contes philosophiques, 11, 12, 15, 16, 26, 31, 35, 55, 59, 60, 84, 104
Rome, 98, 165, 166, 186
Rose, 104
Rosen, E., 182, 184, 186, 197, 198
Rothe, A., 3
Rougon-Macquart, 12, 25, 31
Rousseau, J., 86, 193, 206
Royce, W., ii, 29
rue Joubert, 158
rue de Cluny, 158, 169
rue de Varennes, 158, 161
rue des Cordiers, 158, 169
rue Taitbout, 158
Russe, 114
Russia, 114
Russian, 114, 196
Russie, 209, 210, 217, 218
Ruysch, F., 165

S

Saché (Château de), iii
Saint Antoine, 170
Saint Beuve, C., 104
La Salpétrière, 177
Sand, G., 36, 196
Sanskrit, 43
Sarrasine, 60, 103, 113, 123, 154
Sauveur, 210
Savary, F., 14, 36, 37, 42, 44, 46, 47, 50, 51, 53, 55
La Savonnerie, 144
Saxe, 163
Scènes de la vie privée, 31
Scènes de la Vie de Province, 31
Scènes de la Vie pariesienne, 31
Scènes de la Vie Militaire, 47
Scènes de la Vie de Campagne, 47
Schoch, R., 206
Scott, L., 123
Scott, W., 23, 100
Secrets de la Princesse de Cadignan, 116
Séguin, 152, 178
Seigneur, 210, 223
La Seine (river), 119, 132, 137, 138, 157, 159, 162, 166, 186
Seize Sermons, 75
semiotic, 1, 5, 181
Senatus Populusque romanus, 166
A Sentimental Journey, 65, 73
Seraphita, 120
Sermons of M. Yorick, 126
Sermons of Mr Yorick, 125
Serres, R., 48
Serval, C., 111, 112, 124, 209
Seuils, 2, 3, 4, 5, 6, 7, 11, 12, 18, 20, 25, 27, 31, 47, 52, 58, 59, 130, 207
Shakespeare, W., 197
Shakespearean, 206
Sherman, C., 58, 63, 64
Shklovsky, V., 196
sileni, 102
Sirens, 171, 178
Socratic, 177
Sonnenschein, A., 131, 150

Soulié, F., 198
sous-titre, 6
Spoelberch de Lovenjoul, Charles, 29, 32, 36, 42, 44, 45, 55,58, 60,61, 70, 71, 73, 74, 80, 81, 106, 109, 111, 112, 113, 115, 118, 122, 124, 125, 126, 153, 209, 221, 225
St. Augustine, 193
Staal (lithographer-illustrator), 37, 51
Stendhal, 20, 197
Sterne, 14, 25, 26, 33, 42, 44, 45, 48, 51, 53, 54, 65, 66, 67, 68, 69, 70, 73, 74, 75, 76, 77, 78, 79, 80, 81, 82, 109, 110, 111, 116, 117, 118, 120, 125, 126, 153
Sterne inédit Le Koran, 69
Sternean, 43
Strachey, A., 151
structuralism, 1, 5, 6, 201
structuralist, 2, 3, 4, 5
subtitle(s)/*surtitre*, 3, 4, 12, 13, 17, 30, 37, 43, 44, 58, 59
Sue, E., 198
surtitle (postfixed)/*surtitre ultérieur*, 12
synchronic, 4, 5, 88, 103, 201, 204
synchrony, 203, 207

T

Taillefer, 138, 140, 144, 157, 159, 189, 190, 197
Talbot, E., 198
Le Talisman, 12, 29
Talleyrand, C., 189
Talvart, H., ii, 53, 60, 63
Théâtre des Italiens, 158
Thérien, M., 176
Tilby, M., 25, 26, 65, 68, 69, 73, 75, 76, 79, 80, 81, 82, 125
title(s), 3, 4, 7, 11, 12, 13, 14, 18, 25, 29, 30, 32, 35, 36, 37, 43, 44, 45, 46, 47, 48, 50, 51, 53, 54, 55, 58, 66, 70, 75, 129, 193
titre, 6, 13, 20, 25
titrologie, 7
Tobie, 66, 111
Toby, 67, 70, 71, 75
Todorov, T., 3, 6, 151, 156, 196
Tom, 70, 71
Tomashevsky, B., 196
La Touraine, 13
Tournier., M., 4
Tours, 209
Traité de la vie extérieure, 18
Trim, 70, 71, 72, 75, 81
Tristram, 70
Tristram Shandy, 14, 26, 35, 44, 45, 46, 47, 48, 51, 54, 65, 66, 67, 68, 69, 70, 71, 72, 73, 74, 75, 76, 77, 78, 80, 81, 111

U

ulterior title (*ultérieur*), 12
Undank, J., 64
Ursule Mirouet, 120

V

vagina dentata, 139
Valence, 192
Valens, 192
Valentin, R., 146, 158
Valentinois, 192
Vanoncini, A., 199
La Vendetta, 37
El Verdugo, 98
Vierge Marie, 165, 187
Le Voleur, 104
Vouvray, 214
Voyage sentimental, 75

W

Wadman, 71, 111
Walter (Shandy), 66
Weber, 178, 198
Weinberg, B., 105
Werdet, 35, 58, 60
West, C., 64, 83, 104
Wilhelm, J., 59, 198
Work, J., 68, 80, 81
Wurmser, A., 84, 104

Z

La Zambinella, 103, 154
Zola, E., 105

STUDIES IN FRENCH LITERATURE

1. Gerald Groves (trans.), **Germain Nouveau's Symbolist Poetry 1851 - 1920:** *Valentines*
2. Anne-Marie Brinsmead, **Strategies of Resistance in** *Les Liaisons Dangereuses:* **Heroines in Search of "Author-ity"**
3. Jean-Jacques Thomas (compiler), **Concordance de** *Poemes* **by Yves Bonnefoy**
4. Jean-Jacques Hamm and Gregory Lessard (compilers), **Concordance to Stendhal's** *Armance*
5. Leonora Timm (trans. & ed.), **A Modern Breton Political Poet - Anjela Duval: A Biography and An Anthology**
6. Sharon Harwood-Gordon, **The Poetic Style of Corneille's Tragedies: An Aesthetic Interpretation**
7. M. Adereth, **Elsa Troilet and Louis Aragon: An Introduction to Their Interwoven Lives and Works**
8. Catriona Dinwoodie, **The Fusion of the Spoken and the Written in the Fiction of Antonine Maillet**
9. Roxanne Hanney, **The Invisible Middle Term in Proust's** *A La Recherche Du Temps Perdu*
10. Michael G. Paulson, **A Critical Analysis of de La Fayette's** *La Princesse de Clèves* **as a Royal Exemplary Novel: Kings, Queens, and Splendor**
11. Jeri Debois King, **Paratextuality in Balzac's** *La Peau de Chagrin: The Wild Ass's Skin*
12. Emile Zola, **My Hatreds/***Mes Haines*, translated and with an introduction by Palomba Paves-Yashinsky and Jack Yashinsky